LEARNING TO
COOK VEGETARIAN

LEARNING TO
COOK VEGETARIAN

ROSE ELLIOT

PHOENIX ILLUSTRATED

To Kate, Meg and Claire, with love and thanks

First published in Great Britain in 1998
by Weidenfeld & Nicolson

This paperback edition first published in 1999 by
Phoenix Illustrated
Orion Publishing Group, Orion House
5, Upper St. MartinÕs Lane
London WC2H 9EA

A CIP catalogue record for this book is available from the British Library
ISBN 0 753806908

Photography by Philip Webb
Food stylist Pete Smith

Editorial Director Susan Haynes
Art Director David Rowley
Editor Maggie Ramsay
Designed by Nigel Soper and The Senate
Indexer Hilary Bird

Typeset in LinoLetter and Neue Helvetica

contents

introduction

I grew up in a family in which all the adults close to me were keen vegetarian cooks. The centre of our house was a large kitchen that was always warm from the Aga and often full of delicious cooking smells. So I began to cook by watching (and helping!) my parents from an early age; I loved to experiment and was encouraged to do so.

That, surely, is the ideal way to learn, watching and absorbing techniques and recipes almost unconsciously, then being able to try things without fear of failure, which in turn gives the confidence to experiment in the kitchen. I know that I was lucky and that many people do not have the chance to learn to cook in this easy and natural way. I also know, from talking to the people I meet at book signings and demonstrations, that many people lack confidence in their ability to cook and that this is intensified when they want to make vegetarian dishes and they don't know what to cook either!

This book is for them. It's a book on how to cook and how to become a vegetarian – either, or both. It's written from my experience of cooking and demonstrating for many years, and teaching my three daughters to cook.

So, let's begin. First of all, let's clarify the terms used. According to the Vegetarian Society, a vegetarian is someone who does not eat fish, fowl or animals but does eat dairy produce. A vegan takes it a step further and doesn't eat anything produced by animals, so that means no eggs, no milk or products made from it, no honey. Of course there are individual quirks within these categories; for instance, one of my daughters is a non-egg-eating vegetarian. Some people describe themselves as 'vegetarian' then in the next breath say that they eat fish – but vegetarians don't eat any creature that has been killed or, as Linda McCartney put it 'anything that has a face'. The majority of the recipes in this book are suitable for both vegetarians and vegans: wherever possible I have suggested non-dairy substitutes for milk and butter.

One of the best pieces of advice I can give to any cook is always to read a recipe through before you attempt it. You need to be certain that you have all the ingredients, equipment and time that you need to do the dish justice – even if that means deciding to substitute an ingredient for one that is not available. Having all your ingredients and equipment set out before you begin may seem like unnecessary fuss, but it will allow you to sail confidently through any recipe.

what do vegetarians eat?

Some people like to go vegetarian overnight, others prefer a more gradual approach, starting by making one meal each day completely vegetarian, then increasing the number of vegetarian meals each week until they've cut out all meat and fish. The important thing is to go at a pace that suits you and your lifestyle.

Going vegetarian is surprisingly easy. For instance, you might have an egg and toast for breakfast, a bean burger on a bun with salad for lunch, and pasta with fresh tomato sauce and a different salad in the evening, with yogurt for a pudding or snack and milk or soya milk in tea or coffee or as a milk shake. Fill in any gaps with fruit and vegetables – these are a cornerstone to healthy eating, whether you are a meat-eater or a vegetarian. Vegetable or salad accompaniments to main meals can be as generous as you like, and for snacks, treat yourself to some unusual varieties of apples, a bunch of grapes, or a fresh mango or papaya.

In place of meat and fish, vegetarians eat:

Main protein foods
2–3 servings a day
These foods also provide energy, fibre, iron, zinc, calcium and vitamins B and E as well as essential fats:

• Eggs (1 serving = 1 or 2 eggs)
Free-range eggs are recommended because of the cruelty involved in battery egg production.
• Beans, peas or lentils (1 serving = 175 g/6 oz cooked weight)
• Nuts and/or seeds, nut or seed butters or pastes, for example tahini/sesame seed paste (1 serving = 50 g/2 oz)
• Vegetarian protein foods such as tofu (1 serving = 150 g/5 oz), tempeh (50 g/2 oz), seitan (50 g/2 oz), textured vegetable protein (TVP) mince or chunks (25 g/1 oz dry; 50 g/ 2 oz fresh), Quorn (50 g/2 oz). The Vegetarian Society has not approved Quorn because it contains whites from eggs that are not free-range. For more information and recipes using these foods, see pages 138–145.

Milk products and alternatives
2–3 servings a day
These provide additional protein as well as energy, calcium, zinc and vitamins A and B:

• Milk or calcium-enriched soya milk (1 serving = 200 ml/7 fl oz)
• Hard, firm and semi-soft cheese such as Cheddar, Brie (1 serving = 40 g/1½ oz)
• Soft cheese such as cottage cheese, fromage frais (1 serving = 100 g/3½ oz)
• Yogurt (1 serving = 100 g/3½ oz)

Carbohydrates
At least 5 servings a day
These provide energy, fibre, protein and minerals such as iron and magnesium, and B vitamins:

• Breakfast cereals (1 serving = 50 g/2 oz)
• Bread (1 serving = 1 slice, or 1 roll)
• Potatoes (1 serving = 1 medium potato)
• Grains, pasta, rice (1 serving = 2 tablespoons cooked)

Fruit and vegetables
At least 5 servings a day
These provide vitamin C, beta-carotene (vitamin A), folic acid, magnesium, iron and calcium as well as fibre:

• Vegetables, including some dark green leafy vegetables every day (1 serving = 2–3 tablespoons)
• Fruit (1 serving = 1 apple or orange, or 2–3 tablespoons fresh, frozen or dried fruit) or fruit juices, including some citrus fruit

Fats
Small quantities of butter, margarine or vegetable oils provide some oil-soluble nutrients and vitamins such as vitamins A, D and E.

Almonds provide protein, calcium and B vitamins. Enjoy them as snacks, in cakes and puddings, and in savoury dishes

getting all the nutrients you need

Can a vegetarian diet supply all the essential nutrients? This is an important question and obviously of concern to anyone embarking on a vegetarian or vegan way of life. The answer is a reassuring yes: a vegetarian diet, either with or without dairy produce, can supply all the nutrients needed for health and vitality. This applies to everyone: children, teenagers, pregnant women, physically active men and women, older people.

Supplements such as multivitamin pills may suggest that they are designed specially for vegetarians or vegans, but if you are eating a well-balanced diet they are not really necessary. Some vitamins may be toxic if taken in excess. Always seek medical advice before taking such supplements.

Studies have shown that vegetarians have similar patterns of growth to people who eat meat and fish; and vegetarians (adults and children) are no more likely to suffer from vitamin and mineral deficiencies. This has been confirmed by numerous authorities. Dr Michèle Sadler, senior nutritionist at the British Nutrition Foundation, said in an interview with *The Guardian* (3 June 1997) that 'there is adequate evidence of normal health and development even in vegan children, if parents provide a diet rich in calories and micronutrients, particularly calcium, vitamin D and vitamin B12.'

In fact there is increasing evidence that vegetarian diets are often healthier than those that include meat. Research has shown, for instance, that vegetarians are five times less likely to be admitted to hospital than meat-eaters; that a vegetarian diet can significantly reduce the incidence of heart disease, cancers, hypertension, diabetes and other afflictions. However, there are certain worries that crop up time and again, so let's look at these now.

Dried apricots are a good source of iron in a vegetarian diet

Can a vegetarian diet supply enough protein?
This is usually the first thing people worry about. However, for most of the Western world, it simply isn't a problem; we nearly all eat more protein than we need (0.75 g a day per kg of body weight, or 43 g for a 9 stone woman, 57 g for a 12 stone man). Remember that, besides the main protein foods, we also obtain protein from other sources, such as bread, breakfast cereals and pasta.

Good vegetarian sources of protein

Food (average serving)	g protein/serving
Tofu (150 g)	15
Red kidney beans (175 g)	13
Peanut butter (50 g)	11
Cheddar cheese (40 g)	10
Almonds (50 g)	10
Baked beans (175 g)	9
Egg (1)	7.5
Yogurt (150 g)	7.5
Milk (200 ml)	7
Pasta (50 g dry weight)	6

Neither is it necessary to worry about 'complementary proteins' or protein balancing, despite the commonly held belief that you have to eat certain mixtures of foods at a meal in order to get the full range of amino acids (the 'building blocks' that make up the protein needed by the human body). In 1993 the authoritative American Dietetic Association stated: 'Plant sources of protein alone can provide adequate amounts of the essential and nonessential amino acids, assuming that dietary protein sources from plants are reasonably varied and that caloric intake is sufficient to meet energy needs. Whole grains, legumes, vegetables, seeds and nuts all contain essential and nonessential amino acids. Conscious combining of these foods within a given meal, as the complementary protein dictum suggests, is unnecessary. Additionally, soya protein has been shown to be nutritionally equivalent in protein value to proteins of animal origin and thus can serve as the sole source of protein intake if desired.'

Getting enough B vitamins

Most of the B vitamins present no problems for either vegetarians or vegans. However, vegans do need to watch their intake of riboflavin (which is found in milk, cheese and yogurt). Useful sources are: almonds, cashews, pecans and pine nuts; sesame, sunflower and pumpkin seeds; dried apricots and prunes; quinoa, millet, wheatgerm, barley; molasses, mangetout and mushrooms. Some breakfast cereals are fortified with riboflavin: a 30 g/ 1 oz serving can provide more than half of the suggested daily intake. Nutritional yeast flakes (which can be blended with fresh fruit and milk in a milk shake) and yeast extract (e.g. Marmite) are also rich sources.

Vitamin B12 is found only in animal products, but vegetarians can get this vitamin from dairy foods and eggs, and vegans from any of the increasing range of foods that are fortified with this vitamin, such as yeast extract, some soya milks, breakfast cereals and textured vegetable proteins (TVP).

Getting enough vitamin D

Vitamin D is produced in the body by the action of sunlight on the skin, and is no more of a problem for vegetarians than anyone else. Supplements may be advisable for infants between six months and three years (because of the depletion of vitamin D supplies used in the process of bone formation), for pregnant and breastfeeding women, for anyone over 65, and for people of Asian origin living in northerly countries, who have been found to be at risk of vitamin D deficiency.

Many breakfast cereals are fortified with vitamin D (check the label), and it is also found in fortified margarines and spreads, and in eggs and dairy produce.

Vitamin D is often included in multivitamin preparations, but make sure you're not getting it in any other supplement you're taking, as it is toxic when taken in excess.

Getting enough iron

Iron deficiency is a common cause of anaemia in the British diet. Symptoms of anaemia include fatigue and a general 'run-down' feeling, but scientific studies have shown that vegetarians are no more likely to suffer than meat-eaters (probably because they are aware of the potential problem and take steps to compensate). However, of all the nutrients, iron is the one that is most likely to be lacking in a vegetarian diet. Meat is a good source of easily absorbed iron, whereas the iron in vegetarian foods is not as easily absorbed.

Eating iron-rich foods at the same meal as foods containing vitamin C will ensure that the iron present is utilized to the full. Start the meal with grapefruit or orange juice, serve a salad made from fruit and vegetables rich in vitamin C such as oranges, raw red or green peppers, and leafy vegetables, or finish with strawberries, kiwi fruit or oranges.

Good sources of iron in the vegetarian diet include: fortified breakfast cereals; pumpkin, sesame and sunflower seeds; cashew nuts, almonds, hazelnuts, walnuts, Brazil nuts and pecans, peanuts and peanut butter; lentils, chickpeas and hummus, soya beans, tofu and soya flour, red kidney beans and other beans; wheat bran, wheatgerm and wholemeal flour; quinoa; dried figs, raisins, apricots, peaches and prunes; black treacle and molasses.

Good vegetarian sources of iron

Food (average serving)	mg iron/serving
Cooked lentils (175 g)	6.12
Bran flakes (30 g)	6.00
Cashew nuts (50 g)	3.10
Baked beans (175 g)	2.45
Dried figs (50 g)	2.00
Wholemeal bread (2 slices, 70 g)	1.89
Tofu (150 g)	1.80
Dried apricots (50 g)	1.70
Cooked spinach (100 g)	1.60
Pumpkin seeds (2 tablespoons, 15 g)	1.50

Recommended daily intake of iron

Age	mg/day
Women, 11–49	14.8
Women, 50 and over	8.7
Men, 11–18	11.3
Men, 19 and over	8.7

Getting enough calcium

Since there is virtually no calcium in meat, this concern would be addressed in the much the same way whether or not you are vegetarian. One of the major sources of calcium in any diet is dairy produce such as milk, cheese and yogurt. A well-balanced vegetarian diet provides adequate calcium from milk and cheese, and although vegans don't eat these, strangely, there isn't evidence of calcium deficiency among vegans. Apparently, although they consume less calcium, their bodies use and store it far more efficiently than meat-eaters.

Good sources of calcium are: milk and calcium-enriched soya milk, cheese, yogurt, leafy green vegetables, broccoli, figs, sesame seeds and tahini. These foods, together with the grains, wholewheat bread, nuts, fruits, pulses and vegetables that make up the day's meals will ensure that your needs are met.

Good vegetarian sources of calcium

Food (average serving)	mg calcium/serving
Pizza with cheese (500 g)	1050
Tofu, firm (150 g)	765
Tahini/sesame seed paste (50 g)	340
Yogurt or calcium-enriched soya yogurt (150 g)	300
Cheddar cheese (40 g)	290
Milk or calcium-enriched soya milk (200 ml)	240
Cooked spinach (100 g)	160
Dried figs (50 g)	120
Fromage frais (100 g)	85
Almonds (25 g)	60

Recommended daily intake of calcium

Age	mg/day
Teenage	1100
Adult	800
Pregnancy	1000
Breastfeeding	1200
Women over 50 with HRT	1000
Women over 50 without HRT	1500

A vegetarian diet during pregnancy

During pregnancy your nutritional needs increase considerably. You need more iron, B vitamins – especially folic acid and B12 – vitamins A, D and C, and your need for both protein and calcium increases, but most of the time you don't need many more calories than normal, only about 200 extra calories a day during the last three months. So make sure that what you do eat is really nutritious. Eat a variety of foods, including plenty of fresh fruit and vegetables, especially dark green leafy vegetables, wholegrain bread and other foods high in the important nutrients discussed above, and you'll be fine.

It's a good idea to improve your diet along these lines several months before you get pregnant, concentrating especially on foods that are good sources of folic acid – dark green leafy vegetables, whole grains such as brown rice, wholewheat bread and pulses. For detailed information on how the vegetarian diet can meet the needs of pregnancy, breastfeeding and young children, see *Rose Elliot's Mother, Baby and Toddler Book* (HarperCollins, 1996).

A vegetarian diet for breastfeeding

This is when you do need extra calories – about 500 more than normal every day. Again, make sure these are coming from foods that are full of nutrients for you and your growing baby. Pulses, whole grains like brown rice, nuts and seeds, and dried fruits are especially good at this time when you'll probably feel ravenously hungry but have little or no time to look after yourself!

Make sure you have something good and filling when you get up, like a big bowl of porridge topped with flaked almonds and milk or soya milk. Then, during the day, grab a handful of nuts and raisins, fill a wholewheat pitta bread with Hummus (page 46), munch some raw vegetables with Tahini dip (page 46), whiz some tofu in the food processor for a savoury dip or sweet cream (pages 40 and 161) or stir-fry vegetables with tofu and sprinkle with roasted sesame seeds; have a bowl of Fruits baked with orange and ginger (page 162), perhaps with a spoonful of molasses stirred in for extra iron, calcium and B vitamins; whiz up a thick shake in the blender, using milk or soya milk, some yogurt or soya yogurt and fresh or frozen strawberries, raspberries or banana; make a big panful of iron-rich Lentil soup (page 33) to last you several days; pressure-cook brown rice (page 115) so it's soft and soothing and eat with cooked spinach or Spinach dal (page 126), or with raisins and chopped figs stirred in, like porridge.

Vegetarian food or babies and children

As babies and children fill up quickly, the main concern is to see that their foods provide concentrated nourishment. For the first six months, breast milk or infant formula milk supplies all a baby needs. Start weaning around six months or a little earlier (but not before four months) by introducing fruit and vegetable purées and rice cereal.

As your baby gets used to these, stir in a small amount of iron-rich foods such as tahini (sesame seed purée), puréed pulses, for example baked beans (the low-sugar kind from the health shop), mashed tofu or hard-boiled egg yolk, or Lentil soup (page 33) – a particularly good first food. Unless your baby is having formula milk give also the vitamin A, D and C drops recommended by the Department of Health.

Gradually progress from puréed to more coarsely mashed foods and include some wholewheat bread and well-cooked brown rice (page 115), pasta and potatoes. Make sure that they're getting plenty of the concentrated sources of nutrients described above, and include finely grated cheese (Parmesan is good), finely grated nuts and nut butters. Until they are five or six years old, give them full cream milk (not skimmed or semi-skimmed) to drink, or infant formula soya milk, and avoid low-fat spreads. For snacks, focus on fresh and dried fruits, raw vegetables such as carrot sticks, wholewheat bread or toast.

Vegetarian teenagers

Teenagers need plenty of carbohydrate-rich foods such as pasta, potatoes, rice and pulses, as well as concentrated sources of calcium for growing bones. Pizza and pasta are actually good food for this age group, particularly if the pizza is homemade with a good tomato topping and plenty of grated cheese. Dairy or soya yogurts make good snacks because of the calcium they contain.

Teenage girls need to keep up their iron levels, so include good sources of this nutrient every day. Lentils and pulses such as baked beans, Lentil soup (page 33), Red bean chilli (page 129) and Bean burgers (page 129) are very good, as is tofu in any form – and it's low in fat, so learning to love this wonder food is a good idea. Try the ready-marinated chunks that you can buy (which do have some added fat) or marinate your own (page 141). Tofu can be deep-fried or stir-fried with vegetables, or made into sweet or savoury dips or toppings – there are plenty of recipes in this book.

If you're older

Foods that provide concentrated sources of nutrients are the key, because if you're less active you need fewer calories, but you still have the same nutritional requirements. Make sure you are eating plenty of fresh fruit and vegetables (in the form of juice if you find them difficult to chew). Yogurt or soya yogurt are good sources of protein and calcium.

Other easy-to-eat nutrient-rich foods include tofu, tahini, hummus, eggs (well cooked to avoid salmonella poisoning), finely grated nuts or nut butters, puréed or mashed pulses – Lentil soup (page 33) is a great stand-by and can last several days. Pressure-cooked brown rice (page 115), soft and soothing, can be sprinkled with ground roasted sesame seeds (page 18) and served with stir-fried tofu or Baked marinated tofu (page 141) and steamed vegetables. Make sure you're drinking enough water which, together with the fibre from vegetables and pulses, will prevent constipation.

If you're unwell

You need tempting and building up, with small, frequent meals or snacks. Listen to your body – what you fancy may well be a clue to what your body needs to heal itself. The guidelines given for babies and children and for older people really apply here, too, because you need foods that are going to give maximum nourishment for minimum bulk.

Soothing foods like Lentil soup (page 33) or mashed potatoes, which you can fortify with mashed tofu, finely grated cheese or skimmed milk powder are good choices. Pressure-cooked brown rice (page 115) can be made into a deliciously creamy rice pudding by adding milk or soya milk and perhaps a few raisins or sultanas.

Pasta is a good source of energy

menu planning

Does it take longer to cook?
Cooking vegetarian dishes is a new skill and may seem time-consuming at first. This is not because it's more complicated than cooking meat or fish, it's just that following a recipe you're not familiar with always takes longer. Vegetarian food suffers from its reputation as a 'bean-heavy' style, but in this book I will show you that there's far more to it than bean stews and nut loaves. There are plenty of quick, easy and nutritious dishes you can make – with or without a recipe – when you're pressed for time. Here are some suggestions for meals without meat:

Eggs
Make into omelettes (page 64) and either eat fresh from the pan, or slice and mix into rice or vegetable dishes.

Boil or poach and serve with wholemeal toast.

Scramble and add chopped fresh tarragon, chives or parsley. Better still, add some freshly cooked asparagus tips.

Put a layer of freshly cooked spinach in an ovenproof dish, break an egg on top and pour over some cream and grated cheese. Bake in a hot oven for 10–15minutes.

Beans, peas or lentils
Drain canned beans, mash roughly and spread thickly on toasted bread or rolls. Top with slices of tomato, shredded lettuce and mayonnaise.

Drain canned beans and add some dressing (pages 54–56) or simply a splash of balsamic or wine vinegar and olive oil to make a salad; serve with warm pitta bread or garlic bread.

Whiz canned beans or chickpeas in a food processor with enough of their liquid to make a creamy purée, add crushed garlic and/or chopped herbs and serve as a dip with pitta bread, with salad, or spooned (hot or cold) over baked potatoes or cooked vegetables.

Thin puréed canned beans with water or stock to make a creamy soup. Heat through with some herbs, sprinkle with grated cheese and serve with garlic bread or warm rolls.

Heat canned chilli beans and serve as a topping for baked potatoes, or add some chopped avocado and fill ready-made tortilla pancakes; serve with grated cheese and soured cream.

Drain red kidney beans and mash with fried onion and chopped tomatoes; serve with sliced avocado, salad and tortilla chips.

Add drained chickpeas to a mixture of fried onion, spices and tomatoes. Top with fresh coriander for a simple curry to serve with rice.

Make dried lentils into a quick dal (page 126) and serve with steamed vegetables and cooked rice; or make them into an easy soup (page 33) and eat with crusty rolls.

Nuts and seeds
Add whole or chopped nuts or seeds to muesli, or sprinkle over salads.

Sprinkle finely chopped or ground nuts over yogurt or fruit salad.

Stir nuts or seeds into hot cooked rice, couscous or bulgar wheat, with some fried onions and mushrooms or lightly steamed vegetables and chopped herbs.

Add blanched or flaked almonds, pine nuts or roasted cashew nuts to stir-fried vegetables.

Spread nut or seed butters or pastes (like tahini, made from sesame seeds) on top of crisp biscuits, toast or bread and top with sliced tomato, cucumber, lettuce or grated carrot – or olives and fresh herbs.

Stir-fried vegetables can be made into a nutritious meal with the addition of cashew nuts and almonds

Mix chopped or ground nuts and chopped fresh herbs into mashed potatoes, form into flat 'cakes', coat with flour, then shallow-fry.

Use peanut butter to make a quick satay sauce (page 84) and serve with steamed or stir-fried vegetables, tofu, rice or boiled potatoes.

Make gomasio, a nutritious sesame seed topping from Japan, to sprinkle over stir-fried or steamed vegetables, salads, tofu or rice. The dull, matt brown sesame seeds are better than the white ones, which have been processed in brine or with chemicals. All you do is put 3 tablespoons of sesame seeds into a dry saucepan with 1 teaspoon of sea salt and stir over a moderate heat for a couple of minutes until the seeds start to pop and jump around and smell toasted. Remove from the heat, leave to cool, then grind to a powder in a coffee grinder or with a pestle and mortar.

Tofu

Ready-marinated tofu chunks are very tasty and easy to use straight from the packet. To marinate your own, slice firm tofu, then sprinkle with a good soy sauce (see page 27), add some grated ginger and crushed garlic if you like and leave for at least 30 minutes. Mix with steamed or stir-fried vegetables or cooked rice. For a crisp texture, sprinkle the tofu with cornflour and shallow-fry until crisp on both sides.

Put pieces of tofu into a shallow casserole dish, sprinkle with soy sauce, a little grated fresh ginger and crushed garlic and bake for about 20 minutes in a moderate oven until heated through. Serve with noodles and beansprouts, and a dish of braised, steamed or stir-fried vegetables.

Smoked tofu is good cut into very thin slices and fried until crisp – some people say it's a bit like bacon.

For a savoury dip, whiz tofu in a food processor with crushed garlic, seasoning and some fresh herbs such as parsley and chives and serve with raw vegetable sticks, or with steamed or roasted vegetables.

Whiz tofu to a creamy consistency in a blender, adding water or soya milk as necessary, then flavour with a little sugar, honey or fresh fruit for a nutritious yogurt-like topping or pudding.

Tempeh or seitan

Slice and fry in a little olive oil, then toss with stir-fried vegetables.

Serve with fried onions, mushrooms and gravy (page 83), or a tomato sauce (page 82).

Quorn

Sprinkle Quorn chunks with soy sauce, dry sherry or wine, crushed garlic and/or herbs such as thyme and leave for at least 30 minutes for the flavours to develop, then use in a stir-fry.

Textured vegetable protein (TVP)

Dried TVP needs to be hydrated by simmering for 2–3 minutes in liquid – stock, water or wine, or a mixture. Use the hydrated or frozen chunks as described for Quorn.

Add TVP mince to a rich tomato sauce or gravy (page 83) and serve over pasta or top with mashed potato for shepherd's pie.

Cheese

Grate or flake vegetarian Cheddar or Parmesan on top of steamed vegetables, vegetable soups, cooked rice or pasta for extra flavour and nourishment. Vegan cheese, made of soya milk, makes an acceptable substitute for cheese in uncooked dishes but doesn't respond well to heat.

Stir grated cheese into creamy mashed potatoes and brown under a hot grill.

Mash blue cheese with low-fat soft cheese to make a dip to serve with raw vegetables. Alternatively, spread on crusty bread or spoon over steamed vegetables.

Fry feta or halloumi cheese in olive oil (page 76) and serve with something piquant like black olives or gherkins, and plenty of good soft bread to mop up the juices.

Melt rounds of goats' cheese on toast under the grill – on foil or on rounds of bread – and add to a green salad.

Mix cottage cheese with cooked, well-drained spinach, top with grated Parmesan and brown under a hot grill.

Dairy or soya yogurt
Stir chopped chives or other herbs and salt and pepper into plain yogurt for a dressing/dip/sauce that goes with many dishes.

For a quick pudding, put thick, creamy yogurt into a shallow dish, sprinkle the top thickly with soft brown sugar mixed with ½–1 teaspoonful of ground cinnamon, cover and chill for 1–24 hours.

Bread
There are many delicious breads, flavoured with herbs, olives, walnuts, cheese, dried fruit, mixed grains and seeds, to make generous sandwiches: eat cold or toasted.

Fill a pitta pocket with salad, grilled or roasted vegetables (page 103) and top with hummus (page 46), yogurt dressing (page 56) or aïoli (page 56).

Split a baguette and fill with tomatoes, Mozzarella cheese, black olives, fresh basil and olive oil.

Spread pizza bases with thick tomato sauce, drained canned artichoke hearts, sliced peppers, sweetcorn, fried onions, herbs and grated cheese, then pop into a hot oven for 15–20 minutes.

Potatoes
Baked potatoes (page 94) are cheap, easy and nourishing. Top with grated cheese, tahini dip (page 46), dairy or soya yogurt with chopped chives, cottage cheese, canned chilli beans or baked beans.

Boil, then mash (page 96). Stir in some tofu, chopped spring onions and parsley, form into flat 'cakes', coat with flour and shallow-fry until golden.

Pasta and noodles
Drain and toss with extra virgin olive oil, chopped garlic and parsley, and black olives if you like them.

Serve with a good tomato sauce (page 82) or other vegetarian sauce and sprinkle with freshly grated Parmesan cheese.

Drain, return to the pan and stir in a small carton of double cream and some crumbled Gorgonzola cheese for a luxurious dish.

Drain and add chopped skinned ripe tomatoes and avocados, or sliced canned artichokes with some chopped parsley and olive oil, or canned beans, heated through in their liquid then drained.

Soak rice noodles for 4 minutes, then stir-fry with chopped spring onions, red pepper and thinly sliced mushrooms and/or broccoli, grated fresh ginger and crushed garlic. If you like, add marinated tofu chunks. Sprinkle with soy sauce.

Rice, couscous and bulgar wheat
Cook as described on pages 114–115 and serve with stir-fried or roasted vegetables, or a curry or other dish with a good sauce.

Stir in nuts or seeds, drained canned beans or artichoke hearts, chopped vegetables such as spring onions, red, green or yellow pepper or radishes, lightly steamed vegetables such as asparagus, fried button mushrooms or onions, chopped herbs, black or green olives, crushed garlic, slivers of dried apricots, raisins.

Polenta
Use the quick-cooking variety and prepare as described on page 114. Flavour the resulting porridgy mixture with salt, pepper, freshly grated Parmesan cheese, chopped parsley, crushed garlic, chopped olives. Serve with a salad, grilled vegetables or fried wild mushrooms (this is especially good).

What do I serve for special occasions?
Vegetarian food is not relentlessly brown and stodgy; there are plenty of excellent dishes you can make for special occasions. Here are a few tips and suggestions:

If you're planning a meal of three or more courses, aim for variety and contrast of colour, shape and texture between the courses.
For instance:
• don't have too many creamy or puréed dishes
• avoid pastry in more than one course
• contrast something rich like, for instance, the Cheese and walnut terrine (page 74), with a main-course grain or vegetable-based dish such as the Wild rice pilaf (page 116). I try to restrict cheese to one course – usually the main course – and balance it with a starter and/or pudding that is low in fat.

Get a special meal off to a good start by choosing first courses with vivid colours and flavours. Serve a dip with a pretty selection of crudités (page 38), or an attractive salad like Grilled pepper salad (page 44), Leeks vinaigrette (page 47), Hot oyster mushroom salad (page 44) or Pink grapefruit and fennel (page 42). Well-made soups are always popular and look especially attractive with a swirl of cream or yogurt and a sprinkling of chopped fresh herbs: try Roasted red pepper and sweet potato soup (page 32), Carrot and dill soup (page 34) or, in the summer, Fresh tomato soup (page 33) or Chilled cucumber soup (page 35).

Favourite special occasion main courses in my family include: Goats' cheese in puff pastry (page 155) with Cranberry sauce (page 84); Deep-fried Camembert (page 76) with Apricot sauce (page 84); Cheese fritters (page 75) with Parsley sauce (page 80); Spanakopita (page 154) with a Tomato salad (page 59); Spinach lasagne (page 111); Chilli lentil koftas (page 127); Wild mushroom ragout (page 99) with Saffron rice (page 116).

Gratin dauphinoise (page 97) always goes down well – I usually serve this with a green salad or simple steamed vegetables.

A Soufflé or Roulade (pages 67–68) looks impressive, as does a Gougère – a cheesy choux pastry ring (page 154). Guests usually appreciate it if you take the time to make crêpes (page 70), with fillings such as Brie and broccoli or Stilton and spinach. I hope you will find your own favourites throughout the book.

Like the starter, the pudding is best planned to fit in with the main course, although for a special occasion I'm not as fussy about restricting fat as usual. However, a pudding doesn't have to be high in fat and sugar to be good: Ginger poached pears (page 161) or Fruits baked with orange and ginger (page 162), for instance.

Chocolate pots (page 167), Raspberry ice cream (page 174) or Yogurt, honey and dates (page 161) are good simple ways to conclude a meal. For something more flamboyant, Chocolate roulade (page 166) and Summer pavlova (page 173) are always popular, not to mention homemade pies (page 165) and crumbles (page 162), Tarte Tatin (page 168) or a classic Lemon tart (page 173).

For Christmas I love to try different ideas, but these have to be for Christmas Eve or Boxing Day; for the actual 'meal of the year' on Christmas Day my family always ask for the White nut roast with herb stuffing (page 137), which is as much a tradition in our family as turkey is in most families. I make the vegan version of the recipe so that everyone can eat it. For the rest of the meal it's easy to make vegetarian/vegan gravy, Christmas pudding and mince pies, by replacing traditional stock and fats with vegetarian versions.

Summer pavlova (page 173)

useful equipment

Cutting, chopping, grating

• Top of the list comes a chopping board and a sharp knife. You need a board that's sturdy but also light enough to lift when making pastry (see page 148). A good size is 40 x 30 cm/16 x 12 inches and 2.5 cm/1 inch thick. I prefer a wooden one to a plastic one. Mark one side of the board and always use that side for savoury items; the smell of onions and garlic permeates any chopping board, so use the other side of the board for slicing bread and rolling pastry.

• It's worth spending as much as you can on a basic set of knives because good ones can save hours and last for years. For an all-purpose knife I like a traditional French Sabatier with a 12 cm/5 inch blade; this is made of carbon steel, which can be sharpened on a steel; buy this when you buy your knife. Keep the knife in a block or on a magnetic knife rack on the wall.

You will also find it useful to have a serrated stainless steel knife with a 12 cm/5 inch blade. This is perfect for cutting delicate fruits such as peaches, mangoes and avocados, which would be tainted by the carbon steel knife. I also use this knife for inserting into foods while they are cooking, to check whether they're tender, though you could use a skewer for this purpose.

For slicing bread – and for larger vegetables such as cabbages and aubergines – you will need a knife with a serrated 20–25 cm/8–10 inch blade. These are now available in stainless steel with a lifetime guarantee – they are incredibly sharp, and safer for you to use because you don't need to press hard, so there's little danger of the knife slipping. It's worth buying a good one, but be very careful when using it, and keep it away from children.

• A pair of sharp, stainless steel kitchen scissors is essential for snipping herbs, cutting paper to line baking tins and a hundred and one jobs around the kitchen – don't let anyone remove them!

Lemon zester

• I wouldn't be without my vegetable peeler: I prefer the type with a long handle and a sharp swivel blade.

• A peppermill is essential. A top quality wooden one will outlast many a cheaper one and be worth its weight in gold – after all, like a kitchen knife, it's something you'll probably use several times every day.

• You also need a sturdy grater; I like the box type that you can stand on your chopping board and that has holes of different sizes on each side, including some slits for slicing. (I find this preferable to a mandoline, which is a special piece of slicing equipment that I've never got to grips with.)

• A tiny nutmeg grater – I've got one that has a compartment to hold a nutmeg – is useful.

• If you haven't got a food processor (see page 25), a little rotary hand grinder is useful for grinding nuts finely. It's also good for grating small quantities of cheese.

• A zester – a small gadget with sharp little holes at the top for running down the skin of citrus fruits to remove long, curly pieces of peel without cutting into the white pith – is cheap and surprisingly useful.

• Buy an apple corer if you like baked apples.

• Don't forget a can opener.

Mixing, mashing, whisking

• You'll need large, medium and small bowls – I prefer clear glass because they're easy to clean, heatproof and versatile.

• Some wooden spoons are essential; I have three long ones for stirring mixtures in pans and a smaller, flatter one which is light to use. I use a wooden fork for fluffing up rice gently after cooking.

• You also need some tablespoons and teaspoons for the kitchen.

• You need a metal spoon with a long handle for basting food in the oven, a metal fork for pricking pastry and mashing small amounts of food, and a draining spoon, also known as a slotted spoon (with holes in it) for lifting foods out of liquid. These often come in a set that you can hang on the kitchen wall, along with a potato masher and a fish slice for lifting and turning food in a frying pan; I use it, blade down, to chop spinach as it cooks in the pan. Choose one with a slim, flexible blade – there are some very rigid ones that don't do their job well. A metal spatula is also useful for lifting and turning food as it cooks.

• You will also need a spatula with a flexible plastic blade for getting mixture out of a bowl.

• Some people find a pair of kitchen tongs essential, though I rarely use them, except for turning vegetables on the barbecue.

• When it comes to whisks, everyone has their own preferences. Once you've used an electric whisk, you'll wonder how you ever did without one. Failing that, I think a rotary whisk is the most efficient type. It's also useful to have a simple balloon whisk – not too big – for jobs like whisking sauces and batters to remove lumps.

• A pestle and mortar – a heavy bowl with a rounded tool that you use to pound, crush and mix ingredients in the bowl – is useful for crushing spices and seeds, but I wouldn't put it on the list of essentials.

• I think garlic presses are a waste of time – you can do the job much more quickly by crushing the garlic with a knife on a board. But they do save you from 'garlic fingers'.

Sieving, straining, squeezing

• I have two sieves: a large metal one for sifting flour and straining hot liquid, and a large plastic one for sieving delicately flavoured acidic ingredients (such as raspberries, to remove the seeds) which might otherwise take on a metallic taste.

• You also need a colander for straining and draining both hot and cold ingredients, so a metal one, which will stand in the sink and can cope with boiling liquid, is best. You can use a colander for drying salad leaves – just leave them to drain in it after washing them – but I find a salad spinner invaluable; I use it every day. It consists of a plastic basket inside a container with a lid that you turn two or three times to remove the water from the salad leaves centrifugally. Get a large one.

• A lemon squeezer is another essential. I like the type that has a jug to collect the juice, but best of all is an electric one, ready on the work surface to produce lemon juice in seconds.

Pots and pans

Another area where personal preference will guide your choice. I choose stainless steel or enamel-coated cast-iron pans over aluminium because all the naturopaths and natural healers I've ever met warn against the effects of aluminium on health, especially when salt is used when cooking in them. I'm not very fond of nonstick, which I find do not last well. If you get a new pan, do follow the manufacturer's instructions for seasoning it before you use it for the first time – this means the pan will do its job better.

• Buy a range of sizes including a large one, about 2.75 litres/5 pints, for cooking pasta, stews and stir-fries. If this has a steamer pan to fit on top, you will have an extremely versatile and useful piece of equipment. For example, you can cook potatoes or carrots in the steamer, then put cabbage into the lower part later, to cook quickly on the same burner. A couple of medium-sized pans and a small one are probably all you'll need.

• When it comes to frying pans, I think that heavy, cast-iron pans are best. Ideally you need a small frying pan for omelettes (see page 64) and a bigger one, about 25 cm/ 10 inches across, for general frying.

• A stainless steel pressure cooker is another piece of equipment that I find indispensable – well worth the small amount of time it takes to get to know how to use it. It's wonderful for making soups in about 5 minutes and for cooking brown rice so that it's soft and delicate. You can also use it as a large saucepan when you want to cook pasta for a crowd or make a big stir-fry. In fact, I use mine instead of a wok.

• A heat diffuser is useful: this is a metal disk that you put over the burner to reduce the heat for really gentle cooking.

• You'll need a couple of roasting tins: 18 x 28 cm/7 x 11 inches is a good size for making Yorkshire pudding; a larger one will be needed for roast potatoes and other vegetables. This might be supplied with your oven and simply slide in like one of the shelves. If not, buy a really strong one, 2 cm/ ¾ inch deep.

• You'll need casseroles and heatproof dishes in several sizes. The ones I find the most useful are: a white 30 cm/12 inch pizza plate, which I use both in the oven and as a serving plate; a flameproof casserole – at least 2.4 litres/4½ pints – that you can use on top of the stove as well as in the oven; a large ovenproof oval dish; and three rectangular gratin dishes at least 5 cm/2 inches deep and measuring 22 x 20 cm/9 x 8 inches, 18 x 28 cm/7 x 11 inches and 30 x 25 cm/12 x 10 inches.

• In addition it's useful to have some small ovenproof ramekins, which can double up as serving bowls for pâtés and dips. A large soufflé dish, with deep, straight sides, can also be used for serving puddings and fruit salads.

Baking

When buying baking tins, quality counts, because they're things that you'll never need to replace if you buy the best you can.

• An essential basic is a good solid baking sheet, the largest size that will fit your oven. This conducts heat well, so if you bake pastry cases on it they will cook crisply; they will also be easier to take out of the oven. It is also needed for baking biscuits and scones.

• Particular recipes specify certain tin sizes in which they undoubtedly work best, but for a basic set of baking tins I suggest the following: two 450 g/1 lb and one 900 g/2 lb loaf tins; a 20 cm/8 inch round tart tin, at least 2.5 cm/1 inch deep; a 20 cm/8 inch square tin; two 18 cm/7 inch round sandwich tins; a 20 cm/8 inch round deep cake tin for baking fruit cakes (if it is a spring-clip tin it can be used for cheesecakes too); a pie plate, 24 cm/ 9½ inches across; two shallow Swiss roll tins, measuring 18 x 28 cm/7 x 11 inches and 22 x 33 cm/9 x 13 inches. As you extend your repertoire you might buy a 22 cm/9 inch or a 25 cm/10 inch round tart tin; an 18 cm/7 inch round flan ring; and six or eight individual, 10 cm/4 inch round tart tins.

• A wire rack is usually essential to allow cakes and biscuits to cool after you have taken them out of the oven.

• You need a good rolling pin: I prefer a simple wooden one without handles, about 36–40 cm/14–16 inches long.

• Finally, you'll need a set of pastry cutters of different sizes: sharp metal ones that fit inside each other for storage are best.

Measuring and timing

• Of the many different kitchen scales available I prefer the type with a large bowl for weighing the ingredients and a dial that you can reset, so that you can add one ingredient after another. I prefer mechanical to battery-operated scales.

• In addition, you'll need a measuring jug, marked in millilitres and fluid ounces, and a set of standard measuring spoons: 15 ml/ 1 tablespoon, 10 ml/1 dessertspoon/ 2 teaspoons, 5 ml/1 teaspoon and 2.5 ml/ ½ teaspoon; these are essential for accuracy in baking, and you might be surprised how far your idea of 1 tablespoon differs from the standard measurement. If you want to follow American recipes, you will find a set of US measuring cups very useful.

• Also invaluable are a kitchen timer – it's all too easy to burn things – and a cooking thermometer (sometimes called a sugar thermometer, because it is often used for making sweets and jam), which is useful for making sure oil is at the right temperature for deep-frying. Put it in the pan when the oil is cold and let it heat up with the oil, otherwise it is likely to crack.

Blenders, food processors and mixers

A food processor is a very useful piece of equipment in the vegetarian kitchen; it will save you a great deal of time and effort. I recommend getting a large one and keeping it out on the work surface, ready for action, if space permits. A blender is a good alternative, but not as versatile. Both will make breadcrumbs, grind nuts and blend soups and purées; the food processor will, however, do many other jobs, such as chopping, grating and slicing vegetables, and will handle larger quantities at a time.

• An electric coffee grinder, often sold as a blender or food processor attachment, means you can enjoy freshly ground coffee and is also useful for grinding small quantities of nuts, seeds and spices to a powder.

• A food mixer isn't as versatile as a food processor, though it's good for whisking and for mixing cakes. I think the best combination of these electrical appliances is a food processor and an electric hand whisk.

notes on ingredients

You will find information about specific foods in the relevant sections – beans in the pulses section, vegetables in the vegetable section and so on – but here are some general notes about ingredients used throughout the book.

Fats and oils
For health as well as flavour, olive oil is best. I use a light, relatively inexpensive one for cooking and a good quality extra virgin one for salads, where the delicious flavour can shine through.

For cooking at high temperatures, whether frying or in the oven, it's better to use another type of oil. Groundnut (also known as peanut), soya and rapeseed (this is often sold as 'vegetable oil') oils are recommended, because they're the most chemically stable at high temperatures, and therefore less likely to produce free radicals (trouble-making loose molecules that can be damaging to health).

For the same reason, I think butter is preferable to margarine or white vegetable fat for cooking and it certainly tastes better. If you're vegan, or prohibited butter for medical reasons, buy the best quality unhydrogenated vegetable margarine that you can afford.

Dairy and soya products
I always use free-range eggs, preferably organic. Vegetarians are concerned about animal welfare, and I also wonder about the feed given to battery hens.

I prefer soya to dairy milk, I use soya cream in place of single cream, and soya yogurt when I can get a plain, unsweetened one. However, I do use Greek yogurt, double cream, soured cream, crème fraîche and fromage frais occasionally. If you're new to soya milk I suggest you try the vanilla-flavoured one that you can get at health food shops – it's delicious as a cold drink.

Herbs and spices
Starting with the basics, salt and pepper, I like to use a good sea salt and my favourite is Maldon, which comes in crunchy flakes you can crush with your fingers. Black peppercorns, in a peppermill, are a must; aromatic, freshly ground pepper makes such a difference to the flavour of food. Most dishes are best seasoned shortly before you serve them: any other flavours will be fully developed, and you can taste and add the salt and pepper you think you need.

Ready ground white pepper has a different flavour; I use it in a spicy vegetable mixture to serve with couscous (page 123).

Fresh ginger and garlic are used in many recipes. Look for firm, smooth-skinned ginger roots, which will keep for several weeks in the refrigerator. I wash ginger before use and I find no need to peel it before grating. Garlic bulbs should feel firm when you buy them. Store them in a cool, dark, well-ventilated place; an earthenware garlic pot is ideal.

Parsley is the most useful fresh herb; it's also incredibly nutritious, so use it generously. I find that flat-leaf parsley has a better flavour than the curly type. Fresh herbs, such as coriander, basil, chives, mint and dill, make a wonderful contribution to vegetarian cookery, in soups, salads, sauces and as garnishes. Rosemary, oregano, sage and thyme are good in winter recipes, since they keep their flavour well in their dried form. Dried bay leaves have a more intense flavour than fresh ones.

Mustard has many culinary uses. The seeds (white or black) flavour Indian food, the powder can be added to sauces and cheesy bakes, and the made-up form – such as smooth or grainy Dijon or Meaux mustard – can be used in the kitchen or at the table.

There are many varieties and forms of chilli, ranging from fresh green and red chillies, little dried whole red chillies that keep well in a jar, chilli flakes (crushed dried chillies), hot and spicy ground chillies and cayenne pepper, and the milder paprika, which can be sprinkled on food to add a splash of colour.

Coriander and cumin are available in both seed and ground forms, with slightly different flavours. I also keep turmeric (always sold ground) and whole cardamom pods.

Cinnamon, cloves and saffron are useful in

Vanilla pods   Capers

both sweet and savoury dishes. I keep both whole cinnamon sticks and ground cinnamon. Saffron strands need soaking in a little liquid before you add them to the recipe.

I also keep mixed spice for baking, curry powder, which needs to be well cooked, and garam masala, which is added towards the end of the cooking time. A jar of curry paste is occasionally useful for instant curry flavour.

Lemongrass has a lovely lemony flavour; it looks a bit like a dry spring onion. Peel off any really tough layers and slice or chop it; large slices can, like bay leaves, be fished out of soups or sauces, while very finely chopped lemongrass, in stir-fries, can be eaten.

Buy whole nutmegs and grate just before you need them, for the best flavour.

Long, dark brown vanilla pods can be infused in milk to add their flavour when you make sweet sauces and ice cream, then washed, left to dry and used again. Bury a vanilla pod in a jar of caster sugar for deliciously flavoured sugar. Real vanilla extract is very concentrated, the more widely available vanilla essence is milder; a small bottle of either lasts for ages. Artificial vanilla flavouring is not worth buying.

Sauces and other flavourings

With vinegar, as with olive oil, you get what you pay for. Balsamic vinegar is concentrated and needs to be used sparingly. For everyday I use a supermarket red wine vinegar or, my favourite because it is so light and sweet, a brown rice vinegar that you can buy from macrobiotic or Japanese shops, some supermarkets and health food shops. Rice vinegar is good for dressings because you can use more of it in proportion to the oil, making a lighter dressing.

Tabasco sauce is a hot chilli sauce, useful for adding a dash of chilli heat without the bother of chopping chillies.

Soy sauce has a distinctive flavour that is useful for far more than just shaking over Chinese food. I recommend naturally brewed soy sauces such as shoyu, or the wheat-free version called tamari, which you can get from health shops; Kikkoman is a brand of naturally brewed soy sauce that is quite widely available.

Useful in some recipes is creamed coconut, sold as a hard white block, which keeps for months in the refrigerator.

Other storecupboard ingredients

Black and green olives are good for pasta dishes, pizza toppings, or on their own as appetizing nibbles. For the best flavour, I prefer to buy them loose at a delicatessen, and with their stones still in rather than pitted.

Capers and baby gherkins add piquancy to many dishes, and sun-dried tomatoes (preserved in oil) have a lovely rich flavour.

Dried porcini mushrooms (ceps) may seem expensive, but you don't need many; soak them in hot water for 20 minutes and add them to ordinary mushrooms for a really luxurious taste.

I use dried breadcrumbs in a number of recipes, for example to coat the outside of fritters and burgers. You can buy them at any supermarket or health food store; I prefer the natural type without added colouring. It's quite easy to make your own, by leaving a few slices of bread to dry out in the oven after you have switched it off. Then whiz them in the blender or food processor until you have fine crumbs. Store them in an airtight container for up to two months.

soups

Making soup is one of the best things to start with when you're learning to cook. It's very simple and quick – you can make a good soup in around 30 minutes – and you can choose your own combinations of vegetables, herbs, spices and even fruit. If you serve it with bread and follow it with cheese, salad and fruit, soup becomes a satisfying meal.

You don't necessarily need a food processor or blender to make soup, but if you do have one it opens up more options, since it's then easy to make smooth, creamy soups as well as chunky ones – or in-between ones in which you purée about half of the mixture, giving a smooth, slightly thickened soup with some texture. Don't fill the blender too full, or the liquid could force the lid off, covering you in a jet of hot soup.

I find that people are often discouraged from making soup because they haven't any stock. In fact I very rarely use stock; I generally just use water because I prefer the clear flavour of whatever vegetable I am using. Also, like most people, I don't often get around to making stock and I don't much like the taste of most of the vegetable stock cubes on the market. However, I have included a recipe for vegetable stock in this chapter – it's worth using for a soup with many complex flavours or for a lentil or bean soup.

I nearly always start a soup by heating a little butter or olive oil in a large saucepan and frying a chopped onion over a low heat so that the onion softens gently. After 5–10 minutes I add the other vegetables, cut into even-sized pieces, including a potato for thickening unless it is a bean or lentil soup. Stir them in and cook for a further 5 minutes or so, then add the liquid, cover, and let the soup simmer until the vegetables are tender. I find a pressure cooker perfect for making soups because it cuts the simmering time down to 5 minutes or so for most soups. But a largish saucepan will do just as well – you usually need to allow 15–20 minutes simmering time. After that you simply purée the soup, return it to the pan, add more liquid – water, milk or cream – and any extra flavourings if necessary, season to taste, reheat and serve.

Some fresh herbs snipped over the soup are a nice finishing touch, or you can add a garnish such as toasted flaked almonds, grated cheese (which makes it into more of a meal) or croûtons (see next page). Garlic bread also goes well with soup; it's easy to make and I think there are few things more appetizing than the smell of garlic bread wafting through the house: a recipe follows.

Roasted red pepper and sweet potato soup (page 32)

Croûtons

Slice your bread quite thickly, then cut it into little cubes. Heat a layer of olive oil in a frying pan until it is quite hot, then add the bread cubes and fry for a few minutes until they are golden brown and crisp, stirring them around to brown all the sides. Drain on paper towels.

Garlic bread

To serve 4–6 people you need a large baguette, 125 g/4 oz of softened butter, 2–4 garlic cloves, crushed, and a tablespoon or so of chopped parsley and chives.

Beat the butter and garlic together with a spoon or whiz them in a food processor (in which case you don't need to crush the garlic first) until the butter is light and creamy; mix in the herbs. Cut the bread diagonally, almost through to the crust, into slices about 2.5 cm/ 1 inch wide, then spread the garlic butter in the cuts. Wrap the bread in foil (you may need to halve the baguette and make two parcels).

Heat the oven to 200°C/400°F/Gas Mark 6. Just before you want to eat the garlic bread, pop it in the oven for about 20 minutes. If you want it to be golden and crisp, unwrap it for the last 5–10 minutes. Serve at once, while it is hot and buttery.

Vegetable stock

The vegetables suggested here make a good all-purpose stock. Other vegetables, such as tomatoes, cabbage or broccoli, will have a more pronounced effect on colour and taste – which would be fine for a soup with mixed or strong flavours, You can also add the liquid strained from cooked vegetables to the stockpot, to make the most of their flavour and the water-soluble vitamins B and C.

MAKES ABOUT 1 LITRE/1¾ PINTS
900 g/2 lb mixed vegetables and trimmings
  (onions, celery, carrots, leeks)
4–5 garlic cloves (no need to peel them)
several parsley stalks
2–3 bay leaves
a sprig of thyme
1 tablespoon peppercorns
a strip of lemon peel

Put all the ingredients into a large saucepan and add about 1 litre/1¾ pints of cold water, or enough to just cover the vegetables. Bring to the boil, then put a lid on the pan and simmer gently until the vegetables are very soft, which will take about 20–30 minutes.

Leave to cool, then strain. Stock can be kept in a covered container in the refrigerator for 2–3 days. It can also be frozen in small containers such as ice cube trays, then popped out into a polythene bag.

Mushroom stock
For a dark, richly flavoured stock, add some mushroom trimmings, chopped whole mushrooms or a few dried mushrooms to the saucepan.

Potato and fresh herb soup

The flavour of this soup will vary, depending on the herbs you choose. Chopped fennel, dill, spring onions and lovage are all effective.

SERVES 4
25 g/1 oz butter or vegan margarine
1 onion, peeled and chopped
450 g/1 lb potatoes, peeled and diced
1 litre/1¾ pints vegetable stock or water
2 tablespoons chopped fresh parsley
2 tablespoons chopped fresh chives
2 tablespoons double cream or soya cream
  (optional)
salt and freshly ground black pepper
freshly grated nutmeg

Melt the butter or margarine in a large saucepan or pressure cooker; don't let it brown. Add the onion, give it a stir, then cover the pan and leave it to cook over a low heat, without browning, for 5 minutes.

Add the potatoes, stir well, cover and cook over a low heat for a further 5–10 minutes.

Pour in the stock or water and bring to the boil, then reduce the heat, cover the pan and leave to simmer until the potatoes are tender; this takes about 15 minutes, or 5 minutes in a pressure cooker.

Pour the soup into a blender or food processor and whiz until smooth. Pour the

Potato and fresh herb soup

soup back into the pan, add the chopped herbs and the cream if you are using it. Season to taste with salt, pepper and nutmeg and reheat gently. Serve in warmed bowls.

Delicate mushroom soup

If possible, use mushroom stock (page 30) to make this soup.

Cook the soup as described. While it is simmering, slice 225 g/8 oz mushrooms – little button ones or mixed wild mushrooms – and fry them gently in a little butter for 4–5 minutes, until they are tender. You could add a crushed garlic clove and finish with a squeeze of lemon juice.

Add the mushrooms and their buttery juices to the soup after you've liquidized it. Some chopped parsley or chives look good on top.

Creamy onion soup

Cook the soup as described. While it is simmering, fry another chopped onion very gently in a little butter for 10 minutes, until it is soft and golden but not browned.

Liquidize the soup, then stir in the fried onion (leave out the herbs). The cream is optional.

Watercress soup

Cook the soup as described then, when you put it into the blender or food processor, leave out the herbs and add a bunch or packet (75–100 g/ 3–3½ oz) of fresh watercress (first setting aside four nice-looking sprigs for the garnish). Liquidize to produce a beautiful green soup.

Serve in warmed bowls, and, if you like, top each bowl with a swirl of cream and one of the reserved sprigs of watercress.

Roasted red pepper and sweet potato soup

A lovely soup for a chilly day: warming and cheering in colour and in flavour.

SERVES 6
2 tablespoons olive oil
1 onion, peeled and chopped
2 garlic cloves, crushed
700 g/1½ lb sweet potatoes, peeled and diced
1.5 litres/2½ pints vegetable stock or water
2–3 sprigs of fresh thyme
3 large red peppers
salt and freshly ground black pepper
cayenne pepper
2–3 tablespoons fresh lemon juice
TO GARNISH
150 ml/5 fl oz soured cream
  or soya cream (optional)
sprigs of fresh thyme

Heat the oil in a large saucepan or pressure cooker and add the onion. Give it a stir, then cover the pan and leave it to cook over a low heat, without browning, for 5 minutes.

Add the garlic and potatoes, stir well, cover again and cook over a low heat for a further 5–10 minutes.

Pour in the stock or water, add the thyme and bring to the boil. Reduce the heat, cover the pan and leave to simmer until the potatoes are tender; this takes about 15 minutes, or 5 minutes in a pressure cooker.

While the soup is simmering, turn the grill to its highest setting. Cut the peppers in half and remove the seeds and stalks. Put the peppers shiny side up on a grill pan or baking sheet and grill for 10–15 minutes, until they are tender and charred in places. Remove from the grill, leave until cool enough to handle, then pull off the blistered, papery skin and cut the peppers into rough pieces.

Remove the thyme from the soup, then pour the soup into a blender or food processor, add the red peppers, and whiz until smooth. Pour the soup back into the pan, reheat gently and season well with salt, pepper, cayenne pepper and lemon juice to taste. Serve in warmed bowls, topped with some cream if you are using it, and small sprigs of thyme.

Leek and potato soup

Comforting as a hot soup, this can be left chunky if you don't have a blender – or purée half the mixture for an interesting texture. It can also be served chilled, as vichyssoise.

SERVES 4
25 g/1 oz butter or vegan margarine
450 g/1 lb leeks, washed and cut into
  5 mm/¼ inch slices
450 g/1 lb potatoes, peeled and cut into
  1 cm/½ inch dice
2 tablespoons double cream or soya cream
  (optional)
salt and freshly ground black pepper
freshly grated nutmeg
TO SERVE
chopped fresh parsley

Melt the butter or margarine in a large saucepan or pressure cooker. Add the leeks and potatoes and stir until they are all coated in the butter, then cover the pan and leave them to cook over a low heat, without browning, for 5 minutes.

Pour in 900 ml/1½ pints of water and bring to the boil, then reduce the heat, cover the pan and leave to simmer until the vegetables are tender; this takes about 15 minutes, or 5 minutes in a pressure cooker.

Liquidize half or all of the soup if you wish. Add the cream if you are using it, then season to taste with salt, pepper and grated nutmeg. Serve in warmed bowls, sprinkled with a little chopped parsley.

Vichyssoise
For the classic chilled variation, purée the soup in a blender or food processor, then pour it through a sieve for extra smoothness. Leave to cool, then add the cream and chill in the refrigerator. Taste and check the seasoning – it may need more, as chilling dulls the flavour of food – and add a little more cream if you like. Serve ice cold, sprinkled with some chopped chives.

Fresh tomato soup

This soup is best made with fresh tomatoes rather than canned ones. Lovely ripe summer tomatoes are ideal, but I often make it successfully in the winter months. In fact serving this soup in winter seems to bring some summer sunshine with it.

Serves 4

15 g/½ oz butter or 1 tablespoon olive oil
1 onion, peeled and chopped
325 g/12 oz potatoes, peeled and diced
450 g/1 lb fresh tomatoes, sliced but not peeled
900 ml/1½ pints vegetable stock or water
150 ml/5 fl oz single cream or soya cream
  (optional)
salt and freshly ground black pepper
pinch of sugar
chopped fresh herbs (if available)

Warm the butter or olive oil in a large saucepan – don't let the butter brown. Add the onion, stir, cover the pan and leave to cook over a low heat for 5 minutes.

Add the potatoes, stir well, cover again and cook for a further 5–10 minutes, being careful not to let the vegetables brown as this would spoil the delicate flavour.

Add the tomatoes and stock or water, bring to the boil, then reduce the heat, cover the pan and leave to simmer until the potato is tender, about 15 minutes.

Purée the soup in a blender or food processor, then pour it through a sieve back into the pan, to remove the seeds and skins from the tomatoes. Add the cream if you are using it, then season to taste with salt, pepper and a pinch of sugar. Reheat gently and serve with fresh herbs snipped over the top.

Lentil soup

A nutritious soup that can be varied quite a bit by adding different vegetables and spices to the basic mixture. I find the simplest version is a great pick-me-up, especially if sprinkled with plenty of fresh parsley.

Serves 4

1 tablespoon olive oil
1 large onion, peeled and chopped
2 garlic cloves, crushed
1–2 carrots, peeled and diced
225 g/8 oz split red lentils
1 litre/1¾ pints vegetable stock or water
1–2 teaspoons fresh lemon juice
salt and freshly ground black pepper

Heat the oil in a large saucepan, add the onion, stir, then cover and cook over a low heat for 5 minutes. Add the garlic, carrots and lentils and stir for 1–2 minutes, then pour in the stock or water. Bring to the boil, then half cover the pan and leave to simmer gently for 20 minutes, until the lentils are very tender and pale.

Beat the soup with a wooden spoon to break up the lentils and make it smoother, or purée in a blender or food processor. Thin it with extra liquid if necessary, then add the lemon juice and salt and pepper to taste.

Spicy lentil soup

Add 1–2 teaspoons each of ground cumin and ground coriander at the same time as the garlic, carrots and lentils.

Lentil soup with spiced onion topping

Cook the soup as described. While it is simmering, fry a finely chopped onion in 1 tablespoon of olive oil for 5 minutes or until soft. Add 1–2 teaspoons each of ground cumin (or whole cumin seeds) and ground coriander. Add a spoonful of this mixture to each bowl of soup and top with a few fresh coriander leaves.

Carrot and dill soup

Jewel-bright and fresh-tasting, this is one of the most versatile soups in a cook's repertoire because it can be varied in so many ways. Replacing the carrots with other vegetables can extend the repertoire even further.

SERVES 4

25 g/1 oz butter or vegan margarine
1 onion, peeled and chopped
450 g/1 lb carrots, scraped and sliced
225 g/8 oz potatoes, peeled and diced
900 ml/1 ½ pints vegetable stock or water
salt and freshly ground black pepper
150 ml/5 fl oz single cream or soya cream
   (optional)
3–4 sprigs of dill

Heat the butter or margarine in a large saucepan, then add the onion, cover the pan and cook over a low heat for 5 minutes.

Add the carrots and potatoes, stir well, cover again and cook gently for a further 10 minutes, stirring from time to time.

Add the stock or water, bring to the boil, then simmer gently for about 15 minutes, until the carrots are tender.

Pour the soup into a blender or food processor and whiz until smooth. Rinse out the saucepan and return the soup to the pan. Thin with a little water if necessary. Reheat gently and season to taste with salt and pepper. If you wish to make the soup richer, stir in the cream, or ladle the soup into warmed bowls and spoon some cream on top. Top each bowl of soup with a few feathery fronds of dill.

Carrot and coriander soup
Mix in 1 teaspoon of ground coriander with the carrots and potatoes. Snip some fresh coriander leaves over the soup just before serving.

Dill has a subtle flavour, and its feathery leaves make an attractive garnish

Carrot and ginger soup
Add 1–2 teaspoons of grated fresh ginger to the pan along with the carrots and potatoes.

Carrot and orange soup
When you purée the soup, add the grated rind and freshly squeezed juice of 1 orange.

Beetroot soup
Replace the carrots with 225 g/8 oz cooked beetroot – not the sort that has been dressed with vinegar. Serve with a spoonful of soured cream and some chopped fresh dill on top.

Swede or parsnip soup
Replace the carrots with swede or parsnip. Swede soup is good flavoured with ¹/₂ teaspoon of ground cinnamon, added with the potatoes. A curry flavour goes well with parsnips – add 2–3 teaspoons of curry powder with the potatoes. Top either soup with a swirl of yogurt.

Chilled cucumber soup

A no-cook soup that makes a refreshing first course in summer. You will need a blender or food processor for this.

SERVES 6
1 large cucumber, peeled and cut into chunks
1 small onion, peeled and roughly chopped
1 garlic clove, crushed
450 ml/15 fl oz natural yogurt
2–3 tablespoons double cream
1 tablespoon red wine vinegar
salt and freshly ground black pepper
1–2 tablespoons chopped fresh chives or mint

Put the cucumber chunks into a blender or food processor with the onion, garlic and about a third of the yogurt. Blend until smooth, then add the rest of the yogurt and the cream and blend again. Add the vinegar and season carefully to taste, then chill the soup in the refrigerator.

Check the seasoning before serving in chilled bowls, scattered with chopped chives or mint.

Vegetable and bean soup

A vegetable soup is made more substantial by adding some beans or lentils. You can use either canned or dried beans; if you're using dried beans, you need to soak and cook them first (see page 125), so the vegetables in the soup don't get overdone. You can vary the vegetables according to what is available.

This soup reheats well and tastes as good or even better the next day, after the flavours have had a chance to develop.

SERVES 4
2 tablespoons olive oil
1 onion, peeled and chopped
2 garlic cloves, crushed
125 g/4 oz haricot beans, soaked, cooked and drained, or 425 g/15 oz canned cannellini beans, drained
2 carrots, cut into 5 mm/¼ inch slices
2 potatoes, peeled and cut into 1 cm/½ inch dice
3 leeks or courgettes, washed and sliced
400 g/14 oz canned chopped tomatoes
1 litre/1¾ pints vegetable stock
salt and freshly ground black pepper
sprigs of fresh basil (optional)

Heat the oil in a large saucepan, add the onion, stir, then cover and cook over a low heat for 5 minutes. Add the garlic, beans and the vegetables (including the tomatoes) and cook for a further 5 minutes. Pour in the stock, cover and simmer for about 30 minutes.

Season to taste and, if you are using fresh basil, tear it into the soup just before you serve it.

Minestrone
This is substantial enough to be a meal in itself. After you have simmered the soup for about 20 minutes, add 125 g/4 oz of green (French) beans, cut into 2 cm/³/₄ inch pieces, 125 g/4 oz of peas or baby broad beans and 125 g/4 oz of macaroni or other small pasta shapes. Simmer for a further 10–15 minutes, until the pasta is tender. Season to taste, stir in 2 tablespoons of chopped fresh parsley and serve with grated Parmesan cheese.

starters

It seems to me that dips make excellent first courses, being, usually, light, piquant and appetite-arousing. Dips can be served in a bowl with crisp raw vegetables (crudités) to dip into them, and they make good toppings for crostini (page 38) or crackers, fillings for sandwiches or even dressings for salads. They can be made to look pretty on a plate and served with fresh herbs, lettuce hearts, grated carrots, olives, sliced hard-boiled eggs . . . there's plenty of scope.

Many dishes can be served as first courses as long as helpings are quite small so that they don't fill people up too much before the main course. For me, perfect starters need to be simple, light and quick to make, and if I'm serving them for a special occasion I like to be able to get them done and out of the way, so I prefer those that need the minimum of last-minute attention.

There are plenty of other dishes in this book that also make good first courses: soups, of course; salads, such as rocket served with vinaigrette dressing and flakes of good fresh Parmesan cheese, the Carrot, orange, watercress and red pepper salad (page 60), Grilled goats' cheese salad (page 57), or perhaps a selection of three small salads: Mixed bean salad (page 128), Tomato salad (page 59) and grated celeriac mixed with a mustardy mayonnaise (page 56).

In spring and early summer, cooked asparagus served hot with melted butter, good olive oil or Hollandaise sauce (page 84) is another favourite of mine. Or, as far as I'm concerned, there's really nothing to beat a perfect, buttery avocado half, which melts in your mouth, with some good tangy vinaigrette (page 54).

The Cheese and walnut terrine (page 74) was originally a starter, but I more often make it as a main course, to serve with a salad. Italians would also serve risotto (page 118) as a first course. I generally prefer making a cheese, egg, pasta, grain or pastry dish as a main course, because I feel it makes for a better balance in a vegetarian meal, but if you are serving a vegetable-based main course, almost any of the dishes in the Eggs or Cheese chapters are excellent served as a first course: just keep the portions small.

Globe artichokes make a delicious light starter, served with vinaigrette dressing (page 47)

Crudités

Crudités – fresh vegetables, served with the minimum of preparation – are lovely for serving with dips, or just on their own, perhaps with a few juicy olives, as a starter or nibble at any time. The secret of good crudités is to use the freshest vegetables, washed and trimmed as necessary, and a vibrant mixture of colours.

Radishes are great with their green leaves still attached if these are fresh and perky; celery and spring onions just need the bases or roots trimming and perhaps a little off the top; cauliflower and broccoli can be separated into florets, chicory into individual leaves. Cut carrots, beetroot, celeriac and cucumber into batons. Deseed red, green or yellow peppers and cut into chunky strips.

Crudités can be prepared an hour or two ahead and kept in a polythene bag in the refrigerator until just before you want to serve them. Scatter with a few fresh herbs, such as sprigs of mint, parsley and coriander.

Crostini

Crostini are small crunchy circles of bread that can be topped with all kinds of tasty morsels and dips. They make a good accompaniment to soups and an excellent nibble with drinks.

To make crostini, cut a baguette into 5 mm– 1 cm/¼–½ inch slices. You can brush the slices on each side with olive oil if you wish – that's the classic way – but if the bread is good, you can make a lighter version without the oil. Lay the slices of bread on a baking sheet and place in a cool oven, 150°C/300°F/Gas Mark 2, for 15–20 minutes or until they are dry and crisp, turning them over after about 10 minutes when the tops are dry. Leave to cool on a wire rack. They will keep for a day or so in a tin, but they are at their best when freshly made.

Put the toppings on the crostini just before you serve them, so that they remain crisp.

Bruschetta

This is a more rustic version of crostini. The bruschetta can be served as it is or topped with delicious morsels. Chopped ripe plum tomatoes, fresh basil and a drizzle of olive oil – sometimes some fresh mozzarella cheese, too – is a popular topping.

To make bruschetta, cut a coarse-textured country-style bread (white or brown) into thick slices. Toast the bread on both sides – in a toaster, under the grill, or in a ridged cast-iron chargrilling pan. Cut a garlic clove in half and rub it all over one side of each piece of toast, then brush the toast with olive oil. Pile on your chosen topping and serve at once.

Toppings for crostini and bruschetta

Roquefort dip (page 40) with fresh walnuts, olives and parsley.
Tofu dip (page 40) with olives and sun-dried tomatoes.
Guacamole (page 41) with fresh coriander and a sprinkling of paprika.
Hummus (page 46) with olives, paprika and a drizzle of good olive oil.
White bean pâté (page 46) with black olives and parsley.
Thin circles of goats' cheese with Black olive pâté (page 41).
Cucumber and yogurt dip (page 46) with a sprig of whatever herb is in the dip.
Smooth goats' cheese with sprigs of fresh mint.
Skinned and chopped ripe tomatoes, torn fresh basil leaves and a drizzle of olive oil.
Grilled red and yellow peppers (see page 44), torn fresh basil leaves and crumbled feta cheese.
Sliced ripe avocado tossed in a little lime juice or wine vinegar and olive oil.
Soft white cheese with cooked asparagus tips.
Scrambled eggs and cooked asparagus tips.

Crostini with Guacamole (page 41), Roquefort dip and Tofu dip (page 40)

Roquefort dip

This is excellent served with crostini (page 38) or crudités or, for a more dressed-up first course, you could spoon it on top of peeled and sliced ripe pears and decorate with some sprigs of watercress and fresh walnut halves.

SERVES 4
100 g/3½ oz Roquefort cheese
225 g/8 oz smooth low-fat cheese
   such as quark
salt and freshly ground black pepper

Roquefort cheese is often sold in a pack that contains a little water, so first drain this off, then crumble the cheese roughly into a food processor or bowl. Add the low-fat cheese and whiz or mash together with a fork until combined. Season to taste – you'll probably only need pepper as the Roquefort is quite salty. Pile the mixture into a serving bowl.

Variation
You can use other cheeses instead of the Roquefort: Stilton or Danish Blue, for instance, or a strong goats' cheese, which I think is especially good. Cut the cheese into cubes, including the rind of the goats' cheese, then whiz in a food processor or mash with a fork.

Tofu dip

Tofu makes a good dip but it's quite bland, so it needs some assertive flavourings. Sun-dried tomatoes are ideal, as are black olives and fresh herbs. Here is one of my favourite mixtures. Serve with warm wholemeal pitta bread, wholemeal toast or crudités.

SERVES 4
275 g/10 oz firm tofu
8 sun-dried tomatoes, drained of oil
2 spring onions, trimmed and roughly chopped
2 garlic cloves, crushed
salt and freshly ground black pepper

Tofu is usually packaged or stored in water, so first drain this off and pat the tofu dry on paper towels. Then cut the tofu into rough chunks and put them in a food processor or blender with the tomatoes, spring onions and garlic. Blend to a creamy purée: check to make sure that there are no chunks of garlic left in the mixture, and if necessary scrape around the sides of the blender with a plastic spatula, then blend again. Season to taste, then spoon into a serving bowl.

Tofu and cashew nut dip
Leave out the sun-dried tomatoes and add 100 g/ 3½ oz of roasted salted cashew nuts and a few sprigs of fresh parsley. Blend until fairly smooth, then stir in 2 tablespoons of chopped fresh chives – these are best chopped separately and added last, as they do not chop well in a food processor.

Guacamole

This is an authentic Mexican guacamole. Serve it with tortilla chips or crudités.

The secrets of success are, first, to make sure that the avocados you use are really ripe: press them gently near the stalk to see if they yield. They ripen in a day or so if you leave them at room temperature. Secondly, prepare them not more than about 30 minutes before you want to eat them, otherwise they are likely to discolour. Thirdly, cut and mash them with a stainless steel knife and fork: other metals may leave a metallic flavour.

SERVES 4–6

1 fresh green chilli
4 ripe tomatoes
3 tablespoons chopped fresh coriander
2 large ripe avocados
salt and freshly ground black pepper

Cut the chilli in half lengthways and rinse away the seeds under cold running water. Slice it finely and set aside. Be sure to wash your hands thoroughly to remove all traces of the chilli juice, which can sting.

Wash the tomatoes, then chop them finely and put them into a serving bowl, along with the coriander. Cover the bowl and keep it in a cool place – this can be done in advance.

Just before you want to serve the guacamole, halve each avocado and remove the stone. Use a small spoon to scoop the flesh into the bowl with the tomatoes and coriander and mash well with a fork. Add the chilli a little at a time, tasting to get the right degree of heat for you. Season to taste and serve as soon as possible.

Black olive pâté

A rich-tasting pâté that is good spread on crostini (page 38). You can find the dried chillies with the spices in any supermarket, or you could use a good pinch of chilli powder or cayenne pepper instead. You will need a food processor or blender to make this.

SERVES 4–6

125 g/4 oz pitted black olives
2 tablespoons drained capers
1 garlic clove, roughly chopped
1 dried red chilli, crumbled, or a good pinch of chilli powder
4 tablespoons olive oil
salt and freshly ground black pepper

Put the olives, capers, garlic and chilli into a food processor or blender and whiz until smooth. Then, with the motor running, pour the olive oil in through the top of the processor, to make a thick, shiny purée. Season to taste – you'll probably only need pepper because of the saltiness of the olives and capers. Spoon the mixture into a small serving bowl.

Mushroom and cream cheese pâté

I prefer to use a low-fat or medium-fat soft cheese: curd cheese or one of the smooth packaged varieties. Serve the pâté with crisp toast, or as a sandwich filling. You will need a food processor or blender to make this.

SERVES 4
450 g/1 lb mushrooms, quickly washed and
     drained
50 g/2 oz butter or margarine
2 garlic cloves, crushed
200 g/7 oz soft white cheese
6 good sprigs of parsley, main stems removed
salt and freshly ground black pepper

Slice the mushrooms – there's no need to make them too fine, as they will be puréed later. Melt the butter or margarine in a large saucepan, add the mushrooms and cook over a moderate heat for 15–20 minutes. They will probably produce a lot of liquid and you need to cook them (without a lid on the pan) until all the liquid has disappeared.

Next, tip the mushrooms into a food processor or blender. Add the garlic, soft cheese and parsley and whiz to a purée – make it coarse or smooth, as you prefer. Season to taste, then spoon into a small serving bowl and leave until completely cold – it will firm up slightly.

Variation
For a vegan version, replace the cheese with the same amount of drained tofu.

Pink grapefruit and fennel

If you want a refreshing, taste-bud tingling starter, then this is it; both ingredients are appetite-enhancing. Choose really juicy grapefruit by weighing them in your hand: the heavier, the better.

SERVES 4
2 pink grapefruit
1 medium-sized fennel bulb (about 225 g/8 oz)
a little clear honey or sugar (optional)

Cut the peel and pith off the grapefruit using a sharp knife, cutting around it as if you were peeling an apple and trying to keep the peel in one piece. Hold the grapefruit over a bowl as you work, to catch the juice. Then, still working over the bowl, cut each segment away from the translucent white membranes and put the segments into the bowl. Drain off the excess juice – you don't need it for this recipe.

Trim the leafy bits off the fennel and set them aside. Using a sharp knife, cut away and discard any tough outer layers. Stand the fennel on its base and cut it in half, then cut each half into very thin slices. Add these to the bowl with the grapefruit. Taste and add a little honey or sugar if you think it necessary. Serve in individual plates and top with the reserved feathery fennel leaves.

Pink grapefruit and avocado
Instead of the fennel, use 1 large or 2 small avocados. Halve the avocados, remove the stones and skin and cut the flesh into fairly thin slices. Very gently mix with the grapefruit. A little chopped fresh mint is good with this.

Pink grapefruit and fennel

Grilled pepper salad

In this salad the peppers are grilled and skinned, so they become soft and sweet-tasting. Serve as part of a salad buffet, or as a starter, with bread to mop up the juices.

For a more substantial salad, excellent as a light meal, serve with rocket leaves, or some cooked couscous (see page 114), or a little soft goats' cheese and some black olives.

SERVES 4
2 red peppers
2 yellow peppers
1 tablespoon balsamic or rice vinegar
1 tablespoon olive oil
salt and freshly ground black pepper
1 tablespoon capers (optional)
a few sprigs of fresh basil

Heat the grill to high. Cut the peppers in half and remove the stems, seeds and pale inner membranes, using a sharp knife. Put the peppers, cut side down, on a grill pan or a baking sheet that will fit under your grill. Grill the peppers for 10–15 minutes, turning them from time to time, until the skin blisters and blackens in places. Leave the peppers to cool – to help loosen the skins you can cover them with a plate to keep the steam in.

Remove the skins with a sharp knife and cut the peppers into strips. Put the vinegar and oil into a bowl with some salt and pepper and mix together. Add the pepper strips and the capers if you are using them. Mix gently so that they are all coated with the oil. You can serve this salad immediately, but it's best if you leave it for 1–2 hours to allow the flavours to mingle.

Just before serving, tear the basil leaves over the top.

Hot oyster mushroom salad

I generally make this with oyster mushrooms because they're quite widely available, though you could use other varieties of mushrooms. Serve with some warm bread to soak up the delicious mushroomy juices.

SERVES 4
225 g/8 oz oyster mushrooms
2 tablespoons olive oil
2 garlic cloves, crushed
salt and freshly ground black pepper
about 125 g/4 oz green salad leaves, such as
  rocket or frisée
TO SERVE (OPTIONAL)
a small handful of flat-leaf parsley
a few flakes of fresh Parmesan cheese

Wipe the mushrooms carefully with a damp cloth or give them a quick rinse under the tap and then pat them dry on paper towels. Halve or quarter any large mushrooms.

Heat the olive oil in a large saucepan and put in the mushrooms and garlic. Cook over a fairly high heat, stirring (gently) often, until the mushrooms are tender – about 5 minutes. Season to taste.

While the mushrooms are cooking, arrange a few salad leaves on four plates. Spoon the hot mushrooms on to the leaves, then pour over any juice left in the pan. Snip a little parsley on top or scatter with a few flakes of Parmesan if you wish, then serve immediately.

Hot oyster mushroom salad

Cucumber and yogurt dip

This is my version of the Greek tzatziki. It makes a refreshing starter served with warm pitta bread or crudités, and is also good as part of a salad buffet. It's best not to make it too far in advance because it can become a little watery if left to stand.

SERVES 4–6
1 cucumber
salt and freshly ground black pepper
500 g/1 lb 2 oz Greek strained yogurt
1 tablespoon chopped fresh parsley
1 tablespoon chopped fresh chives
4–6 black olives (optional)

Peel the cucumber thinly, using a potato peeler, then cut it into 3 mm/⅛ inch dice, or grate it coarsely. Put it into a colander or sieve; sprinkle with a little salt and leave until nearly ready to serve. (The salt will draw excess liquid out of the cucumber, preventing the dip from becoming too liquid.)

Pat the cucumber dry on paper towels. Put the yogurt into a bowl, add the cucumber, herbs and some salt and pepper to taste – go easy on the salt, remembering that the cucumber has already been salted. Spoon the mixture into a bowl; or put a spoonful on to individual plates and garnish with a black olive – as served in tavernas in Greece!

Variations
Replace the chives and/or parsley with chopped fresh mint or dill.

For vegans, use plain, unsweetened soya yogurt or silken tofu instead of the Greek yogurt.

Hummus

Although hummus is quite widely available, homemade hummus is really delicious and works out much cheaper than the bought variety. It's very easy to make if you've got a food processor. It's important to use a light tahini (sesame seed paste or sesame cream): the dark one is much too bitter.

Hummus and tahini dip can also be served as sauces with steamed vegetables, or as creamy salad dressings.

SERVES 2–4
400 g/14 oz canned chickpeas
1 tablespoon light tahini
1–2 garlic cloves, crushed
2 tablespoons fresh lemon juice
1 tablespoon olive oil
chilli powder (optional)
salt and freshly ground black pepper
TO SERVE (OPTIONAL)
paprika
extra virgin olive oil
lemon wedges
black olives

Drain the chickpeas, keeping the liquid. Put them into a food processor, along with the tahini, garlic, lemon juice and olive oil and whiz until smooth, then gradually pour in the reserved chickpea liquid until the mixture has the consistency of lightly whipped cream. Add a pinch or two of chilli powder if you wish, then season with salt and pepper.

If you want to dress it up prettily, spread the hummus on a flat plate and sprinkle with a little paprika. Drizzle a little olive oil over the top, then arrange some lemon wedges and black olives around the edge.

Tahini dip
Omit the chickpeas. Put 6 tablespoons of tahini into a small bowl with the garlic, 2 teaspoons of lemon juice and 4 tablespoons of water, and stir. The mixture will be thick and lumpy at first, but don't despair, just keep on mixing and adding more lemon juice and water – it will gradually become smooth and creamy. Add 1–2 tablespoons of olive oil and 1 tablespoon of chopped fresh parsley and stir in, then add more water and lemon juice until you have the consistency and flavour you want, and season to taste.

White bean pâté
Replace the chickpeas with canned (or home-cooked) cannellini, haricot or butter beans and leave out the tahini. Stir in a dash of red wine vinegar or Tabasco sauce at the end.

Leeks vinaigrette

This is best made with tender, small leeks; you can sometimes buy them as thin as a pencil.

SERVES 4
700 g/1½ lb slim young leeks
2 tablespoons wine vinegar
6 tablespoons olive oil
salt and freshly ground black pepper
1–2 tablespoons chopped fresh parsley

Trim the roots off the leeks and cut the green top part to within about 2.5–5 cm/1–2 inches of the white part. Slit the leeks along one side, then wash them under cold running water, gently opening the cut to rinse out any dirt, but making sure the leeks hold together.

Bring a large saucepan of water to the boil, add the leeks and simmer until they are just tender: 7–20 minutes depending on their size. They are done when they can be pierced easily with the tip of a sharp knife. Drain thoroughly – the water makes particularly good stock.

While the leeks are cooking, whisk together the vinegar, oil and some salt and pepper for the dressing.

Put the leeks on a flat plate, pour over the dressing and turn the leeks to make sure they are coated all over with the dressing. Leave to cool, turning them a couple more times. Serve sprinkled with chopped parsley.

Artichokes vinaigrette
Choose green, fresh-looking artichokes. Trim and boil them as described on page 88. When they are tender, plunge them into a bowl of cold water to 'set' the colour, then turn them upside down to drain thoroughly.

Gently separate the outer leaves and pull out the tender leaves in the centre; they will come away in a cone shape, revealing the hairy 'choke', which must be removed. Do this with a sharp-edged teaspoon – make sure you remove every bit of it. Pour a little vinaigrette into the centre of each artichoke.

Asparagus vinaigrette
If the asparagus is untrimmed, gently bend the stem until it snaps off: it will break where the stem begins to get tough. Make sure the asparagus is clean and grit-free. Boil, drain well and dress as for the leeks. Some flakes of fresh Parmesan cheese make a delicious garnish for asparagus.

Broccoli vinaigrette
Use even-sized florets of broccoli, boil and dress as for the leeks. Alternatively, use a mixture of broccoli and red peppers (these are best grilled – see page 44).

French bean vinaigrette
Choose young, tender green beans. Trim them as necessary: you could 'top and tail' them, though I like to leave them whole. Boil them until they are tender, which may be for as little as 2 minutes. Some chopped hard-boiled egg makes a good garnish for these.

salads and dressings

Salads are quick to make and it's easy to create exciting effects with minimum cooking. The colours are fresh and vibrant and you can introduce many different flavours and textures, with interesting dressings using hot chillies, sharp lime, sweet-and-sour balsamic vinegar, pungent garlic, and additions ranging from buttery avocado and sweet fruits to crisp nuts or croûtons. Salads make some of the best first courses, because they are fresh and light, stimulating the taste buds. A salad is also an easy side dish, as well as an excellent main course in itself, with a few additions and accompaniments, such as bread or a baked potato.

The first requirement for any salad is that the ingredients need to be really fresh and of good quality, so look for perky or plump specimens and avoid any that show signs of wilting. Use vegetables in season for variety and flavour all the year round. Lovely firm cabbages for homemade coleslaw in the winter; fragrant, sun-ripened tomatoes in the summer, along with red, yellow and green peppers, cucumbers, tender lettuces, refreshing fennel, radishes, spring onions and fresh herbs; as autumn approaches there are sweet apples and new walnuts to combine with crisp celery to make delicious Waldorf salad.

For leaves or vegetables to be used raw, wash them well in cold water then dry by whirling in a salad spinner or leaving them to drain in a colander. Then you can put them into a polythene bag and leave them to get crisp in the bottom of the refrigerator, ready for when you want to use them.

If you're making a salad from cooked vegetables, be careful not to overcook them. To retain crispness and preserve vitamins you can either parboil them (this is often referred to as blanching), or boil or steam them until they are just tender when pierced with the tip of a knife. It's often a good idea to mix cooked vegetables, such as potatoes or leeks, with the dressing while they are still hot, as they will absorb it well then.

You will find other salads in the chapters on Starters, Pasta, Pulses, and Rice and grains.

Spinach can be served as a salad on its own, or mixed with other salad leaves

salad basics

Asparagus

Break off the woody base of the stalk, if necessary. Lightly boil or steam, then rinse in cold water to 'set' the colour and prevent the asparagus from overcooking; drain well. Serve with rocket and halved cherry tomatoes, with vinaigrette (page 54), and shavings of fresh Parmesan cheese if you like.

Avocado

Slice lengthways, prise out the stone and remove the skin, then place the two halves cut side down on a chopping board and slice. Sprinkle with lemon or lime juice to prevent discoloration, and add to a green salad.

Beans

Small, young green beans add a crunchy texture to salads such as Salade niçoise (page 61). Lightly boil, then rinse in cold water to 'set' the colour and drain well.

Dried beans and lentils make more substantial salads – I've described one on page 128. Cook them yourself (see page 125) or use canned beans; drain and rinse, then mix with vinaigrette, some chopped red or green pepper, and plenty of herbs.

Beetroot

Buy it raw if possible. Peel, grate and toss in some vinaigrette or freshly squeezed orange juice. Serve on lettuce leaves with some fresh mint snipped over.

Alternatively, cook it as described on page 89 (or buy ready-boiled beetroot – but not the sort that is dressed in vinegar) and serve it sliced or cubed, with vinaigrette and perhaps some chopped spring onions, or with Yogurt and honey dressing (page 56).

Cabbage

White, red and green cabbages can all be made into salads. Shred them finely, using a sharp knife or the slicing attachment on a food processor, then mix with vinaigrette or another dressing, which will help to soften the cabbage. Add other ingredients for colour and flavour (see Coleslaw, page 60).

Carrots

Grate and toss with vinaigrette to which you have added the freshly squeezed juice of 1 or 2 oranges. Raisins and toasted flaked almonds are good additions.

Cauliflower

Cut into small florets and serve with Yogurt and honey dressing (page 56).

Celeriac

Peel thickly to remove lumpy skin, then grate coarsely and mix with vinaigrette or mayonnaise (made with Dijon mustard) and chopped fresh chives or other herbs. Or cut it into matchsticks and serve with dips.

Celery

Cut into slices or matchsticks and add to other salad mixtures – it's good with cabbage or beetroot, or with apples, walnuts and mayonnaise. Serve in sticks with dips, or with cheese at the end of a meal.

Chicory

Slice the crisp white buds into quarters or eighths, or cut them across into rings and serve in green salads. Their slightly bitter flavour makes a refreshing contrast to rich food, and goes well with sliced oranges. Separate the leaves to serve with dips.

Chinese leaves

Also known as Peking cabbage or pe tsai, these need a lively dressing to perk them up – try the Thai-style dressing (page 54), Yogurt and honey dressing (page 56), or vinaigrette made with plenty of fresh herbs. Shred the leaves into 5 mm/¼ inch slices, then mix with the dressing. Watercress or grated carrot go well with them.

Courgettes

Slice thinly and toss in a lemon dressing (page 54), with fresh basil, parsley or chives.

Crisp, appetizing radishes

Cucumber

Make sure the cucumber is firm, so that it will be crisp. You can peel the cucumber thinly with a potato peeler, or use it with the skin on, especially if it's young, tender and locally grown. Cut the cucumber into thin slices, little dice or chunky lengths and add to salad bowls or sandwiches, or serve with dips.

Daikon

Also known as mooli, this long white root, about the same circumference as a cucumber, has a hot, radish-like flavour. Slice it thinly, cut it into small dice or into matchsticks. It's nice as a crudité or in an oriental-style salad; try it with Thai-style dressing (page 54).

Endive

Sometimes known as frisée or curly endive, the lacy, crisp, bitter leaves are good as part of a green salad or on their own, tossed in vinaigrette. Remove the tough outer leaves, separate the inner ones, wash thoroughly, then tear or cut into bite-sized pieces.

Escarole

Sometimes known as Batavian endive, this has a very crisp texture, and is slightly less bitter than the very curly endives. Use in a mixed green salad.

Fennel

An ideal salad ingredient because of its crisp texture and refreshing, appetizing, aniseed flavour. Trim off the stalk ends and peel the outside of the white bracts to remove any tough or stringy bits, then slice.

Lambs' lettuce

The tender little leaves of lambs' lettuce (sometimes known as corn salad or mâche) are good on their own with a light vinaigrette dressing or as part of a green salad. Be gentle when washing and drying – use a salad spinner or blot lightly with a clean tea towel.

Lettuce

There are so many varieties – curly, frilly, firm, tender, red, purple, every shade of green – that lettuce need never be boring. I think my favourite is feuille de chêne (oak leaf) in its bronze-purple variety. All lettuce needs very thorough washing, to remove any dirt and bugs if it's organic, or chemical residues if it's not. So swish it around in a deep bowl of cold water then dry it well before tearing the leaves into a bowl with a vinaigrette dressing. Lettuce leaves can also be used to make a base for other salads, such as grated carrot, beetroot or celeriac.

Peppers

Red, green, yellow and orange peppers can be simply chopped or sliced and added to many salads for their bright colours, crunchy texture and fresh flavour. Alternatively, grill them as described on page 44, and serve them on their own or stir them into cooked Puy lentils with some vinaigrette and fresh parsley, for a nutritious salad or starter.

Potatoes

Scrub new potatoes and boil them in their skins. Drain and halve or quarter if large, and toss with a little vinaigrette while they are still warm. Stir in some chopped spring onions and/or snipped fresh chives and plenty of freshly ground black pepper. Add mayonnaise and/or yogurt if you like.

Radicchio

Bitter, purple-red heads of a variety of chicory, which make a pretty contrast to other salad leaves. The leaves can be torn or shredded if they are large. Most people find radicchio rather bitter on its own; instead, try it with something sweet like sliced ripe pears for an interesting salad.

Radishes

These are usually freshest if sold in a bunch with their leaves still attached. With or without the leaves, make sure the radishes themselves are firm, not flabby or wrinkled. Wash and trim the roots but keep the leaves on and serve with dips or just some crunchy sea salt, as an appetizer.

Rocket

Why are these peppery-tasting leaves sold in such small quantities, as if they were a herb? The best place to get them is a Middle Eastern

Rocket leaves have an unusual, slightly peppery flavour

shop, where they come in decent-sized bunches, otherwise grow your own if you have a garden – they're easy to grow but run to seed quickly. Use them whole or tear up larger leaves. Toss in vinaigrette, or just a very light coating of extra virgin olive oil, perhaps with some flakes of Parmesan cheese, or mix them into a green salad.

Spinach
Baby spinach leaves are a delicious addition to a green salad, and are also good as a first course, tossed with garlic vinaigrette and sliced mushrooms, or croûtons (page 30) and crumbled blue cheese or cubes of Gruyère.

Spring onions
Trim off the roots and a little of the green part, then serve whole with a dip, or slice or chop and add to other salads for a fresh, mild onion flavour.

Tomatoes
Plum tomatoes are lovely in the summer, and cherry tomatoes are pretty, though I find they have rather too much skin in proportion to flesh. Skin tomatoes as described on page 93 or keep the skin on if it's unblemished and not tough. Slice into circles or cut in half down through the stalk end, cut away any tough part at the top where the stalk was, then slice the tomato into segments. Fresh basil is the perfect complementary flavour.

Watercress
Watercress can be bought ready washed and trimmed. If it's still in a bunch, remove the tough stalk ends and wash the leaves thoroughly. The hot-tasting leaves don't need much dressing, which is useful if you're cutting down on oil, and they go well with tomatoes, carrots and oranges for a cheering, vitamin-rich winter salad.

dressings

Vinaigrette

Vinaigrette is probably the most useful salad dressing. It is almost infinitely variable, depending on the type of vinegar and oil you use, the proportions and the other flavouring ingredients you add.

Classic proportions are 1 part vinegar to 3 parts oil; some people use 4 or 6 parts oil, especially if the oil is a fruity or peppery extra virgin olive oil. Personally I do not like too oily a dressing, and if I'm using my favourite light brown rice vinegar (sold in Japanese shops and some health food shops) I use a half-and-half mixture.

So feel free to experiment, taste as you go, and find the right proportions to suit you and the particular salad you are dressing.

Serves 4
1½ teaspoons salt
freshly ground black pepper
2 tablespoons red or white wine vinegar,
    balsamic or brown rice vinegar
6 tablespoons olive oil
pinch of caster sugar (optional)

Put the salt, several turns of the pepper mill, the vinegar and oil into a small bowl and whisk together. Alternatively, put the ingredients into a small screw-topped jar and shake well. Taste and, if you like, add a tiny pinch of caster sugar to round out the flavour.

The dressing can be kept in a jar in the refrigerator for about four weeks.

Variations
Finely chopped fresh herbs can be added to the dressing just before you use it.

Light vinaigrette
Make the dressing as described and add the freshly squeezed juice of 1–2 oranges.

Lemon dressing
Replace the vinegar with 1½ tablespoons fresh lemon juice.

Garlic vinaigrette
Add 1–3 crushed garlic cloves to the dressing.

Mustard vinaigrette
Add 1–3 teaspoons of a good mustard – a smooth or grainy Dijon or Meaux mustard.

Walnut vinaigrette
Replace some or all of the olive oil with walnut oil.

Raspberry vinaigrette
Use raspberry vinegar to make the dressing. Some brands are rather sweet, and you may need to add a squeeze of lemon juice to sharpen the taste.

Thai-style dressing

Brown rice vinegar is best for this dressing, but white or red wine vinegar can be used, since there are so many other flavours.

Serves 4
1 green chilli
1 spring onion
1 stalk of lemongrass
1 garlic clove, crushed
3 tablespoons brown rice vinegar,
    or red or white wine vinegar
3 tablespoons water
1 tablespoon caster sugar
1 tablespoon soy sauce
juice of 1 lime
1–2 tablespoons chopped fresh parsley
    or coriander (optional)

Halve, deseed and finely chop the chilli. Trim and slice the spring onion. Remove the hard outer layers of the lemongrass and slice the tender part paper-thin.

Put all the ingredients into a screw-topped jar and shake well, or whisk them together in a small bowl.

This can be kept in a jar in the refrigerator for about two weeks. Shake before serving.

Thinly sliced daikon with Thai-style dressing

Yogurt and honey dressing

A low-fat dressing with a sweet, tangy flavour.

MAKES 200 ML/7 FL OZ
1 tablespoon wholegrain mustard
1 tablespoon clear honey
2 tablespoons white wine vinegar or rice vinegar
150 ml/5 fl oz plain yogurt (dairy or soya)
salt and freshly ground black pepper

Mix the mustard, honey and vinegar together in a small bowl, then add the yogurt and mix until blended. Season to taste.

Creamy tofu dressing

A thick, non-dairy, low-fat dressing that can be used instead of mayonnaise.

MAKES ABOUT 125 ML/4 FL OZ
1 teaspoon mustard powder
150 g/5 oz firm tofu (or half a 285 g packet)
2 tablespoons brown rice vinegar
   or white wine vinegar
salt and freshly ground black pepper

Put all the ingredients into a food processor or blender and whiz to a smooth purée, adding a little cold water if necessary to bring the dressing to the consistency you want.

Classic mayonnaise

You can make mayonnaise very quickly in a blender but it won't have that wonderful thick texture of mayonnaise made by hand. If you're going to the trouble of making it yourself, it seems to me worth doing it properly. It doesn't take much longer, especially if you use an electric whisk. It can be kept in the refrigerator for four weeks.

All the ingredients need to be at the same temperature, so take the egg out of the refrigerator an hour or so before you want to make the mayonnaise. Use groundnut or corn oil rather than olive oil, which gives too strong a flavour.

For a larger quantity just double everything.

MAKES ABOUT 150 ML/5 FL OZ
½ teaspoon sea salt
freshly ground black pepper
1 teaspoon mustard powder
1 large egg yolk
150 ml/5 fl oz groundnut or corn oil
1–3 teaspoons red or white wine vinegar
   or lemon juice

Put the salt, pepper and mustard into a small bowl with the egg yolk and mix together well. Have the oil in a jug with a pouring spout, and begin to add it literally one drop at a time to the egg yolk mixture. Whisk it well before adding the next drop. That is the secret of success with homemade mayonnaise: each drop of oil must be absorbed into the egg yolk before you add the next drop.

After a while, however, the mixture will begin to thicken and from then on you can add the oil in larger amounts.

When you have added half the oil, whisk in 1–2 teaspoons of vinegar or lemon juice, then continue adding the oil until you have added it all and have a very thick mixture. Taste the mayonnaise and add another teaspoon or so of oil, vinegar or lemon juice if it needs it.

Aïoli

For the famous Provençal garlic version, crush 1–2 garlic cloves (or more if you like) with the salt at the beginning of the process. Olive oil would certainly be used in the south of France; replace some or all of the oil with olive oil to get the flavour you want.

Aïoli is particularly good with bean or lentil-based salads and also makes a superb dip for serving with crunchy fresh radishes, florets of cauliflower and other raw vegetables.

Tartare sauce

Stir into the finished mayonnaise a chopped gherkin, 1 teaspoon of chopped capers and 1 teaspoon of chopped fresh parsley or tarragon.

Vegan mayonnaise

This vegan version is surprisingly good (and it is also useful for people who have to be careful about using uncooked eggs). Simply replace the egg yolk with 2 tablespoons of soya milk.

Green salad

A leafy salad seems to go with almost everything, it's easier to prepare than a cooked vegetable, fresh tasting and very healthy. It's also versatile – and it doesn't have to be all green. You can use whatever salad leaves are available and add herbs, nuts, cheese or even fruit to vary the flavours and textures. I've suggested a few ideas below.

SERVES 4
200–225 g/7–8 oz salad leaves (one variety or a
   mixture, which could include lettuces such as lollo
   rosso or lamb's lettuce, radicchio, rocket, tender
   spinach leaves, or dandelion leaves picked from a
   non-polluted place)

FOR THE DRESSING
1 garlic clove, crushed
1 tablespoon balsamic, red wine
   or brown rice vinegar
2–3 tablespoons olive oil
salt and freshly ground black pepper

Wash the salad leaves, drain them in a colander or whirl them in a salad spinner, then keep them in a cool place, ideally in a polythene bag in the refrigerator, until you're ready to make the salad.

About 30 minutes before you want to eat the salad, put the crushed garlic, vinegar, oil and plenty of salt and pepper into a large bowl – you can use the one that you're planning to serve the salad from – and mix together. Cross the salad servers in the base of the bowl, then put the salad leaves on top. Leave the salad like this, with the crossed salad servers keeping the delicate leaves out of the dressing, until just before you want to eat the salad. Then toss the salad with the servers, so that all the leaves are lightly coated with dressing, and serve at once.

Variations
Add 1 diced ripe avocado to the leaves.

Add a 100 g/3½ oz packet of roasted cashew nuts or pine nuts to the salad when you toss it. If the nuts are salted, you won't need to add much salt when making the dressing.

Herb and flower salad
Add an assortment of chopped, torn or whole herbs to the mixture along with some edible flowers, such as nasturtiums, marigolds, borage, chive or other herb flowers.

Rocket salad with Parmesan shavings
For this, use just rocket leaves; put them into the bowl on top of the dressing as described. Cut a 125 g/4 oz piece of Parmesan cheese into flakes using a sharp knife or swivel-bladed potato peeler and add to the rocket. Toss the salad just before serving.

Grilled goats' cheese salad

A wonderful way to turn a green salad into something more substantial, to serve either as a starter or a light main course. You can use a mixture of green salad leaves, or I sometimes make it with one feuille de chêne lettuce.

SERVES 2 AS A MAIN COURSE, 4 AS A FIRST COURSE OR ACCOMPANIMENT
225 g/8 oz salad leaves
1 garlic clove, crushed
1 tablespoon red wine vinegar
2–3 tablespoons olive oil
salt and freshly ground black pepper
2 x 100 g/3½ oz firm goats' cheese logs
a small baguette about the same circumference as
   the cheese, cut into 8 x 7 mm/⅓ inch slices

Wash the salad leaves and put them into a colander to drain.

Mix the garlic, vinegar, oil, salt and pepper in a large salad bowl. Cross the salad servers in the base of the bowl and put the leaves on top – this can be done 30 minutes in advance.

Just before you want to serve the salad, prepare the goats' cheese croûtes. Heat the grill to high. Cut each of the goats' cheese logs into 4 slices. Toast the slices of baguette on one side under the grill, then turn them over and put a slice of goats' cheese on each. Pop them back under the grill for a minute or two until the cheese is flecked with brown and beginning to melt.

Toss the salad, then serve with the goats' cheese croûtes on top.

Tomato salad

This salad benefits from being made ahead of time to allow the flavours to develop. It's nicest made with ripe plum tomatoes in the summer, though I make it all the year round and find it useful for serving with dishes that need a touch of colour or something juicy to go with them. It's also very good on its own with some warm bread (baguette or ciabatta) as a starter or a light meal, perhaps with some soft white cheese, too.

SERVES 2–4
450 g/1 lb tomatoes
salt and freshly ground black pepper
1 teaspoon wine vinegar
2–3 tablespoons olive oil
several fresh basil leaves

Wash the tomatoes, then slice them into rounds or – if you are using plum tomatoes – downwards into long thin slices, discarding any hard pieces of stem or core. Put the tomatoes into a shallow dish and sprinkle with salt and pepper, the vinegar and olive oil. Tear some basil over them, stir gently, then leave in a cool place (not the refrigerator) until you want to eat the salad. Stir again gently just before serving.

Tomato and onion salad
Add a small onion or shallot, peeled and thinly sliced or finely chopped, to the salad. This variation goes particularly well with curries and other spicy dishes.

Tomato salad

Potato salad

A well-made potato salad is a delight, especially if made with small new potatoes. You can use old potatoes, but choose a type with firm flesh that won't break up after cooking: Desiree or King Edward's are good, and other varieties may be labelled as being suitable for salads.

You can adjust the richness of the salad by changing the proportions of mayonnaise and yogurt. Potato salad is also nice with just the vinaigrette dressing – you can stop at this point if you prefer, adding the chopped herbs to the mixture.

SERVES 4
700 g/1½ lb potatoes, ideally scrubbed new
    potatoes
1 tablespoon wine vinegar
3 tablespoons olive oil
salt and freshly ground black pepper
2 tablespoons chopped fresh chives
1 small onion, peeled and finely chopped, or
    2 spring onions, chopped (optional)
2 tablespoons mayonnaise: homemade (page 56),
    or a good-quality bought one (optional)
2 tablespoons plain yogurt or cream (optional)
TO SERVE
a few extra chives

Put the potatoes into a saucepan, cover with cold water and bring to the boil, then reduce the heat and simmer until they are just tender when pierced with a skewer or thin knife; drain in a colander. You can leave the skins on – they're delicious on new potatoes – or, if you are using old potatoes, peel the skins off with your fingers and a sharp knife when the potatoes are cool enough to handle. Cut the potatoes into chunks or dice, as you prefer.

In a large bowl, mix together the vinegar, olive oil and some salt and pepper. Add the still-warm potatoes, the chives and onion and mix gently but thoroughly. Leave until completely cold.

You can serve the salad as it is, or go on and add the mayonnaise, yogurt or cream and mix gently. Taste and add more salt and pepper if necessary. Transfer the salad to a serving bowl and snip some chives over the top.

Carrot, orange, watercress and red pepper salad

This is a light, refreshing salad and as it contains no oil, it's good for serving with something rich like a tart, quiche or deep-fried dish. If you prefer, you could mix the carrots in a vinaigrette dressing or Yogurt and honey dressing (page 56).

SERVES 2–4
4 carrots
2 oranges
1 red pepper
1 bunch of watercress (about 85 g/3 oz)

Scrape the carrots, then grate them coarsely and put them on a plate. Using a sharp knife, remove the peel and pith from the oranges by cutting around them as if you were peeling an apple and trying to keep the peel in one long piece. Hold the oranges over the plate of grated carrot as you do this, so that the carrots catch the juice. Put the oranges on a board and cut them into thin slices, again catching the juice and pouring it over the carrots. Stir the carrots to make sure that they are all coated with orange juice.

Slice the stalk end off the pepper and remove the seeds and core. Cut the pepper into thin rings.

Trim and wash the watercress, then put it on a serving dish, making a space in the centre. Spoon the carrot into the centre of the dish and arrange the orange and pepper rings around the edge. Serve immediately.

Variation
Replace the watercress with 2 Little Gem lettuces, thoroughly washed, trimmed at the base, then cut into quarters or eighths.

Coleslaw

Although you can buy coleslaw at supermarkets and delicatessens, it's usually over-sweetened and synthetic-tasting. This version is easy to make, keeps for at least 24 hours in the refrigerator, and makes an excellent accompaniment to many meals, a topping for baked potatoes or a filling for sandwiches.

You can alter the proportions of the mayonnaise and yogurt to your taste; Greek yogurt is particularly creamy, or you could use low-fat yogurt for a calorie-conscious version.

SERVES 4
325 g/12 oz white cabbage
2 carrots, peeled
1 shallot or small mild onion, peeled
2 tablespoons mayonnaise: homemade
  (page 56) or a good-quality bought one
2 tablespoons plain yogurt
2 tablespoons chopped fresh chives or other herbs
salt and freshly ground black pepper

Wash the cabbage, then shred it fairly finely using a sharp knife or the slicing attachment of a food processor. It does not need to be grated to a mush, as the dressing will soften it if you allow it time to stand. Coarsely grate the carrots. Chop the shallot or onion finely.

Put all the vegetables into a large bowl and add the mayonnaise, yogurt and herbs. Season to taste with plenty of salt and pepper. You can serve it at once but I think it's better if left for at least an hour for the flavours to develop and the cabbage to soften.

Variations
Try adding chopped apple, pear or pineapple; raisins or sultanas; nuts – roasted cashews, roughly chopped walnuts or toasted hazelnuts are particularly good; toasted pumpkin or sunflower seeds; a small diced cooked beetroot, which turns the mixture a rather enticing pink; chopped red or green pepper; chopped, skinned tomatoes; fresh, frozen or canned sweetcorn kernels.

Vegan coleslaw
Use Vegan mayonnaise (page 56) and unsweetened soya yogurt.

Vegetarian salade niçoise

For a vegetarian version of this popular
Mediterranean classic, I replace the tuna fish
with canned artichoke hearts and gherkins,
and the anchovies with strips of grilled or
marinated red pepper.

SERVES 4
Garlic vinaigrette (page 54)
2 hard-boiled eggs, shelled and quartered (page 64)
225 g/8 oz fine French beans, cooked and drained
1 large red pepper, grilled and skinned (page 44),
    or 1–2 marinated red peppers from a jar or can
450 g/1 lb tomatoes
425 g/15 oz canned artichoke hearts, drained
1 lettuce (any variety)
1 tablespoon baby gherkins
2 tablespoons chopped spring onions or
    fresh chives
2 tablespoons chopped fresh parsley
50 g/2 oz black olives

First make the vinaigrette and prepare the
eggs, French beans and red pepper. Cut the
pepper into long strips. Slice the tomatoes and
artichoke hearts.

Wash the lettuce and shake it dry, or whirl
in a salad spinner. Use the leaves to line a
large serving bowl or plate.

Spoon a little of the vinaigrette over the
lettuce leaves, then arrange the beans,
tomatoes, artichoke hearts and eggs on top.
Spoon over a little more dressing and scatter
with the gherkins, spring onions or chives and
parsley. Arrange the red pepper strips over
the top of the salad and scatter with the black
olives. Serve at once.

Vegan salade niçoise
*Rather a long way from the original, but instead
of the hard-boiled eggs try making the salad
using canned butter beans or chickpeas (drain
and rinse them first).*

Vegetarian salade niçoise

eggs

As concentrated sources of protein and other important nutrients, quick and convenient to use, eggs are a useful ingredient in a vegetarian diet. The only reservation is that because they're easy and familiar it can be tempting for new vegetarians to over-use them, especially if they have any lurking doubts about whether they can get enough protein on a vegetarian diet. For a balanced and healthy diet, it is best to eat no more than two to three eggs a week, so enjoy your egg dishes alongside some of the many other vegetable, pulse, pasta and grain dishes in this book.

When preparing eggs for anyone in a vulnerable category – the very old or young, those who are sick or pregnant – make sure that the eggs are very well cooked to prevent any possibility of salmonella poisoning.

Because of the cruelty involved in battery egg production, I will only use free-range eggs from a reliable source, organic if possible. Eggs bought in shops are labelled with a 'best before' date. If you buy them direct from the farm, make a note of the date and try to use them within two weeks.

Eggs are best stored pointed end down, in a cool place – not the refrigerator, although like most people I keep mine there for convenience. Store them away from strong-smelling foods because their shells are porous and easily absorb unwanted flavours.

Many recipes ask you to separate the whites from the yolks. To do this, carefully crack the egg over a bowl, then pass the yolk from one half shell into the other, letting the white drop down into the bowl. If you want to whisk the egg white, make sure that the bowl and whisk are spotlessly clean and grease-free, and that no trace of egg yolk gets in with the white. Do not over-whisk egg whites or the bubbles of air will burst and they will lose volume; stop once the whites stand up in peaks. Extra separated egg yolks and whites can be kept, well-covered, in the refrigerator; whites will keep for seven days and yolks, unbroken and submerged in cold water, for two to three days.

Omelette aux fines herbes (page 64)

basic egg cooking methods

Boiling, coddling and hard-boiling

Everyone has their own favourite way of boiling an egg perfectly. Mine is as follows: take the eggs out of the refrigerator about an hour before you want to use them, to help prevent cracking when the cold egg meets the hot water. Lower the egg gently into a pan of boiling water, turn the heat down and leave to simmer gently for 3½–5 minutes, depending on whether you like your egg just set or firm.

For coddled eggs, once you have put the eggs into the boiling water, put a lid on the pan, remove it from the heat and leave it to stand for 8–10 minutes, after which time the eggs will be lightly set.

To hard-boil eggs, lower them gently into boiling water, turn the heat down and leave to simmer for 10–12 minutes. Then put them immediately into cold water and tap the shells all over to crack them. Leave until they are cold, then remove the shells. This ensures that there will be no dark ring between the yolk and the white.

Poaching

Fill a frying pan with water about 4 cm/ 1½ inches deep and bring to the boil. Turn the heat down so that the water is barely simmering. Break the eggs into the water and set a timer for 3 minutes. As the eggs cook, spoon the water over them to speed up the cooking. When they are done, lift the eggs out of the pan with a draining spoon and put them gently on to a layer of paper towels to blot off the excess water, then transfer them to a warmed plate.

Frying

Heat a little groundnut oil in a frying pan, then carefully break in the eggs. As the eggs cook, spoon some of the oil over the yolks to cook them. When they are done to your liking, lift the eggs out of the pan with a fish slice.

Scrambling

For one person you will need to scramble 2 eggs; for two people, use 3 large or 4 medium eggs. Whisk the eggs with 2–3 tablespoons of milk or water and season them with salt and freshly ground black pepper. Melt a walnut-sized knob of butter in a small saucepan over a gentle heat, then pour in the beaten eggs and keep stirring with a wooden spoon until the eggs begin to thicken. Take the pan off the heat while the eggs are still creamy because they will go on cooking in the residual heat. For luxury, you could stir in a little more butter at this point, then serve the scrambled eggs immediately, on hot buttered toast.

Classic French omelette

For a single omelette, use 2–3 eggs and, if possible, a 12–15 cm/5–6 inch frying pan; for a larger omelette, to serve two people, use 4–6 eggs and an 18–20 cm/7–8 inch frying pan.

Crack the eggs into a bowl, add some salt and freshly ground black pepper and beat very lightly with a fork, just to combine the yolks and whites. Put the serving plate in a warm place.

Put the frying pan over a medium to high heat and add a 15 g/½ oz knob of butter. When it has melted and the froth has just subsided, pour in the eggs. Stir the eggs gently with a fork, and as the bottom begins to set, drag the edges into the centre of the pan and tip the pan to allow the unset egg to run into the space created. Do this until there is no more liquid egg, then let the omelette cook for a few seconds more until it is golden underneath and still creamy on top.

Put your chosen filling (see right) on top of the omelette, then tilt the pan away from you slightly and, using a palette knife or spatula, fold the top third of the omelette down, and at the same time tip the frying pan over the plate, so that the omelette rolls on to the last third and falls on to the plate. Serve at once.

Omelette aux fines herbes

This is a flavouring rather than a filling: add 1–2 tablespoons of chopped fresh herbs – chives, parsley, chervil and/or tarragon – to the beaten eggs. Scatter a few more herbs over the folded cooked omelette.

Asparagus omelette

Cook 3–4 asparagus spears (page 88). Chop them and keep them warm. Spoon them over the omelette before you fold it.

Cheese omelette

Gruyère is especially good. Grate 40 g/1½ oz of cheese; add half to the beaten eggs before you cook them and sprinkle the rest over the top of the omelette before you fold it.

Mushroom omelette

Wash and thinly slice 50 g/2 oz of mushrooms. Fry in a little butter for 4–5 minutes, until tender. Season and spoon on top of the omelette before you fold it.

Tomato omelette

Fry 1–2 skinned (see page 93) and chopped tomatoes in a little butter for 5 minutes, until softened and heated through. Season – add 1 tablespoon of chopped fresh chives if you like – and pour over the omelette before you fold it.

Omelette aux fines herbes

Frittata

A substantial, open-faced omelette can be found in a number of cuisines, including Spanish, Middle Eastern and Italian. This is the Italian version, of which I am particularly fond. You can base it on most types of vegetable, lightly cooked before adding the eggs. For an omelette to serve two people you need about 450 g/1 lb vegetables (prepared weight). Frittata is good hot or cold, cut into sections like a cake.

SERVES 2

3 small carrots, sliced
125 g/4 oz broccoli, cut into small florets
1 courgette (about 125 g/4 oz),
   cut into 5 mm/¼ inch slices
4 eggs
25 g/1 oz Parmesan cheese, grated
salt and freshly ground black pepper
2 tablespoons olive oil
1 bunch of spring onions, trimmed and chopped

First cook the vegetables: bring 5 cm/2 inches of water to the boil in a large saucepan, add the carrots and cook for 5 minutes. Add the broccoli and courgettes and cook for a further 2–3 minutes, or until the vegetables are just tender but still slightly crunchy – test them with a skewer or thin knife. Drain the vegetables in a colander.

Heat the grill. Whisk the eggs lightly, add the cheese and season to taste with a little salt and pepper – not too much salt as the Parmesan is quite salty.

Set a frying pan – ideally a 20 cm/8 inch one – over a moderate heat, then add the oil. In a moment or two, when the oil is hot, add the spring onions and cooked vegetables, stir well, then pour in the egg mixture. Stir gently with a spatula to let the egg run down through the vegetables. After a minute or two, when the bottom of the frittata is set and golden brown, pop the frying pan under the hot grill and leave for a minute or two to set the top. Serve at once, cut in half, or in thick wedges.

Variations

Other vegetables you could use include lightly cooked chopped asparagus or spinach, or grilled peppers (page 44).

Tortilla

This is the basic Spanish omelette; it does not use cheese. Slice a large potato and a large onion and fry in 1–2 tablespoons of olive oil for 15 minutes, or until tender but not browned. Lift out the vegetables with a draining spoon and mix with the beaten eggs. Return the mixture to the pan, turn down the heat and cook gently until the tortilla is set underneath. Grill as for Frittata.

Cheese soufflé

Although it seems complicated and is undoubtedly impressive, a soufflé is actually quite easy to make. The most difficult thing, I find, is getting everyone to the table on time, because a soufflé won't wait! Also, you need to be careful not to over-whisk the egg whites. Apart from that, it's a doddle!

Serves 4

200 ml/7 fl oz milk
1 bay leaf
6 black peppercorns
a slice of onion
a little butter and 1–2 tablespoons finely grated
  Parmesan cheese for preparing the dish
50 g/2 oz butter
2 tablespoons plain flour
2 teaspoons Dijon mustard
pinch of cayenne pepper
pinch of freshly grated nutmeg
4 eggs, separated, and 1 extra egg white
salt and freshly ground black pepper
85 g/3 oz strongly flavoured cheese, grated
  (for example, Gruyère, mature Cheddar, Stilton)

Put the milk into a saucepan with the bay leaf, peppercorns and onion, bring to the boil, then turn off the heat, cover the pan and leave for 30 minutes for the flavours to infuse.

Meanwhile, prepare a 1.5 litre/2½ pint soufflé dish by greasing it evenly with butter. Sprinkle in the Parmesan cheese and tip it around to coat the sides of the dish.

Melt the butter in a saucepan and stir in the flour. Cook for 1 minute, stirring all the time, then remove from the heat and gradually stir in the flavoured milk. Put the pan back on the heat and continue to stir until the mixture has thickened. Remove from the heat and leave to cool until you can put your hand against the pan, then beat in the mustard, cayenne, nutmeg, egg yolks and some salt and pepper. Then scatter all but about a tablespoonful of the cheese over the top. You can now continue or leave the mixture until later.

Heat the oven to 180°C/350°F/Gas Mark 4. Stir the cheese into the sauce mixture. In a clean bowl, whisk the 5 egg whites until they stand in soft peaks. Stir a large spoonful of egg white into the sauce mixture to lighten it, then gently pour the sauce mixture over the remaining egg whites and, using a metal spoon, gently combine the two mixtures: this is done using a technique known as folding – cut the spoon across the centre of the mixture, reaching to the bottom of the bowl, turn the bowl slightly and gently place the spoonful of mixture on top. Continue until no large lumps of egg white are visible, but do not overmix.

Pour the mixture into the prepared soufflé dish and sprinkle with the remaining tablespoonful of cheese. Bake for about 30 minutes, until the soufflé is puffed up and golden brown, doesn't wobble when shaken slightly and a skewer inserted into the centre comes out clean. Serve immediately.

Spinach soufflé

Use only 3 whole eggs plus an extra egg white. Cook 450 g/1 lb spinach as described on page 93; drain and chop thoroughly then put the spinach in a sieve and press to remove all the liquid. Add the spinach to the melted butter in the saucepan, cook for 1 minute, then add 3 tablespoons of flour and continue as above.

Frittata with carrots, broccoli, courgettes and spring onions

Little twice-baked soufflés

You can make these soufflés well in advance, then let them get cold or even freeze them. You reheat them in the oven just before you want to eat them, and when you take them out they are puffed and golden, with a lovely crisp outside. I like them with a tasty, colourful sauce such as tomato (page 82). The mixture is based on soft white cheese rather than a sauce – quicker, easier and lighter.

MAKES 6

a little butter and finely grated Parmesan cheese for
    preparing the dishes
50 g/2 oz curd cheese
175 g/6 oz Gruyère cheese, grated
4 eggs, separated
150 ml/5 fl oz single cream
salt and freshly ground black pepper
50 g/2 oz Parmesan cheese, grated

Heat the oven to 200°C/400°F/Gas Mark 6. Grease six cups, ramekins or individual pudding basins or tins with butter and sprinkle with grated Parmesan.

Put the curd cheese into a bowl with the grated Gruyère, egg yolks, cream and a little salt and pepper to taste and mix together.

In a clean bowl, whisk the egg whites until they stand in soft peaks. Stir a large spoonful of egg white into the cheese mixture, then gently pour the cheese mixture over the remaining egg whites and, using a metal spoon, gently fold the two mixtures together, until evenly combined (see previous page).

Pour the mixture into the prepared cups or dishes and stand them in a roasting tin. Pour almost-boiling water into the tin to come halfway up the sides of the dishes. Put the tin into the oven and bake until the soufflés are risen and a skewer inserted into the centre comes out clean – about 15–20 minutes. Leave the soufflés to cool in their containers – they will sink a good deal.

To serve, heat the oven to 220°C/425°F/Gas Mark 7. Turn out the soufflés and put them into a shallow ovenproof dish. Sprinkle with the grated Parmesan and bake for about 15 minutes, or until risen, heated through and golden brown. Serve from the dish.

Gruyère roulade with red onion and goats' cheese

A roulade is much easier to make than you'd think and makes an impressive main course. As it's easier to manage when it's cold, I usually let the roulade cool before rolling it up, then reheat it in the oven before serving – or serve it cold.

SERVES 6

a little butter and finely grated Parmesan cheese for
    preparing the tin and rolling up the roulade
50 g/2 oz curd cheese or medium-fat smooth white
    cheese
175 g/6 oz Gruyère cheese, grated
4 eggs, separated
150 ml/5 fl oz single cream
salt and freshly ground black pepper
50 g/2 oz Parmesan cheese, grated

FOR THE FILLING

2 tablespoons olive oil
15 g/½ oz butter
450 g/1 lb red onions, thinly sliced
½ lemon
150 g/5 oz soft medium-fat goats' cheese (for
    example, Lingot du Berry)

Heat the oven to 200°C/400°F/Gas Mark 6, and line a 22 x 33 cm/9 x 13 inch Swiss roll tin with nonstick baking paper. Butter the paper lightly and sprinkle with grated Parmesan.

Put the curd cheese into a bowl with the grated Gruyère, egg yolks, cream and a little salt and pepper to taste and mix well.

In a clean bowl, whisk the egg whites until they stand in soft peaks. Stir a large spoonful of egg white into the cheese mixture, then gently pour the cheese mixture over the remaining egg whites and, using a metal spoon, gently fold the two mixtures together, until evenly combined (see previous page).

Pour the mixture into the prepared tin, spreading it gently to the edges. Bake for 12–15 minutes, until firm to the touch. Take the roulade out of the oven, cover with a damp tea towel and leave until completely cold. It will shrink a bit – that's normal.

While the roulade is cooking, make the filling. Heat the oil and butter in a large saucepan, then add the onions. Stir, cover and

Gruyère roulade with red onion and goats' cheese

leave the onions to cook over a gentle heat for 30 minutes, until they are completely tender and sweet. Stir them from time to time and don't let them burn. Then remove them from the heat and add salt, pepper and a squeeze of lemon juice to taste.

To assemble the roulade, sprinkle a piece of cling film with grated Parmesan. Remove the tea towel from the roulade; turn the roulade on to the cling film and peel the nonstick paper off the roulade. Drain off and reserve any liquid from the onions. Beat the goats' cheese with a fork to make it smooth and creamy, adding some of the reserved onion liquid if necessary to give a spreading consistency. Spread the goats' cheese all over the roulade. Put the onions on top of the goats' cheese and spread to within about 1 cm/½ inch of the edges. Starting with one of the long edges, roll up the roulade like a Swiss roll, using the cling film to help.

To serve cold, chill until needed then serve in slices. To serve hot, put the roulade on a heatproof serving plate and bake at 200°C/400°F/Gas Mark 6 for 15–20 minutes, until heated through.

Crêpes with Brie and broccoli

Pancakes with a savoury filling make an excellent main course. Although the instructions seem long, crêpes are simple to make and this dish, once assembled, will happily wait in the refrigerator for 8–12 hours before baking. The pancakes themselves also freeze well and if you separate them with pieces of nonstick baking paper you can take out one or two at a time, add some filling and cook under a hot grill to make a quick meal for one or two.

MAKES 12–14 CRÊPES;
SERVES 4 AS A MAIN COURSE
125 g/4 oz plain flour (white or half white and half wholewheat), sifted
2 eggs
300 ml/10 fl oz milk or soya milk
2 tablespoons melted butter or sunflower oil
groundnut oil for frying
FOR THE FILLING
450 g/1 lb broccoli
225 g/8 oz Brie cheese, cut into thin slices
125 g/4 oz Parmesan cheese, grated (optional)
salt and freshly ground black pepper
TO SERVE (OPTIONAL)
Fresh tomato sauce (page 82)

The easiest way to make the pancake mixture is to put the flour, eggs, milk and melted butter or oil into a food processor or blender and whiz to a smooth batter. Alternatively, put the flour into a large bowl, beat in the eggs, butter or oil and about a third of the milk. Mix until smooth, then gradually beat in the rest of the milk. The consistency should be like single cream.

Put a small frying pan over a low heat and brush it with a little oil: a good way to do this is to make a pad of paper towels, dip this in the oil, then wipe it over the pan. When the pan is hot enough to sizzle when a drop of water is flicked into it, pour 2 tablespoons of batter into the frying pan and swirl it round so that the base is thinly coated.

Fry for a minute or two, until the top is set, then use a palette knife and your fingers to flip the crêpe over and cook the other side for a few seconds.

As the crêpes are done, stack them up on a plate, cover them with another plate and keep them warm over a pan of steaming water.

To make the filling, trim the broccoli, separating the florets from the stems. Peel the stems, then cut them into matchsticks. Cook the florets and stems in a little boiling water until they are tender, about 4 minutes. Drain well and mix with the Brie, half the Parmesan and salt and pepper to taste. Place a heaped tablespoonful of this mixture on to one side of each crêpe and roll it up. Put the crêpes side by side in a shallow ovenproof dish. Pour over the tomato sauce, if you're using it – it looks attractive poured in lines, up and down – then sprinkle with the rest of the Parmesan. The crêpes are now ready to bake.

To finish the dish, heat the oven to 180°C/350°C/Gas Mark 4. Bake the crêpes for 30 minutes, until they are very hot and the tops are lightly browned.

Variations
For alternative fillings, try the Red Bean Chilli mixture (page 129), Ratatouille (page 101), sweetcorn kernels with chopped tomatoes and ricotta cheese, or ricotta with crushed garlic and chopped fresh herbs.

Crêpes with Stilton and spinach
Use 1 kg/2¼ lb of fresh spinach, cooked (page 93) and chopped, and 225 g/8 oz of Stilton cheese, instead of the broccoli and Brie.

Yorkshire pudding

When I was growing up as a vegetarian, our Sunday lunch was often Yorkshire pudding with roast potatoes, vegetables from the garden, and gravy. My father, who was a Yorkshireman, always made the Yorkshire pudding. His secrets were to use a mixture of water and milk for the batter, to use a very hot oven, and to make sure the oil was very hot when adding the mixture – and to make sure we all got to the table the minute it was done, all puffed up and crisp.

SERVES 4
85 g/3 oz plain flour
1 egg
150 ml/5 fl oz milk and water mixed
salt and freshly ground black pepper
2 tablespoons groundnut oil

Heat the oven to 220°C/425°F/Gas Mark 7.

Sift the flour into a bowl, make a well in the centre, crack in the egg and beat, gradually pouring in the milk and water as you do so, until all the liquid is in and you have a smooth mixture. Season to taste.

Pour the oil into a roasting tin – mine is 18 x 28 cm/7 x 11 inches – and pop it into the oven to heat up. After a few minutes, when it's smoking hot, remove it from the oven, stand it over one of the burners of your cooker to keep the oil really hot, and pour in the batter, then put it back into the oven as near the top as you can. (If you're doing roast potatoes too, put them at the very top, with the Yorkshire pudding underneath.) Bake for 25–30 minutes, until it has risen up and is golden brown and crunchy. Serve immediately.

Variations
Add a couple of tablespoons of coarsely grated cheese, cubes of Nut loaf (page 136) or Smoky Snaps (see page 140) to the mixture before baking, for a kind of vegetarian toad-in-the-hole.

Caribbean-style eggs

I am very fond of this combination of sweet and savoury flavours, but if spicy bananas are too much for you, try one of the variations. Serve with warm nan bread or chapattis.

SERVES 4
25 g/1 oz butter
1 tablespoon olive oil
2 onions, peeled and chopped
2 garlic cloves, crushed
2 tablespoons grated fresh ginger
½ teaspoon turmeric
pinch of chilli powder or cayenne pepper
1 large green pepper, deseeded and chopped finely
2 tomatoes, skinned (page 93) and chopped
6 bananas, peeled and chopped
salt and freshly ground black pepper
4 eggs

Heat the butter and oil in a large frying pan, then add the onions, stir, cover the pan with a lid, plate or foil and leave to cook over a low heat for 7 minutes. Stir in the garlic and cook for a further 2–3 minutes. Add the ginger, turmeric, chilli or cayenne and cook for a further 1 minute. Add the pepper, tomatoes and bananas to the pan, stir well, then cover and cook for about 20 minutes, until all the vegetables are tender. Season to taste.

Spread the mixture so that it is level in the frying pan, then make four hollows and break an egg into each. Cover the pan again and cook gently until the eggs are set, about 15–20 minutes. Serve at once.

Variations
As an alternative base for the eggs, you could use Ratatouille (page 101), Leek and potato hotpot (page 97) or Wild mushroom ragout (page 99).

cheese

As cheese can be eaten with no preparation at all, and is extremely tasty in cooked dishes, it's quite easy to eat too much of it, especially when you first give up meat and fish: cheese fills the gaps without difficulty. Cheese is one of the fattier foods in the vegetarian diet, and is best used with discrimination, but it's fine if you also eat a good balance of complex carbohydrates – such as brown rice, pulses, pasta, potatoes and bread – and fresh fruit and vegetables.

In order to make cheese, milk has to be separated into curd and whey. In some cheeses this occurs as a result of the action of lactic acid (from the milk), but in traditional cheesemaking the separation is caused by the addition of rennet, a digestive enzyme obtained from slaughtered young animals. However, in some countries there have always been cheeses made with plant rennets (extracted from thistles, fig leaves and other plants), and cheesemakers today have access to vegetarian or microbial rennet, which is produced from microscopic fungi, and is becoming increasingly widely used.

In the early days of vegetarianism, eating cheese made from animal rennet was a small compromise that had to be made. Then vegetarian rennet was developed and the first vegetarian Cheddar came on to the market. Now, many cheeses are made with non-animal rennet as a matter of course, not just for the vegetarian market. Some cheeses are labelled as suitable for vegetarians, but others are not. When in doubt, ask, because it's good to be able to enjoy a variety of cheeses.

Make sure that the cheese you buy isn't dried out and cracked or 'sweaty', with fat droplets on the surface. A soft cheese such as Brie needs to be neither chalky-firm nor running all over the place. The refrigerator is the best place to store cheese at home, with the cheese well wrapped in greaseproof paper or polythene and kept in the warmest part of the refrigerator – in the door or on one of the lowest shelves. When you want to use the cheese, remember to take it out of the refrigerator about an hour ahead so that it comes back to room temperature, for the best flavour and texture.

Cheese is included in recipes throughout this book, from soups and sauces to desserts and puddings, which just goes to emphasize its versatility and usefulness. Vegan cheese, made from soya milk, doesn't respond well to heat, although it's fine in uncooked dishes.

A selection of blue cheeses: (top to bottom) Stilton, Roquefort and Gorgonzola

Cheese and walnut terrine

This is an adaptation of one of Prue Leith's recipes. Serve as a first course, with toast, bread or crudités; or as a light main course with salad. It is best prepared a day ahead.

SERVES 6
325 g/12 oz Stilton cheese
450 g/1 lb low-fat or medium-fat soft white cheese
125 g/4 oz unsalted butter, melted
85 g/3 oz walnuts
1 glass of port (100 ml/3½ fl oz)
1 tablespoon chopped fresh chives
salt and freshly ground black pepper

TO SERVE
sprigs of watercress

First prepare the tin; line a 450 g/1 lb loaf tin with a strip of nonstick baking paper to cover the base and extend up the narrow sides.

Grate or crumble the Stilton into a bowl and add the soft white cheese. Beat these cheeses together, then pour in the melted butter and mix again. Reserve 6 walnut halves for the garnish and chop the rest with a sharp knife. Stir the chopped walnuts into the cheese mixture, together with the port and chives. Season to taste with a little salt and plenty of freshly ground black pepper, then spoon the mixture into the loaf tin and smooth the top with the back of the spoon. Cover and refrigerate overnight.

To serve the terrine, slip a knife around the sides, invert a plate over the tin, then turn it upside down and the terrine will slip out on to the plate. Strip the paper off and either decorate the terrine with the reserved walnut halves and arrange a few sprigs of watercress around it, or cut it carefully into thickish slices and serve on individual plates with a garnish of watercress on the side.

Walnuts add a wonderful flavour to cakes and savoury dishes

Cheese fritters

These take a bit of time but are well worth the effort. They freeze perfectly and can be fried from frozen, so I generally make up a double quantity. I prefer to use soya milk, but you could use skimmed dairy milk if you prefer.

SERVES 4

600 ml/1 pint soya milk
1 small onion, peeled and stuck with 3–4 cloves
1 bay leaf
125 g/4 oz semolina
125 g/4 oz grated cheese (any variety)
1 teaspoon Dijon mustard
cayenne pepper
freshly grated nutmeg
salt and freshly ground black pepper
1 large egg, beaten with 1 tablespoon water
10 tablespoons dried breadcrumbs
vegetable oil for shallow-frying

TO SERVE

lemon wedges
sprigs of parsley

Put the milk into a saucepan with the onion and bay leaf, bring just to the boil, then turn off the heat, cover the pan, and leave for 30 minutes for the flavours to infuse.

Take out the onion and bay leaf and bring the milk back to the boil. Sprinkle the semolina over the milk in a thin stream, stirring all the time until the mixture is thick. Leave to simmer for about 5 minutes, to cook the semolina, giving it a stir from time to time. Then take it off the heat and stir in the cheese, mustard, a good pinch of cayenne pepper, nutmeg and salt and pepper to taste.

Spread the mixture on an oiled plate or baking tray, to a depth of about 7 mm/⅓ inch, and smooth the top. Leave it to get completely cold and firm.

Put the beaten egg into a bowl and the breadcrumbs into another. Cut the cheese mixture into triangles, fingers or other shapes. Dip the shapes into the beaten egg and then into the breadcrumbs, to coat them evenly.

Heat 5 mm/¼ inch oil in a frying pan and fry the fritters until crisp on both sides; drain well on crumpled paper towels. Serve at once, with lemon wedges and parsley sprigs.

Gnocchi alla romana
Use Parmesan cheese, and add only 2 tablespoons to the cheese mixture. Omit the mustard and cayenne pepper. In addition, you will need to melt 85 g/3 oz of unsalted butter.

Cut out the shapes using a small (liqueur) glass, or the smallest pastry cutter you have, about 4 cm/1½ inches in diameter. Lay the shapes in overlapping layers in a shallow ovenproof dish, sprinkling each layer with a little melted butter and grated Parmesan and finishing with a layer of butter and cheese. Bake in a hot oven, 220°C/425°F/Gas Mark 7, for 15–20 minutes, until a golden crust has formed on top. Serve hot.

Grilled tomatoes and aubergine with mozzarella

A simple dish for lunch or supper, served with some green salad leaves and crusty bread. In smaller portions it makes a substantial starter.

SERVES 4 AS A FIRST COURSE,
2 AS A MAIN COURSE

1 aubergine (about 325 g/12 oz)
2–3 tablespoons olive oil
salt and freshly ground black pepper
450 g/1 lb tomatoes
150 g/5 oz Mozzarella cheese
4 sprigs of basil

TO SERVE

lemon wedges

Turn the grill to high. While it's heating up, slice the aubergine into thin rounds – about 5 mm/¼ inch – discarding the stem, and brush both sides lightly with olive oil. Season with salt and pepper. Lay the slices on a grill pan and grill until they are golden brown and tender, turning them over once.

Meanwhile, cut the tomatoes and Mozzarella into thin slices. Arrange these on top of the aubergine slices, season with salt and pepper, then pop them under the grill for a further 3–4 minutes, until the Mozzarella melts and the tomatoes are heated through. Tear the basil leaves over the top and serve immediately, with lemon wedges.

Deep-fried Camembert

Although you can now buy Camembert coated in crumbs ready for cooking, it's nowhere near as good as the homemade version. Most people serve this as a starter, but I think the meal has a better balance if it's a main course, with a light, vegetable-based starter. I serve the Camembert with a sweet but tangy sauce and a simple salad or steamed vegetables.

SERVES 3 AS A FIRST COURSE,
2 AS A MAIN COURSE
1 egg, beaten
10 tablespoons dried breadcrumbs
6 individual portions of Camembert or a whole
   Camembert cut into 6 portions
vegetable oil for deep-frying
TO SERVE
lemon wedges
Apricot or Cranberry sauce (page 84)

Put the beaten egg into a bowl and the breadcrumbs into another. Dip the pieces of Camembert first in egg, then in breadcrumbs, making sure they're well coated so that the cheese won't ooze out during cooking – you may need to repeat the process to cover them completely. If you have time to chill the crumbed Camembert at this point, so much the better, though it's not essential.

Just before you want to eat the Camembert, heat some oil in a saucepan or deep-fryer (not more than a third full of oil) to 180°C/350°F. If you have a cooking thermometer, put it in the pan when you start heating the oil, to prevent it from cracking in the heat. If you don't have a thermometer, test the temperature by dropping a small cube of bread into the oil; if it rises to the surface immediately and turns golden brown in 1 minute, the oil is hot enough. Lower the Camembert into the oil (you may need to do this in two batches). It will rise immediately to the surface and start browning at once. As soon as it is golden brown all over, remove it from the oil with a slotted spoon and drain well on crumpled paper towels. If necessary, reheat the oil to the right temperature and fry the remaining Camembert. Serve on warmed plates, with lemon wedges and your chosen sauce.

NOTE *Sometimes you may find that, despite all your efforts, one or two of the Camembert begin to leak through the crumbs – so serve and eat them quickly. Occasionally you may get one that, unbeknown to you, leaks out completely in the oil, leaving just the crumb case; however, this is quite rare. Just make sure you have enough Camembert to allow for the odd mishap.*

Halloumi with tomato and caper salsa

Halloumi is a firm, salty white cheese from Greece and Cyprus. It is usually sold vacuum-wrapped, and packets of Halloumi will keep for several weeks in the refrigerator, ready to make a meal in next to no time. Bring out the flavour by frying or grilling it, and I think it needs a piquant accompaniment to set it off and cut the richness. If you haven't time to make this salsa, try serving it simply with a wedge of lemon and some green salad leaves.

SERVES 4
2 packs of Halloumi cheese (about
   250 g/9 oz each)
olive oil for shallow-frying
FOR THE SALSA
450 g/1 lb tomatoes, skinned (see page 93)
2 tablespoons capers, drained
1 lemon, washed and dried
salt and freshly ground black pepper

First make the salsa. Chop the tomatoes quite finely, discarding any tough bits of core. Put the tomatoes into a bowl with the capers. Grate the lemon rind into the bowl, and add a teaspoonful of the lemon juice. Season to taste. All this is best done a few hours in advance, to allow the flavours to develop.

Just before you want to serve the dish, drain the cheese, pat it dry on paper towels and cut it into thin slices. Heat a little olive oil in a frying pan and fry the cheese for a few seconds on each side (you may need to do this in two batches). Drain on paper towels. Serve immediately, with the salsa.

Halloumi with tomato and caper salsa

sauces

The first thing people ask a vegetarian is usually 'what do you have for Christmas dinner?', and the second is 'what do you have instead of gravy?'. Well, for the answer to the first question, have a look at page 20 and I think you'll realize we're spoilt for choice. As far as the gravy is concerned, there's no problem with that, either. You can make a very tasty gravy without any meat fat or juices – the recipe follows, along with some other sauces that are useful basics for any cook.

As an accompaniment, sauces are invaluable with dishes like the Lentil and herb bake (page 127), Bean burgers (page 129), or any of the recipes in the chapter on Nuts.

Sauces are also an easy way to make a selection of two or three simple boiled or steamed vegetables into an interesting meal: most of the sauces in this chapter can be quickly put together while the vegetables are cooking. White sauce and its variations are good mixed with cooked pasta, which can then be spooned into a heatproof dish, topped with grated cheese and breadcrumbs and popped under the grill or into a hot oven for about 15 minutes for a satisfying pasta bake.

Pasta with Fresh tomato sauce (page 82)

White sauce

This simple, flour-thickened sauce is the basis for Béchamel, Cheese sauce and Parsley sauce. These proportions make a medium-thick sauce; you can vary the thickness by adding more or less milk, or for a thinner sauce use just 25 g/1 oz of flour. I prefer to use soya milk to make this sauce, although dairy milk is more usual. I first learnt this 'all in the pan and whisk' method from Delia Smith – it makes sauce-making effortless and foolproof.

MAKES 600 ML/1 PINT
50 g/2 oz butter or vegan margarine
40 g/1½ oz plain flour
600 ml/1 pint milk or soya milk
salt and freshly ground black pepper
freshly grated nutmeg

Put the butter, flour and milk into a saucepan and put it over a moderate heat. Then, using a small balloon whisk, keep whisking the mixture as it heats until it comes to the boil and thickens to a smooth sauce. After that, turn the heat down as low as you can and leave it to simmer very gently for 5–6 minutes to cook the flour. Season to taste with salt, pepper and nutmeg. That's all there is to it – perfect sauce every time. Easy, isn't it?

Béchamel sauce
First flavour the milk by putting it into a saucepan with a slice of peeled onion, a bay leaf and a sprig of thyme if you have it. Bring to the boil, then remove from the heat, cover the pan and leave until cold. Remove the onion and herbs and use the milk to make the sauce as above.

Cheese sauce
After the sauce has thickened, add 1 teaspoon of Dijon mustard and 50–125 g/2–4 oz of grated cheese, such as Cheddar or Gruyère. Be careful not to let the sauce boil after you have added the cheese or it may become stringy.

Parsley sauce
Stir 2–4 tablespoons of chopped fresh parsley into the finished sauce.

Caper sauce
For this tangy variation, stir 1–3 teaspoons of Dijon mustard and 2–3 tablespoons of drained capers into the sauce.

Yogurt and herb sauce

A light, low-fat, no-cook sauce – in a way it's more of a dressing – that I find useful with bean and nut dishes that need a bit of moisture and a fresh, sharp flavour.

MAKES 150 ML/5 FL OZ
150 ml/5 fl oz plain yogurt or soya yogurt
2 tablespoons chopped fresh herbs (chives, parsley, chervil, basil or a mixture)
salt and freshly ground black pepper

Just put the yogurt into a bowl, add the herbs and stir together. Add seasoning to taste.

Yogurt and dill sauce
This is particularly good with lentil burgers, or the koftas on page 127. Use 2 tablespoons of chopped fresh dill instead of the other herbs.

Yogurt and caper sauce
Replace the herbs with capers, or try a mixture of half capers and half chopped gherkins.

Soured cream and herb sauce
For this richer variation, replace the yogurt with soured cream, or use a mixture of the two.

Parsley is very nutritious, so use it generously – in sauces, or sprinkled over almost any vegetarian dish to add a touch of colour

Fresh tomato sauce

One of the most useful sauces – excellent over pasta, steamed vegetables or with many vegetarian savoury dishes. I like it best when made with fresh tomatoes – even winter ones – although you can use canned tomatoes instead. However, it's best to use these when the sauce is going to be part of a cooked dish like a lasagne or aubergine bake.

SERVES 4

1 tablespoon olive oil
1 onion, peeled and finely chopped
700 g/1½ lb fresh tomatoes, skinned (see page 93) and roughly chopped or 400 g/14 oz canned tomatoes, chopped
salt and freshly ground black pepper

Heat the oil in a large saucepan, add the onion, stir, then cover the pan and cook over a low heat for 5 minutes, until the onion has softened but not browned.

Add the tomatoes and stir, then leave the sauce to cook gently for 10–15 minutes, until the tomatoes and onion are soft and the sauce has thickened.

You can serve this sauce as it is, or purée it in a food processor or blender – and even pass it through a sieve after that, to remove the seeds, if you wish – for a really smooth consistency. I prefer the sauce to be left chunky, especially when it's made with fresh tomatoes. In any case, season to taste with salt and pepper before serving.

Variations

There are many ways in which you can give this sauce your own personal touch: when you add the tomatoes, you could also add a clove or two of crushed garlic, a splash of red wine, or a little chopped chilli or chilli powder. At the end, throw in a good tablespoon or two of chopped fresh herbs – basil and oregano are especially good – or chopped black olives.

Fresh tomato sauce

Vegetarian gravy

This is best when made with vegetable stock (page 30) and though I'm generally not very keen on stock cubes and powders, it's one occasion when I think you need to use them if you haven't got any fresh stock. The soy sauce is important, too, adding both flavour and colour. For best results use a naturally brewed one: tamari or shoyu from health shops or Kikkoman from most supermarkets. You can adjust the consistency of this gravy by using more or less liquid.

MAKES JUST OVER 450 ML/15 FL OZ
4 tablespoons vegetable oil
1 onion, peeled and chopped
4 tablespoons plain flour
1 garlic clove, crushed
450 ml/¾ pint stock, or water and a stock cube
  or powder
1 teaspoon yeast extract
1–2 tablespoons soy sauce
salt and freshly ground black pepper

Heat the oil in a large saucepan, add the onion, stir, then cover the pan and cook over a low heat for 5 minutes.

Stir in the flour and cook, uncovered, for a further 5–10 minutes, until the flour and the onion are browned. This is important; they need to be a good nut-brown, but not burnt. Add the garlic, cook for a moment or two, then pour in the stock. Bring to the boil, then simmer for 10 minutes.

You can serve this as it is, or purée it in a food processor or blender – and even pass it through a sieve after that – for a smooth gravy. In any case, stir in the soy sauce and season to taste with salt and pepper before serving.

Wild mushroom sauce

This adds a touch of luxury to anything from pasta to nut loaf.

SERVES 2–4
20 g/¾ oz dried porcini mushrooms (ceps)
450 ml/15 fl oz vegetable stock
50 g/2 oz butter or vegan margarine
300 ml/10 fl oz red or dry white wine
1 tablespoon Madeira or brandy
1 tablespoon double cream or soya cream
salt and freshly ground black pepper

First prepare the porcini by putting them into a saucepan with the stock and bringing to the boil; remove from the heat and leave them to soak for at least 1 hour, or even overnight, to bring out the flavour.

After this, strain the stock into a bowl through a very fine sieve to get rid of any grit that may have been on the porcini. Give the porcini a quick rinse under the tap to remove any further grit, then pat them dry and chop them finely.

Melt the butter in a saucepan and add the porcini; cook over a gentle heat for 5 minutes, then add the strained porcini liquid, together with the wine. Bring to the boil and let the mixture bubble for several minutes, until it is reduced by half. Stir in the Madeira or brandy and the cream and season to taste.

Hollandaise sauce

This is a quick and easy way to make this rich, luxurious sauce. It's particularly good with steamed asparagus.

SERVES 2–4
125 g/4 oz butter, cut into chunks
2 egg yolks
1 tablespoon fresh lemon juice
salt and freshly ground black pepper

Start by putting the butter into a small saucepan and heating it until it melts and comes to the boil, but don't let it get brown.

Meanwhile, put the egg yolks into a food processor or blender with the lemon juice, some salt and a grinding of black pepper and whiz until they are pale and thick – this takes about 1 minute. Next, with the machine running, pour the butter into the machine through the top of the goblet. Do this in a very thin, steady stream and the sauce will thicken. Stop the machine when all the butter is in and leave it to stand for a minute or two, then use it immediately, while it's warm.

If you want to set it aside to use later, you will need to warm it gently by transferring it to a small saucepan and standing that pan inside a larger one of boiling water.

Cumberland sauce

A sweet, tangy sauce that goes well with savoury bean, lentil and nut dishes.

SERVES 4
4 tablespoons redcurrant jelly
rind of 1 orange, thinly pared and cut into
    fine shreds
2 tablespoons orange juice
2 tablespoons port

Put all the ingredients into a small saucepan and heat gently for about 5 minutes, until syrupy. Leave to cool before serving.

Apricot sauce
Use a good-quality apricot jam instead of the redcurrant jelly, omit the orange rind and port, and use lemon juice instead of orange juice.

Simple cranberry sauce
Use a good-quality cranberry jelly instead of the redcurrant jelly.

Satay sauce

This is a spicy, protein-rich, peanut and coconut sauce that can turn a plate of steamed vegetables or simply cooked rice or tofu (or all three together) into a main course. This version is quick and easy to make.

SERVES 4
4 slightly rounded tablespoons smooth peanut
    butter
4 garlic cloves, crushed
1 green chilli, halved, deseeded and chopped
50 g/2 oz creamed coconut (from a block), cut into
    small pieces
1 tablespoon soy sauce
salt and freshly ground black pepper

Put the peanut butter into a small saucepan with the garlic, chilli and 150 ml/5 fl oz water and heat gently, stirring, until the peanut butter is smooth. Stir in the creamed coconut until that too is smooth, then add the soy sauce and season to taste.

Creamy cashew nut sauce

Cashew nuts are very nutritious and can be made into a versatile sauce.

MAKES ABOUT 400 ML/15 FL OZ
2 tablespoons olive oil
1 onion, peeled and chopped
1–2 garlic cloves, crushed
100 g/3½ oz cashew nuts
1 tablespoon fresh lemon juice
1–2 tablespoons chopped fresh parsley
salt and freshly ground black pepper

Heat the oil in a saucepan, then add the onion, stir, cover and leave to cook over a low heat for about 7 minutes. Stir in the garlic and cook for a further 2–3 minutes.

Tip the onion mixture into a blender or food processor and add the cashew nuts and 150 ml/5 fl oz water. Blend thoroughly, until the mixture is creamy, then add another 150 ml/5 fl oz water and whiz again. Stir in the lemon juice and parsley and season to taste. Return the mixture to the pan, reheat gently and serve hot.

Piquant cashew nut sauce
Make the sauce as described. When you return it to the pan to reheat, stir in 2 tablespoons of drained capers.

Cashew and mushroom sauce
Fry 125 g/4 oz of sliced button mushrooms in 15 g/½ oz of butter for 10 minutes, until they are tender and any liquid has boiled away.

Add the mushrooms to the sauce, with or without the parsley.

Cashew and sun-dried tomato sauce
Add 6 sun-dried tomatoes to the sauce with the cashew nuts. Leave out the parsley.

Cashew and vanilla sauce
For this sweet variation, simply blend 100 g/3½ oz of cashew nuts with the water as described, adding 1 whole vanilla pod and 1 tablespoon of caster sugar or honey. When the sauce is smooth and creamy, taste and add a little more sweetening if necessary. Serve hot or cold.

Pesto

While there are some very good fresh versions of this classic Italian herb sauce available from supermarkets, homemade pesto has a wonderful flavour and a more interesting texture. Toss it with freshly cooked pasta, or spread it on crostini (page 38) or grilled large mushrooms.

SERVES 4
50 g/2 oz fresh basil leaves
2 garlic cloves, peeled
8 tablespoons extra virgin olive oil
2 tablespoons pine nuts
50 g/2 oz Parmesan or Pecorino Romano cheese, grated
salt and freshly ground black pepper

Put the basil, garlic, pine nuts and olive oil into a blender or food processor and whiz to a smooth purée. Put the mixture into a small bowl and stir in the cheese. Season to taste.

Variations
Use the same method to create any number of thick herb and nut sauces. For example, you could replace the basil with parsley, or a mixture of parsley and mint. Instead of the pine nuts, you could use walnuts, hazelnuts or cashew nuts.

vegetables

Although there's much more to vegetarian cookery than just vegetables, vegetables have an important part to play – which surely accounts for the health-giving properties of this way of eating. It's certainly not uncommon to have a vegetarian meal consisting of 'veg and two veg': vegetables are used both to make main dishes and to accompany them.

Vegetables are very easy to cook and now that you can get such good fresh ones at most supermarkets, you don't need to be an expert to come home with high-quality produce. As a rough guideline, allow 125–225 g/4–8 oz of vegetables per person; of course this will partly depend on what else you are serving at the meal.

It is best to store vegetables in a cool, dark, dry place – I keep all my vegetables in the refrigerator except for onions and potatoes.

The golden rule to remember when preparing and cooking vegetables is less is best: trim as little as possible, then cook in as little water as possible for the least amount of time – just long enough for the vegetables to become tender but retain their texture. Then, if they're really at their peak, they need little in the way of embellishments – a little sea salt crumbled over them, a grinding of black pepper, a squeeze of fresh lemon juice, a flake or two of unsalted butter, maybe some chopped fresh parsley. The water the vegetables are cooked in is full of flavour and contains soluble vitamins and minerals, so it's worth saving to use as stock (page 30) or in soups or sauces. To retain even more of the flavour, texture and vitamins, keep the vegetables out of the water by steaming them – if you don't have a steamer basket with its own lid, improvise with a metal sieve or colander covered with the saucepan lid. Make sure the water is kept boiling and topped up, as the vegetables will take a little longer to cook.

Stir-frying is another healthy way to cook most vegetables. The amount of oil used is minimal and, since stir-frying is done over a high heat, the vegetables cook very quickly, so they keep their vitamins and their crisp texture. For successful stir-frying, you need to cut all the vegetables into fairly small pieces of a similar size. Heat a tablespoon of vegetable oil in a wok or large saucepan and, if you like, throw in some chopped garlic, ginger and spring onions. After they have sizzled for a few seconds, add the prepared vegetables and keep stirring them over a high heat for about 3–5 minutes, until they are heated through. Shake on some soy sauce and sesame oil, then serve at once.

Beetroot can be eaten raw (see page 50) or cooked in a number of ways, as a side dish or main course

vegetable basics

Artichokes, globe

Choose fresh-looking green or purple-tinged artichokes; avoid any with brownish patches.

The big ones that are the size of large oranges need washing well then trimming. First break off the stem level with the base and slice about 2.5 cm/1 inch off the top leaves, using a sharp serrated knife. Immerse the artichokes in a large saucepan of boiling water to which you have added the juice of 1 lemon, to prevent discoloration (use an enamelled or stainless steel pan because aluminium reacts with artichokes). Boil for 40–45 minutes; the artichokes are ready when you can easily pull off one of the leaves. Turn the artichokes upside down to drain.

To eat the artichoke, pull off one leaf at a time, dip the fleshy part in melted butter, or Vinaigrette (page 54) or Hollandaise sauce (page 84), nibble off the tender part and discard the rest of the leaf. When you reach the central leaves they become too small to handle; pick them up together – they will come away in a cone shape, revealing the hairy 'choke'. This needs to be cut out with a knife or scraped out with a sharp-edged teaspoon – make sure you get rid of it all because if you accidentally swallow some it is extremely irritating. You will be left with the base of the artichoke, which is the real delicacy – cut it into quarters and eat with more melted butter.

If you want to make things easier for your guests, and you have the time, you can remove the choke before serving the artichokes; pull back the leaves until you get to the inner 'cone'. then scrape out the choke as described.

If you can get baby artichokes, about the size of walnuts, simply trim off any tough outer leaves, then simmer them in a little olive oil and water, with some fresh herbs and sliced garlic, for about 30 minutes, or until tender. No need to remove any choke because there isn't one!

Artichokes, Jerusalem

Choose the smoothest, most evenly sized artichokes you can.

Peel the artichokes, being fairly ruthless about the lumpy bits, then boil them, covered in water, in an enamel or stainless steel pan for 20–40 minutes, until they are tender when you test them with a skewer. Don't overcook them, or they will collapse in a watery mess. As an alternative cooking method, melt some butter in a heavy-based saucepan, add the artichokes and toss them in the butter, then put a lid on the pan and leave it over a very low heat until the artichokes are tender.

Asparagus

Choose firm, evenly coloured stalks; avoid flabby ones or those with dark patches.

Break off any thick ends – the stem will break where it starts getting too tough to eat. You can stand the asparagus in a pan of boiling water, like flowers in a vase, and arrange a dome of foil over the top to keep in the steam, but I generally cook it in a frying pan of boiling water, with the stems all lying down. Either way, cook until it's just tender when pierced with a skewer or pointed knife; this will take 3–8 minutes or more, depending on the width of the stems. Drain and serve with extra virgin olive oil and lemon juice, melted butter and lemon juice, or Hollandaise sauce (page 84).

Aubergines

Some recipe books tell you to salt aubergines and leave them to drain before you cook them. That was intended to remove bitterness, but growers have long since conquered that trait, at least in the widely available varieties . . . has anyone come across a bitter aubergine recently? (You can still taste it in the tiny 'pea' aubergines sold in some Indian shops and often used in Thai curries.) All you need to do is wash the aubergine, cut off the stem, then slice the aubergine lengthways, widthways or into cubes, depending on the recipe.

However, salting does make the aubergine less absorbent, so it might be worth doing it if you're going to fry the aubergine, to prevent it from taking up too much oil. Cut the aubergine as required, put it into a colander, sprinkle with salt, put a plate and a weight on top and leave for 30 minutes or so. Rinse in cold water and pat dry with paper towels.

Beans, broad

If you can get really baby ones in tender pods, about 10 cm/4 inches long, prepare and cook them like French beans (see below) – they're delicious. Even when they're a bit older, if the pods are still tender you can leave the beans in their pods, cut the pods into 2.5 cm/1 inch lengths, cook in 5 cm/2 inches of boiling water for 5–10 minutes, then drain and serve with Parsley sauce (page 80).

But the pods of big broad beans are too tough to eat, so take the beans out of the pods, then boil the beans in a large pan of unsalted boiling water for 5–10 minutes, until tender. Drain and serve with butter and chopped herbs. For a really fine flavour, pop the beans out of their grey coats with your fingers and serve just the vibrant green beans. Broad beans also make a good purée, blended in the food processor with some melted butter or olive oil and lemon juice.

Beans, French

Green beans vary enormously in size, from the tiny Kenya beans to the larger, lumpier but tasty beans you may grow yourself.

Trim the ends ('top and tail') if you like, although I prefer to leave them as they are if they are not too coarse. Cook in 1 cm/½ inch of boiling water for 2–7 minutes, until just tender. Drain and serve.

Beans, runner

Top and tail; cut down the sides of the beans to remove any tough strings. Cut the beans into 2.5 cm/1 inch lengths or slice in a bean slicer if you have one. Cook in 1 cm/½ inch of boiling water for 5–7 minutes, until just tender. Drain and serve.

Beansprouts

These have little flavour of their own, but are often added to stir-fries with other vegetables for their light, crunchy texture. Rinse in cold water, drain and stir-fry in 1–2 tablespoons of oil for 1–2 minutes, with crushed garlic, grated fresh ginger and soy sauce to flavour.

Beetroot

A bunch of young beetroots with their leafy tops still attached is one of the delights of early summer cookery. Cut off the leaves about 10 cm/4 inches above the beetroot – if you go too close to the beetroot it will 'bleed' and lose its colour. For this reason, take care not to cut or damage them, just wash them gently, then boil them in water to cover, with a lid on the pan, for 1–3 hours, until they are tender. Slip off the skins, slice or cube as necessary and reheat in butter or olive oil. The tops make a delicious vegetable treat in their own right. Wash them well and cook in 1 cm/½ inch of boiling water for 4–5 minutes, until tender, then drain.

Broccoli

Choose firm heads of broccoli, avoiding any with yellowing florets.

Cut off the stems; separate the florets and cut if necessary so that they are all about the same size. Cut the stem pieces into slim matchsticks, discarding any tough bits. Cook in 1 cm/½ inch of boiling water for 5–7 minutes, until just tender. Drain and serve.

Brussels sprouts

Choose small firm sprouts; larger ones may taste bitter.

Trim off outer leaves and stalk ends. Cook really tiny ones whole and cut larger ones in half before cooking in 1 cm/½ inch of boiling water for 2–5 minutes, until just tender. Take care not to overcook them! Drain and serve.

Determined Brussels sprouts haters may be converted by stir-fried sprouts. Heat a little oil in a wok, add some sliced garlic and tiny sprouts. Toss for 1–2 minutes, then sprinkle with soy sauce and sesame oil. Serve at once.

Cabbage

Trim off outer leaves and stalk ends, then shred, discarding the central core. Cook in 1 cm/½ inch of boiling water for 5–7 minutes until just tender, drain and swirl with butter, salt and pepper, plus other flavourings such as freshly grated nutmeg, chopped fresh herbs, grated lemon rind, crushed coriander seeds or juniper berries.
See also Red Cabbage, page 92.

Carrots

If the carrots are still in a bunch, cut off the leafy tops. Scrub carrots if they're organic, otherwise peel them to remove any chemical residues. Leave small carrots whole; halve, quarter, slice or dice larger ones. Boil in water to cover for 5–20 minutes, until tender.

Cauliflower

Choose creamy-white cauliflowers with tight florets and no brown patches. Break or cut into florets, cut off tough stems, shred any tender leaves. Cook in 1 cm/½ inch of boiling water for 5–7 minutes, until just tender. Drain and serve as it is, or tossed in butter, or cover with White or Cheese sauce (page 80), top with breadcrumbs and pop under a hot grill until crisp and golden on top.

Celeriac

Peel fairly thickly, then slice or dice. Boil in water to cover for 5–20 minutes, until tender. Or steam, if you're just doing a little. Serve with butter and chopped herbs, or make into a creamy purée. Celeriac reacts with aluminium, so use an enamel or stainless steel pan.

Celery

Trim and slice outer sticks, cover with water and boil until tender, 20–30 minutes. Drain (keep the water – it makes excellent stock) and serve with butter.

Chicory

Cook in boiling salted water to which you have added a squeeze of lemon juice and a pinch of sugar. Drain well, then melt a knob of butter in a wide saucepan, add the chicory and cook over a low heat until it is just golden all over – do not let it brown. If you like, add 1–2 tablespoons of double cream, raise the heat and serve when the cream is bubbling.

Chinese leaves

Wash and cut into chunks or shreds. Best stir-fried, as for beansprouts (page 89), but it can also be cooked in 1 cm/½ inch of boiling water for 5–7 minutes, until just tender.

Courgettes

Trim the ends of finger-sized courgettes, slice or dice larger ones. Sauté with a knob of butter and/or a tablespoon or two of olive oil for 3–5 minutes, until just tender. Or cook in 1 cm/½ inch of boiling water for 3–5 minutes, drain well and serve.

Fennel

Trim off the stalk end and trim the outer white bracts to remove any stringy bits. Halve, quarter or slice the bulbs and cook in boiling water until just tender, then drain. Place in an ovenproof dish, season with salt and pepper and sprinkle with grated cheese (preferably Parmesan), then bake in a hot oven for about 15 minutes, until the cheese is bubbling.

Kale

Strongly flavoured but delicious – and high in iron, beta-carotene and folic acid. Trim off outer leaves and stalk ends, then shred. Cook in 1 cm/½ inch of boiling water for 5–7 minutes, until just tender. Drain well, swirl with butter, salt and pepper and serve hot.

Kohlrabi

Peel this delicately flavoured vegetable fairly thickly, to remove the lumpy bits, then slice or dice. Boil in water to cover for 5–15 minutes, until tender. Or steam, if you're just doing a little. Serve with butter and chopped herbs. It's good in a medley of other root vegetables.

Leeks

Trim off the roots and cut the green part down to within about 2.5–5 cm/1–2 inches of the white part, then slit down one side and rinse out the grit under the cold tap, keeping the leek intact. Leave whole, or slice if large. Steam, boil whole as for Leeks vinaigrette (page 47) or cook slices in 1 cm/½ inch of boiling water for 5–8 minutes, until just tender. Drain well, toss with butter, salt and freshly ground black pepper and serve hot.

Mangetout

Top and tail, then stir-fry or cook in 1 cm/½ inch of boiling water for 1–3 minutes; they don't need much cooking, just heating through. Drain and serve.

Perfect, creamy-white cauliflower

Marrow

Rather neglected, in my opinion. Although part of the same family as courgettes, marrow has a different flavour and texture and is delicious in its own right as long as it hasn't been allowed to get too large. A good marrow has a skin and seeds that are tender enough to eat, though you could remove them if you prefer. Cut the marrow into chunks, then steam or – and I think this is best – put into a heavy-based saucepan with a good knob of butter, a bay leaf, salt and pepper and 4 tablespoons of water and cook over a low heat with a lid on the pan until the marrow is translucent and tender, 10–20 minutes.

Mushrooms

Some cooks say it is best not to wash mushrooms, just wipe them with a damp cloth, because they soak up too much water, but this doesn't matter too much if you cook them in the way I recommend. Heat a knob of butter in a saucepan, add the mushrooms and cook over a moderate heat until they are tender and most of the liquid has evaporated.

Okra

Trim off the stalk ends, then cut into 1 cm/ ½ inch slices, or leave whole if they're small. Fry in 2 tablespoons of olive oil with a chopped onion, chopped tomato, crushed garlic, ground coriander and cumin for 10–15 minutes for a delicious, spicy dish.

Onions

Bake in their skins as for baked potatoes (page 94), cut a cross in the top and serve with butter, salt and pepper.

To serve as a vegetable in their own right, peel, cut into even-sized pieces and boil for 15–20 minutes, until tender, or slice and fry in butter or oil for about 10 minutes.

For caramelized onions, begin with twice as many as you think you'll need; cook with a little butter or oil over a low heat for about 30 minutes, stirring occasionally, adding a splash of water or sherry to prevent sticking, and adding a pinch of sugar near the end of cooking time.

For crisp onion rings, dip raw onion slices in milk and flour, then deep-fry for 1–2 minutes.

Parsnips

Peel fairly thickly then halve, quarter, slice or dice. Boil in water to cover for 5–20 minutes, until tender. Or, if you're just doing a few, steam them. Serve with butter and chopped herbs, or make into a creamy purée. Parsnips are also excellent roasted in a little hot oil.

Peas

Remove from their pods, then cook in 1 cm/ ½ inch boiling water for 2–5 minutes; they need very little cooking, so be careful not to overcook them or they will be hard and stodgy. Serve with butter and chopped mint.

Peppers

The best way to cook these is grilling (see page 44).

Potatoes

Scrub, scrape or peel potatoes depending on their condition and whether or not they're organically grown. Boil in water to cover for 15–20 minutes, until tender. Or, if you're just doing a few, steam them; they may take a few minutes longer. Serve with butter and chopped herbs – chives and parsley are good. Other ways of cooking potatoes are described on pages 94–97.

Pumpkin

Allow about 225 g/8 oz per person. Cut off the skin and remove the seeds, then slice or dice the flesh. Steam, or boil in water to cover for 10–20 minutes, until tender. Purée or serve with butter.

Pumpkin is also good cooked gently in butter as described for Jerusalem artichokes (page 88); or cut into wedges (with the skin left on) and baked for about 40 minutes; or cut into chunks and roasted in a little hot oil.

Red cabbage

Trim off outer leaves and stalk ends, then shred, discarding the central core.

Delicious cooked in a heavy-based saucepan as described for marrow (above), but allow 1½–2 hours. A chopped onion, crushed garlic, grated nutmeg, stick of cinnamon, chopped apple and a glass of red wine or dry cider are good additions.

Spinach

Wash the spinach very thoroughly: put it into a sinkful of cold water, swish it around, then take it out and repeat twice, using clean water each time.

Remove any substantial stems (most of the spinach sold in supermarkets has tender stems, which can remain), chop them and cook them for 2–3 minutes in 1 cm/½ inch of boiling water before putting in the spinach leaves and cooking for a further 5–7 minutes, until just tender. If the stems are delicate, simply put the spinach, stems and all, with just the water clinging to it after washing, into a dry saucepan and cook over a high heat until the spinach has wilted and is tender, 5–7 minutes. As it cooks, push the leaves down into the pan with the end of a fish slice, chopping them as you do so.

Drain well and chop roughly with the fish slice; or drain into a colander, press out as much liquid as possible, then turn the spinach on to a board and chop thoroughly before returning it to the pan with a knob of butter and reheating gently.

Another way to cook tender spinach is to wilt it in olive oil: heat 2 tablespoons of olive oil in a large saucepan and put in some spinach. Stir-fry over a high heat until it collapses, then transfer it to a warmed dish and repeat until all the spinach is done.

Whichever method you use, season spinach with salt, pepper, freshly grated nutmeg and perhaps some crushed garlic.

Swede

Peel fairly thickly then slice or dice. Boil in water to cover for 10–20 minutes, until tender. Or steam, if you're just doing a little. Serve with butter and chopped herbs or mash – a mixture of half swede and half carrots is excellent – flavouring it with a finely chopped piece of preserved ginger.

Sweet potatoes

Treat these as you would potatoes; scrub and bake, or peel, boil and mash.

Sweetcorn

To cook a whole corn cob, first remove the leaves and silky threads and trim off the stalk. Immerse in a large pan of boiling water and simmer for 4–5 minutes, or until the kernels are tender – don't add salt to the water because this toughens them. Drain, blot dry with paper towels and serve with melted butter, crunchy sea salt and freshly ground black pepper.

Alternatively, you can cut the kernels off the cob: slice off the tip to make a flat end; stand the end on a chopping board and cut downwards with a sharp knife to remove the kernels. Cook them in a little boiling water for 2–3 minutes, then drain and serve. The kernels are also nice raw in a salad.

Swiss chard

You can treat this like spinach with substantial stems (left), cooking the stems in boiling water for 3–4 minutes before adding the leaves.

Or you can treat the green leaves and white stems as two separate vegetables, cooking the green part like tender spinach without stems and the stems as celery, slicing and simmering them in water to cover for 4–7 minutes, until tender. Drain and serve with butter or a sauce.

Tomatoes

Remove the stems, cut a cross in the top, or halve them, and bake them in a moderate oven, 180°C/350°F/Gas Mark 4, or under a hot grill until tender: they take about 15 minutes. Or fry them on both sides in a little hot oil.

Many recipes call for skinned tomatoes. To skin them, cut a cross in the top, then put them into a bowl and cover with boiling water. Leave for about 30 seconds, until the skins loosen, then drain, cover with cold water and peel off the skins, using your fingers and a sharp pointed knife.

Turnips

If the turnips are still in a bunch, cut off the leafy tops. (These can be washed and cooked like beetroot tops, see page 89. They're full of iron and other good things but quite bitter.) Scrub turnips if they're organic, otherwise peel them. Leave small turnips whole; halve, quarter, slice or dice larger ones. Boil in water to cover for 5–15 minutes, until tender. Or, if you're just doing a few, steam them.

six basic potato recipes

Baked potatoes

For really tasty, crisp-skinned baked potatoes you need to bake them in a very hot oven, 230°C/450°F/Gas Mark 8. Scrub one or two large, preferably organic, potatoes per person, prick several times with a fork and bake for 1–1½ hours, until the potatoes feel soft when squeezed and the skins are crisp – turn them and change their position in the oven once or twice so they cook evenly.

   Split open and serve with butter and grated cheese, or cottage cheese, soured cream or Greek yogurt with chopped fresh herbs. For alternative toppings, try one of the dips from the Starters chapter, Wild mushroom ragout (page 99) or Ratatouille (page 101).

Bircher potatoes

This is a delightful cross between a baked and a roast potato. The dish is named after the man who invented them, Dr Bircher Benner, who was also responsible for muesli (in its original form this was very different from the muesli we know today).

SERVES 4
4–6 medium-sized potatoes, scrubbed
olive or groundnut oil

Heat the oven to 200°C/400°F/Gas Mark 6. Brush a roasting tin generously with oil. Cut the potatoes in half lengthways and place them, cut side down, on the oiled tin. Bake the potatoes for about 45 minutes, until they are soft on top and crisp and golden brown underneath. Blot with paper towels to remove any excess oil, then serve immediately.

Chips

For the best potato chips you need to use a floury variety of potato such as Maris Piper, Desiree or King Edward.

SERVES 4
900 g/2 lb potatoes, peeled
groundnut oil for deep-frying
salt

Cut the potatoes into chips – I first cut the potatoes into slices about 1 cm/½ inch thick, then across into 1 cm/½ inch sticks. Rinse them in cold water to get rid of some of the starch, and leave them to soak in a bowl of cold water for half an hour or so, until you're ready to cook them.

   To fry the chips, fill a deep-fat fryer or deep, sturdy saucepan not more than one-third full of oil and heat it to 190°C/375°F. A cooking thermometer is the most reliable way of checking the temperature – you need to put it in the pan when you start heating the oil to prevent it from cracking in the heat. Alternatively, dip the end of a wooden chopstick or wooden spoon into the oil – if bubbles immediately form around it, the oil is hot enough.

   While the oil is heating, dry the chips thoroughly on a clean tea towel. Put the first batch of chips into a chip basket and lower them into the hot oil. If you don't have a chip basket, you will need to use a large metal draining spoon to lift the chips out of the oil. Fry the chips until they are just becoming tender – about 5 minutes. Then lift them out of the oil and set aside – if you're doing more than one batch, get all the chips to this stage.

   Just before you want to serve them, reheat the oil to 190°C/375°F. Plunge each batch of chips into the oil for 1–2 minutes, until they are golden brown and crisp. Put them into a dish lined with crumpled paper towels and serve immediately.

Crisp, golden chips

Mashed potatoes

These are a good accompaniment to many vegetarian dishes. Their creamy consistency means that you don't need to serve a sauce.

SERVES 4
700 g/1½ lb potatoes, peeled and cut into
   even-sized pieces
150 ml/5 fl oz milk, soya milk or single cream
15–25 g/½–1 oz butter or vegan margarine
salt and freshly ground black pepper

Put the potatoes into a saucepan, cover with cold water and bring to the boil. Put the lid over the pan but leave a space for steam to escape. Boil for about 15 minutes, until just tender. Drain the potatoes, then either put them back into the pan and mash very thoroughly with a potato masher, or push them through a sieve or a potato ricer. Don't use a food processor, because it makes the potatoes gluey.

In another saucepan, heat the milk or cream. When it comes to the boil, add it gradually to the potatoes, together with the butter or margarine, beating all the time with a wooden spoon. The potatoes will become fluffy and whiter as you do so; they should have the consistency of lightly whipped cream. Add salt and pepper to taste.

Variations
Use 1–2 tablespoons of extra virgin olive oil instead of the butter. When mashing with either butter or olive oil, you could include 2–4 crushed garlic cloves.

Roast potatoes

The secret of crisp, golden roast potatoes is to put very hot parboiled potatoes into very hot oil (4 tablespoons for each 450 g/1 lb of potatoes), thus sealing the outsides.

SERVES 4
900 g/2 lb medium-sized potatoes, peeled
about 8 tablespoons groundnut oil
salt

Heat the oven to 220°C/425°F/Gas Mark 7. Cut the potatoes into even-sized pieces – I generally cut them lengthways so that there is a nice big area to get crisp, but you could cut them into chunky quarters. Put the potatoes into a saucepan, cover with cold water, bring to the boil and parboil for 10 minutes.

Meanwhile, pour the oil into a roasting tin large enough to hold the potatoes in a single layer, then put the tin into the oven to heat up.

Drain the potatoes (keep the water – it makes excellent stock).

Bring the tin of oil from the oven to the hob and put it over a burner to keep the oil sizzling hot. Put the potatoes into the tin one by one, turning each one in the oil so that it is coated all over. Put the tin back into the oven and bake for about 40–50 minutes, turning them after about 25 minutes, until the potatoes are crisp and golden brown. Serve as soon as possible, and don't cover them once they're cooked, or they will soften.

Rosti

This grated potato cake is delicious as part of a meal or on its own, as a snack.

SERVES 2–4
450 g/1 lb potatoes, peeled
salt
4 tablespoons olive oil

Grate the potatoes coarsely, using a box grater or the grating attachment of a food processor. Don't rinse them, because the starch will help to hold them together as they cook; just season them with a little salt.

Heat the oil in a frying pan, then add the potatoes, either in one large cake or four individual cakes, and press down with a fish slice. Cover the pan, reduce the heat and let the potatoes cook gently until they are tender and browned on the bottom; this will take about 15–20 minutes. Then turn the rosti over, either using a fish slice, or by turning it out on to a plate then sliding it back into the frying pan. Continue to cook until the second side is browned and crisp, then drain on paper towels and serve at once.

Gratin dauphinoise

I have experimented many times with this dish and I have found that a mixture of double cream and water gives the best result: lower fat creams tend to curdle. Although usually served as an accompaniment, it is very rich and I prefer to serve it as a main dish, to give a better balance to the meal. Serve it with simple steamed vegetables.

SERVES 3
450 g/1 lb potatoes, peeled
25 g/1 oz butter
1 garlic clove, crushed
salt and freshly ground black pepper
freshly grated nutmeg
150 ml/5 fl oz double cream

Heat the oven to 180°C/350°F/Gas Mark 4. Cut the potatoes into the thinnest slices you can manage – use a sharp knife, the slicing side of a grater, or the slicing disc on a food processor. Put the slices into a bowl of water, swish them round to wash off some of the starch, then drain them in a colander.

Grease a shallow ovenproof dish with half the butter, then put in the crushed garlic and the potato slices, layering them as neatly as you can and seasoning between the layers with salt, pepper and nutmeg.

Mix the cream with 150 ml/5 fl oz water and pour evenly over the potatoes. Dot the remaining butter in little pieces over the top, and bake, uncovered, at the top of the oven until the potatoes feel tender when you push in a skewer or the point of a knife and the top ones are golden and crisp; this will take about 1½ hours. Serve hot.

Wild mushroom dauphinoise
Put 15 g/½ oz of dried porcini mushrooms into a cup and add just enough boiling water to cover them. Leave to soak for at least 30 minutes, then rinse the porcini under the tap to remove any grit, squeeze dry and chop into small shreds. Strain the soaking liquid and add water to make it up to 150 ml/5 fl oz; use this to dilute the cream. Sprinkle the chopped porcini between the layers of potato; finish and bake as above.

Leek and potato hotpot

An idea which originated from Doris Grant and Jean Joice's book, *Food Combining for Health* (Thorsons, 1984) and a particular favourite of my daughter Claire. It's very easy to make, filling and delicious. We like it with sliced tomatoes and a little watercress.

SERVES 2–3
4 leeks
2 tablespoons olive oil
4 medium-sized potatoes
4 tablespoons evaporated milk, cream or soya cream (optional)
salt and freshly ground black pepper
freshly grated nutmeg
chopped fresh parsley

Trim and wash the leeks as described on page 91, then cut them into 2.5 cm/1 inch lengths. Heat the oil in a large saucepan, add the leeks, stir, then leave to cook over a low heat for 5 minutes.

Meanwhile, peel the potatoes and cut them into 1 cm/½ inch chunks. Add these to the pan with the leeks, stir, then cover with a lid and cook very gently for a further 5 minutes, stirring occasionally. Add 85 ml/3 fl oz water, cover again and cook for a further 10 minutes, or until the potatoes and leeks are tender.

Add the milk or cream if you are using it. Season to taste with salt, pepper and nutmeg, sprinkle with chopped parsley and serve hot.

Beetroot with crème fraîche and dill

Beetroot makes a lovely vegetable dish. You can buy it raw and cook it yourself (see page 89) or, for speed and ease, buy it ready-cooked – just make sure it hasn't been mixed with vinegar. I like this as a light main course, with boiled rice.

SERVES 2–4
700 g/1½ lb cooked beetroots
salt and freshly ground black pepper
squeeze of lemon juice
150 ml/5 fl oz crème fraîche or soured cream
sprigs of fresh dill

If the beetroots are still in their skins, peel it off with your fingers; it will slip off easily. Rinse the beetroots in cold water and cut them into 2.5 cm/1 inch dice or thick slices.

Put the beetroot pieces in a saucepan with 4–5 tablespoons water, cover and cook gently for about 5 minutes, until the beetroot is piping hot. Season to taste with salt, pepper and lemon juice, and serve on warmed plates. Top each serving with a spoonful of crème fraîche and some curly fronds of dill, grind a little pepper over the top and serve at once.

Wild mushroom ragout

Wild mushrooms make an exotic-looking dish, but this is just as rich and luxurious made with ordinary mushrooms, or a mixture of mushroom varieties. In fact, many of the unusual mushrooms sold in supermarkets today are not wild but cultivated. They may not have the depth of flavour of truly wild mushrooms, but they are not expensive, so do experiment with this recipe. It's good served with pasta, or with Saffron or Lemon rice (page 116).

SERVES 4
25 g/1 oz butter
1 tablespoon olive oil
1 onion, peeled and chopped
2 garlic cloves, crushed
1 kg/2¼ lb mushrooms (any variety)
2 teaspoons cornflour
200 ml/7 fl oz crème fraîche
salt and freshly ground black pepper
freshly grated nutmeg
paprika or chopped fresh parsley

Melt the butter with the oil in a large saucepan, add the onion, stir, cover and leave to cook gently for 5 minutes. Stir in the garlic, and cook for a further 2–3 minutes.

While the onions are cooking, wash or wipe the mushrooms, pat them dry on paper towels and cut them into slices about 5 mm/¼ inch thick. Add them to the onions and cook over a moderate heat until the mushrooms are tender and most of the liquid has disappeared; this will take 20–30 minutes.

Stir the cornflour into the mixture, then add the crème fraîche and stir over the heat for a minute or two, until the mixture thickens very slightly. Season to taste with salt, pepper and nutmeg. Serve with rice, sprinkled with paprika or chopped parsley.

Variation
For a lower fat version, use Greek yogurt or fromage frais instead of the crème fraîche.

Beetroot with crème fraîche and dill

Spicy vegetable curry

This simple curry is one of my favourites. The 'heat' of the curry depends on the strength of the chilli. It's a 'dry' curry, good served with either Indian bread (chapatti or nan) or with rice. I often serve accompaniments of sliced tomato and onion, and some mango chutney.

SERVES 2–3
325 g/12 oz even-sized potatoes
225 g/8 oz cauliflower
  (about ½ a small–medium one)
2 tablespoons olive oil
1 large onion, peeled and chopped
1 fresh chilli, deseeded and chopped very finely
1 garlic clove, crushed
1 teaspoon cumin seeds
1 teaspoon ground cumin
½ teaspoon ground coriander
¼ teaspoon turmeric
salt and freshly ground black pepper
2–3 tablespoons finely chopped fresh coriander

Put the potatoes, still in their skins, into a saucepan, cover with cold water and boil until they are tender enough to be pierced with a sharp knife; this will take about 15–20 minutes. Drain and leave to cool, then slip off the skins with a knife and cut the potatoes into 1 cm/½ inch dice.

While the potatoes are cooking, cut the cauliflower into 1 cm/½ inch florets. Rinse the florets and leave to soak in cold water for 30 minutes.

Heat the oil in a large saucepan, add the onion, cover and cook over a low heat for 5 minutes. Add the chilli, garlic and spices, and 1 teaspoon of salt. Stir over a low heat for 1–2 minutes, then put in the cauliflower. Stir to coat the cauliflower with the spicy mixture, then cover and leave to cook over a low heat for about 5 minutes, or until the cauliflower is nearly tender.

Add the potato, stir, and cook for a further 2 minutes or so, to heat the potato through and finish cooking the cauliflower. Taste and adjust the seasoning and serve hot, sprinkled with fresh coriander.

Potato and spinach curry
Replace the cauliflower with spinach. Cook 450 g/ 1 lb of frozen leaf spinach in 1 cm/½ inch of boiling water for 2–3 minutes, then drain thoroughly in a colander, pressing out all the excess water. Add the spinach to the onion and spice mixture in place of the cauliflower.

Sri Lankan curried vegetables

This is quick and easy to make and is delicious with lots of boiled rice to soak up the spicy coconut sauce – brown Basmati is especially good.

SERVES 3–4
1 tablespoon olive oil
1 onion, peeled and chopped
2 garlic cloves, crushed
1 red pepper, deseeded and chopped
  into 5 mm/¼ inch pieces
2 teaspoons hot curry paste
4 courgettes, sliced into 3 mm/⅛ inch rounds
2 tablespoons ground almonds
400 ml/14 fl oz coconut milk
juice of ½ lemon
salt and freshly ground black pepper
1 tablespoon chopped fresh coriander

Heat the oil in a large saucepan, add the onion and fry over a medium heat for 5 minutes, but don't let it brown.

Add the garlic and red pepper and cook, stirring frequently, for a further 5 minutes, then stir in the curry paste. Add the courgettes and cook for a further 4–5 minutes, stirring frequently until the courgettes are just tender.

Stir in the almonds, coconut milk, lemon juice and salt and pepper to taste. Sprinkle with fresh coriander and serve with rice.

Variations
Other vegetables can be used, just chop or slice them and add to the pan after you have cooked the onion; cook until they are just tender. Broccoli, French beans, mangetout, carrot sticks, baby sweetcorn and spring onions are all good.

Vegetables braised in oil and lemon

I serve this dish on its own as a first course or with rice, potatoes or another carbohydrate as a main course.

SERVES 4
225 g/8 oz broccoli
175 g/6 oz mangetout
450 g/1 lb carrots
2 red peppers
225 g/8 oz small white mushrooms
1 bunch of spring onions
1 lemon, scrubbed
85 ml/3 fl oz olive oil
1 bay leaf
1 sprig of fresh thyme or a good pinch of dried thyme
salt and freshly ground black pepper
chopped fresh parsley

Start by preparing all the vegetables. Prepare the broccoli as described on page 89, but cook in boiling water for only 3 minutes, then drain into a colander and rinse in cold water. Pat dry with paper towels and set aside.

Top and tail the mangetout, cook in boiling water for 1 minute, then drain and rinse in cold water to stop them cooking in their own heat and to bring out their colour; pat dry.

Peel the carrots and cut them into pieces the size of your little finger. Deseed the peppers and cut into similar-sized pieces to the carrots. Wipe the mushrooms; leave them whole, or halve or quarter them. Trim and chop the spring onions.

Pare the rind thinly from one half of the lemon, being careful to peel off only the yellow part, not the white pith underneath. Grate the yellow rind from the other half.

Pour the oil into a large saucepan or wok and add 85 ml/3 fl oz water, the pared lemon rind, the bay leaf, thyme, carrots and red pepper and bring to the boil. Cover and simmer for about 4 minutes, or until the vegetables are becoming tender but still have plenty of bite.

Then add the mushrooms, cover and cook for another 3 minutes. Add the broccoli, mangetout and spring onions and cook for a further 2–3 minutes.

Remove from the heat, add the grated lemon rind and enough of the juice to give a pleasant tang. Season to taste with salt and pepper, then serve immediately, sprinkled with chopped parsley.

Ratatouille

This delicious Provençal summer stew is easy to make and very versatile: I often serve it with pasta, polenta, baked potatoes or rice.

SERVES 4
3 tablespoons olive oil
2 large onions, peeled and chopped
3 garlic cloves, crushed
450 g/1 lb red peppers, deseeded and cut into 1 cm/½ inch pieces
450 g/1 lb aubergines, cut into 5 mm/¼ inch dice
450 g/1 lb courgettes, cut into 5 mm/¼ inch dice
700 g/1½ lb tomatoes, skinned (see page 93) and chopped
salt and freshly ground black pepper
chopped fresh parsley or basil

Heat the olive oil in a large saucepan, then add the onions, garlic, peppers and aubergines, stir, cover and leave to cook over a low heat for 10 minutes.

Add the courgettes and tomatoes, stir, then cover the saucepan and cook over a low heat for 20–25 minutes, until all the vegetables are tender. Season to taste and sprinkle with chopped parsley or basil. Serve hot or cold.

Ratatouille with coriander
Coriander seeds make a subtle difference to the flavour: add a tablespoon of the crushed seeds, or ground coriander, to the mixture with the onions. (Crush whole coriander seeds with the back of a wooden spoon or in a pestle and mortar.)

Winter ratatouille
Try using green peppers instead of the red peppers, sliced carrots instead of the aubergines and sliced mushrooms instead of the courgettes.

Roasted Mediterranean vegetables

These are equally good hot, warm or cold; any left over are excellent as a salad the next day, with some Garlic vinaigrette (page 54). I like to serve them with couscous, which is very quick and easy to prepare (see page 114). You can vary the mixture of vegetables according to what is available.

SERVES 3

1 aubergine
3 peppers (red, yellow and green)
3 tablespoons extra virgin olive oil
3–4 garlic cloves
1 tablespoon chopped fresh oregano or marjoram
salt and freshly ground black pepper
425 g/15 oz can artichoke hearts, drained and
    quartered
50 g/2 oz black olives, roughly chopped
2–3 sprigs of basil

Heat the oven to 230°C/450°F/Gas Mark 8. Trim the aubergine and cut into 2.5 cm/1 inch chunks; cut the peppers into similar-sized pieces, discarding the seeds and core. Sprinkle the aubergine and peppers with the olive oil and rub the oil in, using your fingers, to make sure they are well coated. Put them into a roasting tin with the unpeeled garlic cloves, oregano or marjoram and some salt and pepper and roast for 20 minutes.

    Turn the oven down to 180°C/350°F/Gas Mark 4 and bake for a further 10 minutes, then add the artichoke hearts and cook for 10–15 minutes more, until the vegetables are all tender and beginning to brown. Add a little more olive oil during this time if they look at all dry. To serve, scatter the olives and tear the basil leaves over the top.

Roasted root vegetables

A selection of roasted winter vegetables can be eaten as a main course, perhaps with a cooked green vegetable and/or some mashed potatoes to accompany them. You could serve them with grated Parmesan cheese, hummus, yogurt or fromage frais with chopped winter herbs such as sage and thyme.

SERVES 2

2 red onions
2 turnips, scrubbed
2 small red-skinned potatoes, scrubbed
2 parsnips, scrubbed
2 carrots, scrubbed
1 small swede, peeled
2 garlic cloves, crushed
3 tablespoons olive oil
1 tablespoon chopped sage, thyme or rosemary
salt and freshly ground black pepper

Heat the oven to 200°C/400°F/Gas Mark 6. Peel and quarter the onions and turnips; cut the potatoes, parsnips, carrots and swede into 2.5 cm/1 inch chunks.

    Put the vegetables into a bowl and add the garlic, oil, herbs, salt and pepper; using your fingers, rub the oil mixture into the vegetables to make sure they are evenly coated with the oil and flavourings. Put them into a roasting tin and roast for 35–40 minutes, or until they are tender and browned. Serve hot.

Roasted Mediterranean vegetables

pasta

For a quick and easy vegetarian meal, pasta is hard to beat: it is loved by just about everyone, and there are numerous variations, including Italian spaghetti, pasta shapes and stuffed pasta such as ravioli, Chinese egg noodles, and Japanese varieties such as the thick, slippery udon noodles and soba noodles, made of buckwheat flour.

The main key to success when cooking pasta is to use a large enough saucepan. It needs to hold 1 litre/1¾ pints of water for every 125 g/4 oz of pasta – and 125 g/4 oz of pasta is the amount I find is usually right for one person as a main dish.

So, find a large saucepan, fill not more than two-thirds full with water and bring to the boil. When it's boiling vigorously, add a couple of teaspoons of salt, throw in your pasta or, if it's spaghetti or another long dry noodle, hold it in your hand like a bunch of flowers, stand the base of the 'stems' in the water, and gently push them down into the water as they soften, until it's all in. Then give the pasta a quick stir and let it boil, without a lid, until it's done. This may take as little as 3 minutes for fresh pasta and 6–7 minutes or more for dried pasta, depending on the size of the pieces. The packet will usually suggest a time, but take a piece of pasta out with a slotted spoon and bite it just before the time is up, to see how it's doing. It's done when it's tender on the outside but still firm in the middle, with the inside looking slightly white. Because pasta is traditionally tested by biting it to check that it's still firm in the middle, recipes often describe it as being cooked *al dente*, literally 'to the tooth'.

When it's done, immediately drain it into a colander in the sink, then tip the pasta back into the saucepan and add a knob of butter or a tablespoon or two of olive oil and some freshly ground black pepper. Serve at once, before it has a chance to cool down, as it is, or with herbs, cheese or any other trimmings. If you are adding a sauce, such as Fresh tomato sauce (page 82), you can mix it with the pasta in the pan, or serve the pasta on to warmed plates and spoon the sauce on top.

Pasta is now available in a wide variety of colours and flavours

Mediterranean pasta

This brings the flavours of sunshine to the table at any time of year.

SERVES 4
3 tablespoons olive oil
1 onion, peeled and chopped
1 aubergine, cut into 5 mm/¼ inch dice
1 red or green pepper, deseeded and cut into
    5 mm/¼ inch dice
1 garlic clove, crushed
400 g/14 oz can chopped tomatoes in juice
salt and freshly ground black pepper
400 g/14 oz penne or other short pasta
2–3 fresh basil leaves
50 g/2 oz fresh Parmesan cheese, grated or cut into
    thin flakes

First make the sauce. Heat 2 tablespoons of the oil in a large saucepan, add the onion, stir, then cover and leave to cook over a low heat for 5 minutes.

Add the aubergine and pepper, stir, cover and cook gently for a further 10 minutes, stirring occasionally to prevent sticking.

Add the garlic, then the tomatoes in their juice. Bring to the boil, then let the mixture simmer, without a lid, until any wateriness has disappeared, leaving a thick sauce – about 15 minutes. Season to taste.

When the tomatoes are bubbling away, cook the pasta as described on page 105. When it's done, return it to the pan with the remaining tablespoon of oil.

Either serve the pasta on to warmed plates and spoon the sauce on top, or add the sauce to the pasta in the pan and toss gently before serving. Either way, top with some torn basil leaves and Parmesan cheese.

Farfalle with courgettes

In this quick recipe, the courgettes are cooked with the pasta, and flavoured with lemon rind. Farfalle are pasta in the shape of butterflies or, more prosaically, bow-ties.

SERVES 4
400 g/14 oz farfalle
salt and freshly ground black pepper
3 medium-sized courgettes, sliced
200 g/7 oz fromage frais
grated rind of ½ lemon

Bring a large saucepan of water to the boil and add 2 teaspoons of salt. Add the pasta, let the water come back to the boil, give it a quick stir, then leave it to cook for 6 minutes.

Add the courgettes and cook for a further 2 minutes, until both the pasta and courgettes are just tender. Drain the pasta and courgettes, then tip them back into the pan and add the fromage frais and lemon rind. Season to taste and serve immediately.

Pasta with asparagus
Instead of the courgettes, use 450 g/1 lb of asparagus, trimmed and cut into 2.5 cm/1 inch lengths. Allow a little longer for the asparagus to cook – add it 3–4 minutes before the pasta should be ready.

Pasta with peas and mint
Instead of the farfalle, a ribbon pasta like fettuccine is nice for this variation. Instead of the courgettes, add 450 g/1 lb of frozen petit pois or trimmed mangetout 1 minute before the pasta is ready. Omit the lemon rind and add 2–4 tablespoons of chopped fresh mint.

Farfalle with courgettes

Macaroni cheese

Not the most original vegetarian dish in the world, but so popular with all the vegetarians I know that I felt I had to include a recipe. The secret of a good macaroni cheese is to make the sauce quite thin because it thickens up considerably as it cooks.

SERVES 4–6
50 g/2 oz butter, plus a little extra for the topping
40 g/1½ oz flour
900 ml/1½ pints milk or soya milk
175–225 g/6–8 oz Cheddar cheese, grated
1 tablespoon Dijon or English mustard
dash of Tabasco sauce
salt and freshly ground black pepper
freshly grated nutmeg
225 g/8 oz quick-cook macaroni
100 g/4 oz fresh wholemeal breadcrumbs

First make the sauce. Put the butter, flour and milk into a saucepan and place over a moderate heat. Using a balloon whisk, keep whisking until the mixture comes to the boil and thickens to a smooth sauce. Turn the heat down as low as you can and leave to simmer very gently for 5–6 minutes to cook the flour. Stir in two-thirds of the cheese, the mustard, and Tabasco, salt, pepper and nutmeg to taste.

Heat the grill, or heat the oven to 200°C/400°F/Gas Mark 6. Grease a heatproof dish.

Cook the macaroni as described on page 105 until just tender, about 8 minutes. Drain well, then mix the macaroni with the cheese sauce. Add more salt and pepper to taste, then spoon the mixture into the heatproof dish and sprinkle with the breadcrumbs, the remaining cheese and a few flakes of butter. Bake in the oven for about 20 minutes, or grill for 10–15 minutes, until the top is browned and crisp.

Cauliflower cheese
Instead of the pasta, use a medium to large cauliflower; break into florets and cook in boiling water for about 5 minutes, until just tender. Drain well. Make the sauce a little thicker by using 150 ml/5 fl oz less milk, because the cauliflower has the opposite effect to the macaroni, and the sauce tends to thin as it cooks.

Fusilli with cream cheese and herbs

Fusilli are little spiral or corkscrew-shaped pasta. You can use either a medium-fat cream cheese or a reduced-fat type for this recipe.

SERVES 4
400 g/14 oz fusilli
salt and freshly ground black pepper
300 g/11 oz cream cheese with garlic and herbs

Bring a large saucepan of water to the boil and add 2 teaspoons of salt. Add the pasta, let the water come back to the boil, give it a quick stir, then leave it to cook for 6–8 minutes or until the pasta is just tender.

Drain the pasta, then tip it back into the pan and add the cream cheese. Stir gently, season to taste and serve immediately.

Variation
Add 175–225 g/6–8 oz of frozen peas to the water 1 minute before the pasta is done.

Tagliatelle with lentil sauce

This is a very filling and nutritious sauce, which can be made with split red lentils, or brown, green or Puy lentils (see below). The sauce also freezes well.

SERVES 4
3 tablespoons olive oil
1 large onion, peeled and chopped
2 garlic cloves, crushed
½ teaspoon ground cinnamon
225 g/8 oz split red lentils, washed
400 g/14 oz canned tomatoes
salt and freshly ground black pepper
400 g/14 oz tagliatelle
flaked or grated Parmesan cheese (optional)

First make the sauce. Heat 2 tablespoons of the oil in a large saucepan, add the onion, stir, then cover and leave to cook gently for 5 minutes. Then add the garlic and cook for a few seconds before adding the cinnamon, lentils, tomatoes and 400 ml/15 fl oz water. Stir, then leave to cook, uncovered, stirring occasionally to prevent sticking, until the lentils are tender and any wateriness has disappeared, leaving a thick sauce – about 30 minutes. Season to taste.

When the sauce is almost ready, cook the pasta as described on page 105. When it's done, return it to the pan with the remaining tablespoon of oil. Either serve the pasta on to warmed plates and spoon the sauce on top, or add the sauce to the pasta in the pan and toss gently before serving. Either way, top with some Parmesan if you like.

Variations
Try using other spices or herbs, or replace a little of the water with a glass of red wine.

Tagliatelle with green, brown or Puy lentils
Using these lentils gives a result similar to a 'bolognaise' spaghetti sauce, which I've found popular with new vegetarians and meat-eaters.

It's best to cook these lentils in water for about 30 minutes, until they are almost tender, before adding them to the onions, because the acid in the tomatoes prevents them from softening properly.

Noodle stir-fry

Once all the vegetable preparation is done, this is quick to cook, and good hot or cold.

SERVES 2
225 g/8 oz egg noodles
1 tablespoon sesame oil
2 spring onions, chopped
1 garlic clove, crushed
2.5 cm/1 inch piece of fresh ginger, grated
50 g/2 oz broccoli, divided into florets and sliced
1 carrot, cut into slim matchsticks
50 g/2 oz mangetout, halved lengthways
50 g/2 oz baby sweetcorn, halved lengthways on the diagonal
50 g/2 oz button mushrooms, sliced
2 tablespoons soy sauce
salt and freshly ground black pepper
2 tablespoons chopped fresh coriander

Cook the noodles according to the packet instructions, either by soaking them in boiling water or by cooking them in boiling water for 4–6 minutes. Drain.

Meanwhile, heat the oil in a large saucepan or wok. Add the spring onions, stir, then add the garlic and ginger and cook for 1 minute. Add the broccoli, carrot, mangetout, sweetcorn and mushrooms and stir-fry over high heat for 3–4 minutes. Add the soy sauce, drained noodles and salt and pepper to taste. Sprinkle with coriander and serve.

Spinach lasagne

This is an easy lasagne that makes a satisfying and simple supper, needing only a salad to go with it.

SERVES 6

900 g/2 lb frozen spinach, thawed
250 g/9 oz ricotta cheese
125 g/4 oz Parmesan cheese, grated
175–225 g/6–8 oz oven-ready lasagne
150 ml/5 fl oz soured cream

FOR THE TOMATO SAUCE

2 tablespoons olive oil
1 onion, peeled and chopped
1 garlic clove, crushed
2 x 400 g/14 oz cans tomatoes in juice
salt and freshly ground black pepper

First make the tomato sauce. Heat the oil in a large saucepan, add the onion, stir, then cover and leave to cook gently for 5 minutes. Then add the garlic and tomatoes, stir, then leave to cook, uncovered, stirring occasionally to prevent sticking, until any wateriness has disappeared, leaving a thick sauce – about 15 minutes. Season to taste with salt and pepper.

Heat the oven to 200°C/400°F/Gas Mark 6. Grease a large, shallow ovenproof dish.

Drain the thawed spinach in a large sieve or colander, pressing out the excess water. Then put the spinach into a bowl and add the ricotta and half of the Parmesan. Mix well and season to taste.

Cover the base of the ovenproof dish with sheets of lasagne and spread with half of the tomato sauce. Follow with a layer of half the spinach mixture, then repeat the layers, ending with a final layer of lasagne. Pour the soured cream over the top, then scatter with the remaining grated Parmesan. Bake for 40–45 minutes. Serve warm.

Vegetable lasagne

An unusual and fresh-tasting lasagne.

SERVES 6

2 carrots, cut into 5 mm/¼ inch dice
2 small courgettes, cut into 5 mm/¼ inch dice
225 g/8 oz frozen peas
several sprigs of mint, chopped
250 g/9 oz ricotta cheese
175–225 g/6–8 oz oven-ready lasagne
50 g/2 oz Parmesan cheese, grated

FOR THE TOMATO SAUCE

2 tablespoons olive oil
1 onion, peeled and chopped
1 garlic clove, crushed
2 x 400 g/14 oz cans tomatoes in juice
salt and freshly ground black pepper

First make the tomato sauce. Heat the oil in a large saucepan, add the onion, stir, then cover and leave to cook gently for 5 minutes. Then add the garlic and tomatoes, stir, then leave to cook, uncovered, stirring occasionally to prevent sticking, until any wateriness has disappeared, leaving a thick sauce – about 15 minutes. Season to taste with salt and pepper.

Meanwhile, put 2.5 cm/1 inch of water into a saucepan and bring to the boil. Add the carrots, cover and cook for 10 minutes, until the carrots are almost tender, then add the courgettes and peas to the pan, cover and cook for a further 3–4 minutes, until the vegetables are all done. Drain the vegetables, add the mint and season to taste.

Mix the ricotta cheese with 150 ml/5 fl oz of water to make a creamy mixture.

Heat the oven to 200°C/400°F/Gas Mark 6. Grease a large, shallow ovenproof dish. Cover the base of the dish with sheets of lasagne and spread with one-third of the tomato sauce. Follow with a layer of half the vegetable mixture, then half the ricotta mixture. Repeat the layers, ending with lasagne and a final layer of tomato sauce. Scatter with grated Parmesan. Bake for 40–45 minutes. Serve warm.

Spinach lasagne

rice and other grains

Grains are important foods, rich in nutrients including protein, but we don't always give them the respect they deserve. Rice makes a filling and nourishing main course in many cuisines, from Chinese stir-fried rice to Italian risotto. Brown rice is often associated with vegetarian cooking, but most vegetarians don't use it exclusively or excessively. (Having said that, I must admit that for me it is very much a staple; I find that it has a balancing, calming effect, unlike any other food.) Brown rice is simply rice that has not had its outer layers polished off, so it retains more nutrients and fibre, as well as a nutty flavour. Its only drawback is that it takes longer to cook than white rice – but it doesn't need constant attention, so you can get on with something else while the rice cooks.

Other grains can just as easily take the leading role. They are not at all difficult to cook and they complement many other foods, which may be why we are inclined to think of them as supporting cast rather than as the star. Perhaps the recipes in this section will help to redress the balance.

Pumpkin risotto (page 118)

guidelines on using grains

Barley

Two types of barley are used in cooking: pot barley (the unprocessed grains) and pearl barley, which looks a bit like brown rice, and is available from any supermarket or grocer. (Although pearl barley has been processed it provides more fibre than brown rice.)

Pot barley needs to be soaked overnight, then simmered for about 1 hour or until tender. Pearl barley doesn't need soaking and cooks in about 30 minutes. Barley can be added to a vegetable soup or stew to make it more substantial, or it can be used to make a chewy, nutty-flavoured pilaf or salad, as a change from rice.

Buckwheat

Not a true grain, but the three-sided seeds of a dock-like plant, buckwheat has a distinctive nutty flavour, especially when roasted. It can be bought ready roasted (and is sometimes labelled kasha) or you can roast your own by stirring the buckwheat in a dry, heavy-based saucepan for 5–8 minutes, until it smells toasted. After roasting, buckwheat is cooked by simmering for 15–30 minutes, until tender. It can be served as an accompaniment or pilaf. Buckwheat flour is used to make crêpes in Brittany and blinis in Russia.

Bulgar, burghul, bulgur or cracked wheat

This is wheat that has been cooked then dried and crushed to produce golden grains, which look a bit like demerara sugar. Because of its pre-treatment it's quick to prepare – just soak it in double its volume of boiling water for about 10 minutes until it has absorbed it all. It can be used without further cooking as the basis for salads, or heated through and served hot. Bulgar wheat makes a pleasant change from rice and is quicker to prepare; it can be used in most of the same ways – in salads (for example Tabbouleh, page 121), as a stuffing for vegetables like peppers, or as an accompaniment to casseroles.

For a basic pilaf, fry some onions in olive oil, add a little garlic and the soaked bulgar wheat and heat through.

Couscous

Couscous is not a grain but a wheat product, made from tiny particles of semolina (which is hard durum wheat) processed into little pellets. Preparing couscous used to be a time-consuming process, but the couscous that is now widely available is pre-cooked so it can be prepared quickly and easily. I treat it in the same way as bulgar wheat – soak it in double its volume of boiling water for about 10 minutes – and find the two pretty well interchangeable, though couscous has a less 'wheaty' flavour. You can heat the soaked couscous in a steamer basket or metal sieve above a pan of simmering vegetable stew, where it will absorb some of the flavour, then serve the two together.

Millet

These round, golden grains cook more quickly than brown rice – just simmer for 8–10 minutes – and can be used in similar ways, for example as Pilau rice (page 116), which you would cook for 15–20 minutes. However, it's a good idea to increase the flavour by toasting the grains in a dry pan before adding them to the onions. Millet can be cooked with milk to make a nourishing 'porridge' for breakfast, or a creamy pudding.

Oats

Whole grain oats look like unprocessed grains of wheat and are very chewy – they need to be soaked overnight, then simmered for about 1 hour. Far better known and more useful forms of oats are medium and fine oatmeal (for porridge, oatcakes and Parkin, page 186) and the familiar flat rolled oats (used in muesli, porridge, biscuits and crumbles).

Polenta

This is corn (maize) that has been ground to a meal of varying degrees of fineness. Coarse polenta may be as coarse as bulgar wheat, while fine polenta is sometimes labelled maize flour. It's cooked by sprinkling it on to boiling water and simmering for 5–40 minutes, depending on whether it has been pre-treated to make it cook quickly – check the packet for details. Serve it 'wet', as a golden purée, mixed with butter and grated cheese, or leave it to set. It can then be sliced and grilled, fried or layered with a sauce, rather like lasagne.

Quinoa

A little round grain that looks very like millet before it's cooked, after which it has a pretty spiral shape. It's a nutritious grain with a pleasant 'grassy' flavour and makes a good pilaf or salad. It's important to wash quinoa thoroughly under the cold tap before you cook it to rinse off the natural bitter coating on the grains. Cook as for rice, allowing about 20 minutes, or in Summer millet pilaf (page 117).

Rice

Both brown and white rice are available in short (or round), medium and long grain varieties. Long-grain types include Patna and Basmati, the latter having slim pointed grains and being particularly quick to cook and fragrant. The grains in long-grain varieties of rice stay separate when cooked; with short-grain rice, the grains stick together more, as with Italian arborio or 'risotto' rice. So choose the type of rice according to the effect you want to achieve.

There are two basic ways of cooking rice and in either case you need to allow about 50 g/2 oz of rice per person if you're serving it with something else or 125 g/4 oz if it's a main course. With the exception of Basmati rice, most rice has already been cleaned and does not need washing before cooking.

For the first method, which I call the 'pasta' method, you throw the rice into lots of boiling water, simmer until tender (bite a grain to test – check packet for details of timing), then drain and rinse under hot or cold water (depending on whether you want to serve it hot or cold).

For the second method you cook the rice over a low heat in just enough water to be absorbed during the cooking time (for example as in Pilau rice, page 116).

I used to prefer the latter method, but now I nearly always use the 'pasta' method unless I'm cooking the rice with other ingredients.

You can also use a pressure cooker for brown rice. I use this method when I want to make very soft rice that is soothing to eat. Simply put in a cupful of rice and 2½ cupfuls of cold water or, for creamy, very soft rice, 5 cupfuls of water. Put the pressure cooker on a heat diffuser (see page 24) over a low heat so that it comes up to pressure slowly, then cook under full pressure for 45 minutes. After that, turn off the heat and leave it to come back to normal pressure naturally as it cools. The creamy rice makes a nice pudding or breakfast dish, particularly if you stir in some sultanas or raisins – they plump up with the moisture of the rice – and serve it with a scattering of flaked almonds and perhaps some soya cream on top.

Semolina

Semolina is a flour consisting of fine grains of durum wheat. It is used to make dried Italian pasta, but is very difficult to work with, so homemade pasta is usually made with a high proportion of bread flour or strong plain flour. I use semolina mainly for Cheese fritters (page 75), but it can also be made into puddings or used in cakes and biscuits such as Shortbread (page 182).

Wheat

Most often used in the form of flour, wheat can also be bought as whole grains, sometimes known as wheat berries. Soak these overnight, then cook for about 1½ hours or until tender. Drain and mix with vinaigrette to make a very chewy salad – a little goes a long way. Kibbled (cracked) wheat grains can be bought to scatter on homemade bread.

Wild rice

Not a true rice but a nutritious grass that grows alongside lakes and rivers in north America. It has a chewy texture and a smoky flavour and although it is expensive, you don't need to use much: 125 g/4 oz will serve up to 6 people, or even more if mixed with other types of rice, which I think is best. Cook wild rice in plenty of water for about 45 minutes until tender, then drain and mix with equal quantities of cooked brown and white long-grain rice.

Pilau rice

You can use brown or white long-grain rice for this delicately spiced pilau. It's good with spicy vegetable mixtures or even on its own, with a tomato and onion salad and some mango chutney, for a simple meal.

SERVES 3–4
2 tablespoons olive oil
1 small onion, peeled and finely chopped
1 garlic clove, crushed
1 teaspoon turmeric
2 cardamom pods, crushed
1 teaspoon cumin seeds
½ cinnamon stick
1 bay leaf
225 g/8 oz long-grain rice
salt and freshly ground black pepper
600 ml/1 pint boiling water

Heat the oil in a heavy-based saucepan (you need one with a close-fitting lid), add the onion and cook for 3–4 minutes, just to soften it, then stir in the garlic, turmeric, cardamom, cumin, cinnamon stick and bay leaf and stir over the heat for 1 minute.

Add the (uncooked) rice and stir over the heat for a few seconds to get it well coated with the onion and spices. Add a little salt and pepper, then pour in the boiling water – the mixture will probably boil up fiercely as you do, so stand well back. Put the lid on the pan, adjust the heat so that the mixture simmers very gently, then leave it undisturbed until it's done: 15 minutes for white rice, 40 minutes for brown.

After this time, tip the pan to see if any liquid runs out; if so, leave it on the heat for another couple of minutes. Then gently tip it into a warmed serving dish (or it will go on cooking in the hot pan) and 'fluff' it by lifting it gently with a fork.

Coconut rice
For this fragrant variation, use a 400 ml/14 fl oz can of coconut milk made up to 600 ml/1 pint with water, instead of the boiling water. You can omit some of the spices, according to your taste and what you want to serve with the rice.

Saffron rice
Leave out the garlic and spices. Soak ½ teaspoon of saffron threads in 1 tablespoon of boiling water for 2–3 minutes; add to the softened onion.

Lemon and turmeric rice
Leave out all the spices except the turmeric. After the rice is cooked, stir in 2 tablespoons of fresh lemon juice: this will intensify the golden colour of the rice.

Vegetable rice
Leave out the spices and instead fry a small chopped red or green pepper with the onion. Other vegetables, for example leeks or mushrooms, can be used instead; you need about 125 g/4 oz for this quantity of rice.

Wild rice pilaf

This mixture of rices sets off the flavour of wild rice to its best advantage.

SERVES 4
2 tablespoons olive oil
1 small onion, finely chopped
2 garlic cloves, crushed
125 g/4 oz brown rice
50 g/2 oz wild rice
450 ml/15 fl oz boiling vegetable stock or water
50 g/2 oz Basmati rice
salt and freshly ground black pepper
225 g/8 oz oyster mushrooms, washed or wiped
225 g/8 oz baby sweetcorn, halved lengthways
2–3 tablespoons chopped fresh parsley

Heat 1 tablespoon of the oil in a heavy-based saucepan, add the onion and cook for 3–4 minutes, then stir in half the garlic, all the brown rice and wild rice and stir for a few seconds to get the rice well coated with the onion and garlic. Add a little salt and pepper, then pour in the boiling stock or water. Put the lid on the pan, turn the heat down low and leave to simmer very gently for 40–45 minutes, until all the water has been absorbed and a grain of rice is tender when you bite it.

About 20 minutes before the rice is ready, wash the Basmati rice in a sieve under the cold tap until the water runs clear. Fill a saucepan with water and bring to the boil, then add the rice. Let the rice boil, uncovered, for about 10 minutes, or until it is just tender. Drain into a sieve and rinse with hot water.

Heat the remaining oil in a saucepan and add the remaining garlic, stir for a few seconds, then add the mushrooms and cook for 4–5 minutes over a medium heat, stirring often until they are tender. Finally add the sweetcorn and stir-fry for a minute or two.

Tip the wild rice mixture into a large warmed serving dish and add the Basmati rice; mix gently with a fork, then fork in the vegetables and the parsley. Taste and adjust the seasoning and serve immediately.

Summer millet pilaf

The light flavour and texture of millet makes it a perfect grain for warm weather, as in this pilaf flavoured with fresh herbs and summer vegetables. A yogurt sauce and a green salad go well with it.

Serves 4
300 g/11 oz millet
2 tablespoons olive oil
1 large onion, peeled and chopped
2 small carrots, cut into 5 mm/¼ inch dice
1 garlic clove, crushed
salt and freshly ground black pepper
1 courgette, cut into 5 mm/¼ inch dice
1 bunch of spring onions, trimmed and chopped
225 g/8 oz shelled fresh peas or frozen petits pois
2–3 tablespoons chopped fresh mint

Put the millet into a large, heavy-based saucepan over a moderate heat and stir constantly for 3–4 minutes, until it begins to smell roasted and some of the grains start to pop. Remove from the heat and tip the millet into another container.

Heat the oil in the saucepan and fry the onion for 5 minutes, then add the carrots and garlic and stir over the heat for a further 30 seconds. Then add the toasted millet, together with 750 ml/1¼ pints of water and some salt and pepper. Stand back as you add the water because it may bubble up vigorously. Put a lid on the pan, turn down the heat and cook very

gently for 15–20 minutes, until all the water has been absorbed and the millet is tender.

Stir in the courgette, spring onions, peas and a little more salt and pepper and cook for 2–3 minutes, just to heat the vegetables through. Taste and adjust the seasoning, stir in the mint, and serve hot.

Layered wheat grain salad

This looks best if you make it in a glass bowl to show off the different layers. You need to soak the wheat grains the day before.

Serves 4
125 g/4 oz wheat grains
2 tablespoons olive oil
2 tablespoons red wine vinegar
salt and freshly ground black pepper
400 g/14 oz canned red kidney beans, drained
1 teaspoon tomato ketchup
1 small–medium lettuce, cut into shreds
Potato salad (page 59)
½ cucumber, cut into 5 mm/¼ inch cubes
3 carrots, grated
4 tomatoes, sliced
2 raw beetroots, peeled and grated
6–8 tablespoons mayonnaise
1 punnet of mustard and cress

Put the wheat grains in a bowl, cover with cold water and leave to soak overnight.

The next day, drain and rinse them, put them in a saucepan or pressure cooker and cover generously with cold water. Boil for 1¼ hours, or 25 minutes in a pressure cooker. Leave them to cool.

Drain the wheat grains and mix with 1 tablespoon of the oil and 1 tablespoon of vinegar and salt and pepper to taste. In a separate bowl, mix the red kidney beans with the remaining oil and vinegar, and the tomato ketchup. Season to taste.

To assemble the salad, put the lettuce into the base of a salad bowl. Spoon the wheat salad on top in an even layer. Then add the potato salad, the kidney beans, then the rest of the vegetables in layers, ending with the beetroot. Swirl the mayonnaise over the top, then sprinkle with mustard and cress.

Mushroom risotto

This is a simplified version of the authentic Italian risotto, but I find it works fine.

SERVES 4

2 tablespoons olive oil
25 g/1 oz butter
1 onion, peeled and chopped
3 garlic cloves, crushed
325 g/12 oz arborio rice or other risotto rice
pinch of saffron threads (optional)
salt and freshly ground black pepper
4 tablespoons dry white wine
750 ml/1¼ pints vegetable stock
450 g/1 lb mushrooms, wiped and sliced
2 tablespoons chopped fresh parsley
50 g/2 oz Parmesan cheese, cut into flakes with a
   potato peeler or sharp knife

Melt the butter and oil in a large, heavy-based saucepan, then add the onion and garlic and cook gently for 2–3 minutes.

Add the rice, saffron (if you are using it) and some salt and pepper and stir to coat the rice with the butter and oil. Add the wine, stir, then add the stock and bring to the boil, stirring frequently. Cover and leave to simmer for 5 minutes, or stir continually if you have the time, because the more the risotto is stirred, the creamier and better it will be.

Add the mushrooms, give the risotto another stir, then let it cook for a further 6–7 minutes. Stir as often as possible, until the rice is tender and most of the liquid is absorbed. Add a little more stock towards the end of the cooking time if the mixture looks a little dry; it needs to be quite moist. Stir in the chopped parsley, taste and adjust the seasoning, top with flakes of Parmesan and serve at once.

Asparagus risotto
Replace the mushrooms with 450 g/1 lb of asparagus spears, washed, trimmed and halved.

Pumpkin risotto
Replace the mushrooms with 450 g/1 lb of peeled pumpkin, cut into 2.5 cm/1 inch chunks.

Pumpkin risotto

Microwave risotto

I have adapted this recipe from one by microwave expert Barbara Kafka.

SERVES 2

25 g/1 oz butter
1 tablespoon olive oil
1 onion, peeled and chopped
3 garlic cloves, crushed
175 g/6 oz arborio or other risotto rice
50 g/2 oz Parmesan cheese, cut into flakes with a
    potato peeler or sharp knife
salt and freshly ground black pepper

You need a deep, microwaveable casserole dish. The risotto is cooked uncovered, on Full power throughout.

Put the butter and oil into the casserole and microwave for 2 minutes. Add the onion and garlic, stir, then microwave for 4 minutes. Add the rice, stir, then microwave for 4 minutes.

Pour in 750 ml/1¼ pints of boiling water or stock and microwave for 9 minutes. Stir well, then microwave for a further 9 minutes.

Remove from the microwave and leave to stand, uncovered, for 5 minutes, so that the rice absorbs the rest of the liquid – stir it several times. Stir in the Parmesan and season to taste. Serve immediately.

Leek and barley risotto

Pearl barley makes a very pleasant 'risotto', and this is also good cold, as a salad.

SERVES 4

4 medium-sized leeks
2 tablespoons olive oil
225 g/8 oz pearl barley
1 garlic clove, crushed
salt and freshly ground black pepper
12 sun-dried tomatoes in oil, drained and chopped
4 tablespoons finely chopped fresh parsley
50 g/2 oz black olives (optional)

Trim and wash the leeks as described on page 91, then cut them into 2.5 cm/1 inch lengths. Heat the oil in a large saucepan, add the leeks, stir, then cook gently for 5 minutes.

Add the barley, garlic, 750 ml/1¼ pints of water and 1 teaspoon of salt. Bring to the boil, then cover and leave to cook gently for 45 minutes, or until the barley is tender. Tip the pan to make sure there is no water left; if there is, put the lid back on and leave the pan to stand for a further 10 minutes.

Stir in the sun-dried tomatoes, chopped parsley and the olives if you are using them. Season to taste and serve hot or cold.

Buckwheat with beetroot and dill

Buckwheat is something of an acquired taste: I think it goes best with wintry flavours and is enhanced by something sweet, such as beetroot. Serve this dish with some soured cream and big grilled mushrooms.

SERVES 4

2 tablespoons olive oil
1 large onion, peeled and chopped
1 garlic clove, crushed
225 g/8 oz buckwheat, roasted (see page 114)
salt and freshly ground black pepper
450 g/1 lb cooked beetroot (page 89), skinned and
    cut into 1 cm/½ inch cubes
2 tablespoons chopped fresh dill or mint

Heat the oil in a large saucepan and fry the onion for 5 minutes, then add the garlic and cook for a further 30 seconds. Add the roasted buckwheat, together with 750 ml/1¼ pints water and some salt and pepper. Stand back as you add the water because it may bubble up vigorously. Put a lid on the pan, turn down the heat and cook very gently for 15–20 minutes, until all the water has been absorbed and the buckwheat is tender.

Stir in the beetroot and cook for a further 2–3 minutes, just to heat the beetroot through, then taste and adjust the seasoning. Stir in the dill or mint, and serve hot.

Variation
Buckwheat cooked as above but without the beetroot makes a good accompaniment to Roasted root vegetables (page 103), turning them into a substantial meal.

Spicy rice salad with fruit and nuts

The flavour of rice blends with many different ingredients, so there is plenty of scope when making a rice salad.

SERVES 4–6

1 tablespoon olive oil
25 g/1 oz butter
1 onion, peeled and chopped
125 g/4 oz mushrooms, sliced
275 g/10 oz long-grain brown rice
½ teaspoon turmeric
1 teaspoon ground coriander
1 teaspoon ground cumin
50 g/2 oz sultanas
salt and freshly ground black pepper
50 g/2 oz flaked almonds

Heat the oil and butter in a large saucepan, add the onion, stir, then cover and cook over a low heat for 5 minutes. Add the mushrooms, stir again, then cook, uncovered this time, for 4–5 minutes. Meanwhile, wash the rice in a sieve under the cold tap.

Add the turmeric, coriander and cumin to the pan, cook for 30 seconds, stirring, then add the rice and stir for 1–2 minutes, so that it gets coated with the spices. Add the sultanas, some salt and pepper and 450 ml/15 fl oz of water. Bring to the boil, then cover the pan, turn the heat down low and leave the rice to cook until it is tender and all the water has been absorbed, 40–45 minutes. Turn off the heat and let the rice stand, covered, for a further 10 minutes.

Meanwhile, toast the flaked almonds under the grill until they are golden brown and crisp: keep your eye on them as they only take a minute or so and burn easily.

Turn the rice into a serving bowl and leave to cool. Just before serving, taste and adjust the seasoning and stir in the flaked almonds.

Mediterranean rice salad

In this recipe the rice and other ingredients are cooked separately and then combined to make a glorious, rich-tasting mixture that is good hot, warm or cold.

SERVES 4–6

275 g/10 oz long-grain brown rice
2 tablespoons olive oil
1 onion, peeled and chopped
1 aubergine, cut into small dice
1 red or green pepper, deseeded and cut into small dice
1 garlic clove, crushed
400 g/14 oz canned chopped tomatoes
8 sun-dried tomatoes in oil, drained and chopped
50–125 g/2–4 oz black olives
a few drops of Tabasco sauce
salt and freshly ground black pepper
2–3 fresh basil leaves

Bring a large saucepan of water to the boil, add the rice, stir, and let it boil, without a lid, for about 30 minutes, or until it is tender when you bite it. Drain the rice, rinse it under the cold tap, drain well and put it into a bowl.

Meanwhile, prepare the vegetable mixture. Heat the oil in a large saucepan, add the onion, stir, then cover and cook over a low heat for 5 minutes. Add the aubergine and pepper, stir, cover again and leave to cook gently for a further 10 minutes, stirring occasionally to prevent sticking.

Add the tomatoes in their juice and the sun-dried tomatoes and bring to the boil, then let the mixture simmer, without a lid, until any wateriness has disappeared, leaving a thick sauce – about 15 minutes.

Add the rice to the vegetable mixture, together with the black olives. Add Tabasco and salt and pepper to taste. Serve warm or cold, with the basil leaves torn over the top.

Tabbouleh

Use plenty of parsley, mint and lemon juice, so that the tabbouleh is really refreshing. Serve it as a salad, with some Cos or iceberg lettuce to scoop it up, or as an accompaniment to a vegetable stew. You don't need to let the wheat cool before you serve it, though the longer it is left the more the flavours develop.

SERVES 4–6
225 g/8 oz bulgar wheat
300 ml/½ pint boiling water
4 tablespoons fresh lemon juice
2 tablespoons olive oil
8 tablespoons chopped fresh parsley
4 tablespoons chopped fresh mint
1 bunch of spring onions, trimmed and chopped
4 tomatoes, skinned (see page 93) and chopped
salt and freshly ground black pepper

Put the wheat into a large bowl and pour in the boiling water. Leave for 10–15 minutes for the wheat to absorb the water. Add all the other ingredients, mix well and season to taste. Leave in a cool place for up to 24 hours.

Variations
Add chopped cucumber, sliced avocado, green or black olives, or grilled red pepper (see page 44).

Polenta slices with olives and Parmesan

Polenta can be served 'wet', as a warm purée, or left to set, then cut into slices and fried or grilled, as here. I've used quick-cooking polenta, which is widely available and takes only 5 minutes to cook. If you can't get this, or want to use the traditional type, simply extend the cooking time to 30 minutes.

SERVES 4

225 g/8 oz instant polenta
125 g/4 oz Parmesan cheese, grated (optional)
50 g/2 oz pitted black or green olives, chopped
salt and freshly ground black pepper
olive oil for shallow-frying

Put the polenta into a saucepan and mix to a smooth paste with some cold water taken from 1 litre/1¾ pints, then gradually stir in the rest of the water. Put the pan over a medium heat and stir gently until the mixture comes to the boil, and is thick and smooth. Let the polenta cook over a low heat for about 5 minutes, stirring from time to time, until it is very thick and comes away from the sides of the pan.

Then add the cheese (if you are using it), the olives and salt and pepper to taste. Mix well, then spread the mixture out on a flat plate, baking tin or tray, to a depth of just under 1 cm/½ inch. Leave the mixture to get completely cold.

Just before you want to serve the polenta, cut it into slices. Heat a little olive oil in a frying pan and fry the slices of polenta until they are crisp and golden on one side, then turn them over and fry the other side (you may need to do this in batches). Drain on paper towels, and if necessary keep warm, uncovered, until all the polenta is done.

Polenta slices with olives and Parmesan

Polenta with mushrooms

For this version serve the polenta as a purée, as soon as it is cooked, accompanied by Wild mushroom ragout (page 99).

Polenta with ratatouille

Serve the polenta as a purée, with Ratatouille (page 101).

Polenta with roasted vegetables

Serve the polenta as a purée, with Roasted Mediterranean vegetables (page 103).

Polenta with tomato sauce

Make the polenta as described above – with or without the Parmesan and olives. Spread it out thinly to about 5 mm/¼ inch deep and leave to get completely cold.

Make a double batch of Fresh tomato sauce (page 82). Cut the polenta into pieces, then put a layer in the base of an ovenproof dish and cover with a layer of tomato sauce. Continue until all the polenta is used up, finishing with tomato sauce and a good sprinkling of grated Parmesan if you like. Bake in a moderate oven, 180°C/ 350°F/Gas Mark 4, for 30–40 minutes, until golden brown.

Couscous with spiced vegetables

The fragrant vegetable mixture is reminiscent of the north African origins of this dish.

Serves 4

3 tablespoons vegetable oil
1 large onion, peeled and chopped
225 g/8 oz carrots, peeled and cut into 3 mm/
⅛ inch slices
225 g/8 oz turnips, peeled and cut into 5 mm/
¼ inch dice
2 garlic cloves, crushed
1 teaspoon ground ginger
¼ teaspoon ground cinnamon
¼ teaspoon ground white pepper (optional)
175 g/6 oz baby sweetcorn, halved
125 g/4 oz sultanas (optional)
400 g/14 oz canned chickpeas, drained
salt
325 g/12 oz couscous
40 g/1½ oz butter or vegan margarine
chopped flat-leaf parsley or fresh coriander

Heat 2 tablespoons of the oil in a large saucepan and add the onion, stir, then cover the pan and leave to cook gently for 5 minutes. Add the carrots and turnips, cover and leave to cook gently for 10 minutes.

Stir in the garlic and spices, then add the sweetcorn and sultanas, chickpeas and 1 litre/ 1¾ pints of water. Bring to the boil, then leave to simmer for about 30 minutes, or until the vegetables are tender and the liquid has reduced and thickened slightly.

Meanwhile, prepare the couscous. Put the remaining oil into a large saucepan with 375 ml/12 fl oz of water and 1½ teaspoons of salt and bring to the boil. Add the couscous, remove from the heat and leave to swell for 2 minutes. Add the butter or margarine and reheat the couscous gently, stirring with a fork, for about 3 minutes.

Check the seasoning of the stew, sprinkle with parsley or coriander, serve with couscous.

Variation

Serve the couscous with Roasted Mediterranean vegetables (page 103), hot or cold, with Garlic vinaigrette (page 54).

pulses

Pulses – dried beans, lentils and peas – are an important ingredient in vegetarian cookery. They provide protein and are rich in useful vitamins, minerals and fibre, with virtually no fat. A wide range of beans and lentils is available, many of them canned, ready for use. This means you don't have to go through the soaking and cooking routine if you don't want to – though I maintain that the difficulty of this is overstated. All you need is a bit of forethought and, if you've got a freezer, you can stow away your own cooked beans for another time.

To prepare dried beans, peas and lentils, allow 40–50 g/1½–2 oz per person. Wash the pulses in cold water, then place them in a bowl and add enough cold water to cover them to twice their depth. Leave to soak for 8–12 hours or overnight, or to speed things up, bring them to the boil, boil for 3 minutes, then remove from the heat, cover and leave to soak for 1–2 hours.

After soaking, drain and rinse the pulses, then put them into a saucepan and again cover them to twice their depth with fresh water. Do not add salt, or the beans will harden again, and never cook properly. Bring to the boil, then reduce the heat and simmer gently until the pulses are tender. This takes about 35–40 minutes for black-eyed and flageolet beans; 45–50 minutes for whole lentils; about 1¼ hours for other types of beans; and up to 3 hours for chickpeas. Test the beans by biting one, or see if you can crush one easily between your finger and thumb. The time they take to cook depends on the size and variety, and also on the age of the bean or lentil; the longer they have been stored, the longer they will take to cook. Although they look as though they can be kept indefinitely, after a year they become so dry that it is difficult to get them to cook tender – so keep an eye on your storecupboard, and make a note of purchase dates if necessary.

To freeze cooked beans, you can open-freeze them by spreading them in a single layer on a tray until frozen, then transferring them to a polythene bag from which you can take out whatever amount you need. Alternatively, divide the cooked beans into portions and freeze in small bags. If you soak and cook a 500 g/1 lb 2 oz bag of dried beans, then divide them into five equal portions, each will be equivalent to the contents of a 425 g/15 oz can.

When following or converting a recipe, allow a 425 g/15 oz can, drained, for every 100 g/3½ oz of dried beans or lentils.

Unless you use the canned variety, chickpeas need to be soaked before use

Dal

This basic dish of split lentils or split peas is useful for serving with steamed vegetables and/or cooked rice to turn them into a nutritious meal; you can make it thick or thin according to your taste.

SERVES 4

1 onion, peeled and chopped
125 g/4 oz split red lentils
2.5 cm/1 inch piece of fresh ginger, grated
1–2 garlic cloves, sliced
½ teaspoon turmeric
1 green chilli, deseeded and chopped
1 teaspoon ground coriander
1 teaspoon cumin seeds or ground cumin
salt and freshly ground black pepper

Put the onion into a large saucepan with the lentils, ginger, garlic, turmeric and 1 litre/ 1¾ pints of water and bring to the boil. Add the chilli, then leave the mixture to simmer for 20–30 minutes, or until the lentils are soft and pale. If the mixture is too thin, boil hard for a few minutes to reduce the liquid.

Just before the lentils are ready, put the coriander and cumin into a small pan (with no oil or water) over a moderate heat and stir for a few seconds, until they smell fragrant. Add them to the lentil mixture, stir, then season to taste with salt and pepper.

Variations

For a richer version, while the dal is cooking, fry a chopped onion in 1 tablespoon of vegetable oil until the onion is soft and beginning to brown. Instead of dry-frying the coriander and cumin, add these to the onion, stir over the heat for a few seconds, then add to the dal.

Dal with coconut cream

Stir 25–50 g/1–2 oz of chopped coconut cream into the dal at the end.

Spinach dal

Follow the recipe above, then add 450 g/1 lb of shredded fresh spinach or thawed frozen spinach and cook for about 10 minutes, or until the spinach is tender.

Lentil and vegetable casserole

A comforting, warming dish that you can vary according to the vegetables available. I like to use a mixture of split red lentils and whole green or brown lentils.

SERVES 4–6

3 tablespoons olive oil
3 onions, peeled and sliced
2 garlic cloves, crushed
450 g/1 lb carrots, peeled and cut into 5 mm/ ¼ inch slices
325 g/12 oz turnips, peeled and cut into 1 cm/ ½ inch dice
325 g/12 oz leeks, trimmed, thoroughly washed and cut into 5 mm/¼ inch slices
175 g/6 oz split red lentils
50 g/2 oz whole green or brown lentils
750 ml/1¼ pints vegetable stock
450 g/1 lb mushrooms, washed and cut into quarters
salt and freshly ground black pepper
2 tablespoons chopped fresh parsley

Heat 2 tablespoons of the oil in a large saucepan, add the onions, cover and cook for 5 minutes. Add the garlic, carrots, turnips and leeks, stir, then cover and cook for 10 minutes.

Add the lentils, stir, then pour in the stock and bring to the boil. Reduce the heat, cover the pan and cook for 45 minutes or until the lentils and vegetables are tender.

Meanwhile, heat the remaining oil in a frying pan and fry the mushrooms, uncovered, for 5–6 minutes, until they are tender. Add the mushrooms and any liquid they have produced to the lentil mixture. Season well, scatter with the parsley and serve hot.

Lentil and herb bake

This is simple and tasty, good with Vegetarian gravy (page 83) and some Cranberry or Cumberland sauce (page 84).

SERVES 4
3 tablespoons olive oil
2 large onions, peeled and finely chopped
1 large garlic clove, crushed
2 x 425 g/15 oz cans green lentils, drained, or
   200 g/7 oz green or brown lentils, soaked and
   cooked until tender (see page 125), drained
2 tablespoons chopped fresh parsley
1 teaspoon mixed dried herbs
2 tablespoons soy sauce
salt and freshly ground black pepper
25–50 g/1–2 oz fresh breadcrumbs

Heat the oven to 180°C/350°F/Gas Mark 4. Heat 2 tablespoons of the oil in a large saucepan, add the onions and fry for 10 minutes until soft and lightly browned, stirring from time to time.

Add the garlic, lentils, parsley, mixed herbs and soy sauce. You now need to mash everything thoroughly, to make the mixture hold together. You can do this by hand with a potato masher, or purée roughly in a food processor or blender. Season the mixture generously, then transfer it to a shallow ovenproof dish and level the top. Sprinkle with the breadcrumbs and the remaining tablespoon of oil and bake for about 20 minutes. Serve hot.

Chilli lentil koftas with dill sauce

Crisp lentil croquettes have the perfect accompaniment in a cool yogurt sauce. In addition, you could serve baked potatoes, rice or warm pitta bread, plus a green salad or tomato salad.

MAKES 8
1 tablespoon vegetable oil
1 onion, peeled and finely chopped
1 garlic clove, crushed
1 green chilli, deseeded and chopped
4 teaspoons curry powder

200 g/7 oz whole green lentils, soaked and cooked
   until tender (see page 125), drained, or
   2 x 425 g/15 oz cans green lentils, drained
2 tablespoons chopped fresh coriander
salt and freshly ground black pepper
a few fresh breadcrumbs (optional: if necessary)
a little flour
1 egg
10 tablespoons dried breadcrumbs
vegetable oil for shallow-frying, or soya or groundnut
   oil for deep-frying

TO SERVE
Yogurt and dill sauce (page 80)

Heat the oil in a large saucepan, add the onion and leave to cook gently, covered, for 10 minutes. Stir in the garlic, chilli and curry powder and cook for a minute or two longer.

Remove the pan from the heat and add the lentils, coriander and some salt and pepper to taste. Mix all the ingredients well, mashing them with the spoon so that they hold together. If the mixture is a little on the soft side, add a few fresh breadcrumbs, so that you can mould it into shapes.

Sprinkle a little flour on a board, then with floured hands divide the lentil mixture into eight equal portions and form them into rounds, pressing the mixture together firmly.

Put the egg into a small bowl and beat with 1 tablespoon of cold water. Put the dried breadcrumbs into another bowl. Dip the lentil rounds into the beaten egg mixture and then into the crumbs, coating them well.

Fry the koftas in a little oil in a large frying pan until they are crisp and brown on one side, then turn them over and fry the other side: this will take about 5–6 minutes in total.

Alternatively, you could deep-fry them. The method for deep-frying is described under Deep-fried Camembert on page 76. Don't put in too many koftas at once, because it's important that the oil stays really hot. Fry until they are crisp underneath – about 1–2 minutes – then turn them over and fry the other side for a further minute or so. Drain them on paper towels and keep them warm but don't cover them or they'll go soggy. Continue until all the koftas are done, then serve them at once, while they are still crisp. Serve with Yogurt and dill sauce.

Purée of white beans

This is a simple but versatile recipe – the puréed beans go well with many other ingredients: steamed or roasted vegetables, polenta, bulgar wheat or rosti potatoes. They are also good served very simply with some hot toast or even with chips.

SERVES 4

2 tablespoons olive oil
1 onion, peeled and chopped
2 garlic cloves, crushed
2 x 425 g/15 oz cans butter beans or cannellini
  beans, or 200 g/7 oz dried beans, soaked and
  cooked (see page 125), drained, reserving liquid
salt and freshly ground black pepper
1–2 tablespoons chopped fresh parsley

Heat the oil in a large saucepan, add the onion, cover and cook for 10 minutes, stirring occasionally, until the onion is soft but not browned. Stir in the garlic and the beans, together with 300 ml/10 fl oz of the reserved bean liquid. Leave to simmer gently, uncovered, for about 10 minutes, until the beans are very soft and the liquid reduced in quantity and slightly thickened. Mash with a potato masher or purée in a food processor, then season to taste. Serve sprinkled with chopped parsley.

Mixed bean salad

This is a filling salad that can be served in small helpings as a starter – it's also a good dish for a buffet party. As a main course, you could serve another salad of leaves or tomatoes alongside it, as well as some bread, rice or potatoes.

I find that a 425 g/15 oz can of beans serves 2–3 people, so the more people you're making this for, the greater the variety of beans you can use.

SERVES 6–8

3 x 425 g/15 oz cans beans (red kidney beans,
  black-eyed beans, flageolet beans, cannellini or
  haricot beans, butter beans, borlotti beans,
  chickpeas, pinto beans)
1 garlic clove, crushed
2 tablespoons wine vinegar
6 tablespoons olive oil
salt and freshly ground black pepper
3 tablespoons chopped fresh herbs (parsley, chives,
  mint, tarragon, dill, coriander, a little rosemary)
1 small onion, peeled and finely chopped, or
  3–4 spring onions, chopped (optional)

Tip the beans into a sieve or colander. Leave them to drain while you put the garlic into a large serving bowl with the vinegar, oil, salt and pepper – this dressing should be well seasoned – and mix together.

Add the drained beans, the chopped herbs and the onion if you're using it. Mix gently and, ideally, leave for about 1 hour before serving, to allow the flavours to develop. It will keep for 2 days in the refrigerator.

Variation

I sometimes add a tablespoon of tomato ketchup to the dressing – it adds a subtle sweetness and tang without being at all obvious.

Bean burgers

You can use any canned beans or lentils for these; a mixture of cannellini beans and brown lentils is good, as are red kidney beans.

MAKES 8

1 tablespoon olive oil

1 onion, peeled and chopped

1 carrot, peeled and grated or cut into 3 mm/
⅛ inch dice

½ green pepper, deseeded and cut into 3 mm/
⅛ inch dice

1 garlic clove, crushed

¼–½ teaspoon chilli powder

1 teaspoon ground coriander

2 tablespoons chopped fresh parsley or coriander (optional)

2 x 425 g/15 oz cans beans, drained, or
200 g/7 oz dried red kidney beans, soaked and cooked (see page 125) and drained

50 g/2 oz fresh wholewheat breadcrumbs

salt and freshly ground black pepper

10–12 tablespoons dried breadcrumbs

vegetable oil for grilling or shallow frying

Heat the oil in a large saucepan, add the onion, cover and cook for 5 minutes. Add the carrot, green pepper, garlic and chilli powder, stir, then cover and cook for 10 minutes.

Stir in the ground coriander and cook for a further 1–2 minutes, then remove from the heat and add the fresh parsley or coriander, beans and fresh breadcrumbs. Mix well and season generously.

Divide the mixture into eight equal portions and form them into burgers. Coat on both sides with dried breadcrumbs, pressing the mixture together well – this is important, so be firm!

To cook, either brush the burgers lightly on both sides with oil and put under a hot grill until brown on both sides, or shallow-fry, turning the burgers to brown both sides. Drain on crumpled paper towels and serve hot, in soft rolls or with a sauce.

Red bean chilli

Very easy to make and universally popular, this is good with brown rice, a baked potato or crusty bread and a leafy salad. You could replace one of the cans of red kidney beans with another type such as flageolet beans.

SERVES 4

1 red pepper

1 green pepper

2 tablespoons olive oil

1 onion, peeled and chopped

1 garlic clove, crushed

2 small carrots, scrubbed or scraped and cut into
5 mm/¼ inch dice

2 x 400 g/14 oz cans tomatoes

2 x 425 g/15 oz cans red kidney beans, or
200 g/7 oz red kidney beans, soaked and cooked (see page 125)

1 dried red chilli, crumbled, or chilli powder to taste

salt and freshly ground black pepper

This is nicest made with grilled peppers, so start by heating the grill to high. Cut the peppers in half and remove the stems, seeds and pale inner membranes, using a sharp knife. Put the peppers, cut side down, on a grill pan or a baking sheet that will fit under your grill. Grill the peppers for 10–15 minutes, until the skin blisters and blackens in places, turning them as necessary. Leave the peppers to cool – you can cover them with a plate to keep the steam in and help to loosen the skins if you like. Then remove the skins with a sharp knife and cut the peppers into strips.

Meanwhile, heat the oil in a large saucepan, add the onion, cover and cook for 5 minutes. Add the garlic and carrots, stir, then cover and cook for 10 minutes. Stir the tomatoes into the mixture, chopping them up with the spoon once they're in the pan. Simmer gently, uncovered, for 10–15 minutes, or until the carrots are tender.

Add the beans and a piece of the red chilli or ¼ teaspoon of chilli powder, simmer for a few minutes, then taste. Repeat the process until the chilli flavour is hot enough for your taste. Add the grilled pepper strips and leave the mixture to cook gently for a further 5–10 minutes. Season to taste and serve hot.

Spicy chickpea ragout

A simple but delicious dish, excellent with couscous, rice or bread – perhaps a chapatti (page 178).

SERVES 4

2 tablespoons olive oil
2 large onions, peeled and finely chopped
2 garlic cloves, crushed
2.5 cm/1 inch piece of fresh ginger, finely grated
½ teaspoon turmeric
1 teaspoon garam masala
2 tomatoes, skinned (see page 93) and chopped
1 green chilli, deseeded and sliced
2 bay leaves
2 x 425 g/15 oz cans chickpeas or
    200 g/7 oz dried chickpeas, soaked and cooked
    (see page125)
salt and freshly ground black pepper
½ lemon
4 tablespoons chopped fresh coriander

Heat the oil in a large saucepan, add the onions, cover and cook gently for 5 minutes. Add the garlic and ginger, stir, cover and leave to cook for a further 5 minutes.

Add the turmeric, stir for a moment or two, then add the garam masala, tomatoes, chilli, bay leaves and the chickpeas, together with 150 ml/5 fl oz of their liquid (or fresh water). Cover the pan and leave the mixture to simmer gently for about 30 minutes, until the liquid has reduced and the chickpeas are bathed in a purée. Season to taste and sharpen with a squeeze of lemon juice. Sprinkle with fresh coriander and serve hot.

Red bean potato moussaka

This is a big, filling dish. Serve it with a lightly cooked green vegetable such as broccoli, cabbage or spinach.

SERVES 6

1 kg/about 2 lb even-sized potatoes, scrubbed
1 tablespoon olive oil
1 onion, peeled and chopped
1 carrot, peeled and grated
1 garlic clove, crushed
¼–½ teaspoon chilli powder
1 teaspoon ground coriander
400 g/14 oz canned tomatoes, chopped
425 g/15 oz canned red kidney beans, drained, or
    100 g/3½ oz dried red kidney beans, soaked and
    cooked (see page 125), drained
salt and freshly ground black pepper
250 g/9 oz fat-free fromage frais
150 ml/5 fl oz milk or soya milk
1 egg
50 g/2 oz cheese, grated

Boil the potatoes until just tender, drain and leave to cool slightly, then peel off the skins and cut the potatoes into 5 mm/¼ inch slices.

Heat the oven to 200°C/400°F/Gas Mark 6. Heat the oil in a large saucepan, add the onion, cover and cook for 5 minutes. Add the carrot, garlic and chilli powder, stir, then cover and cook for 10 minutes.

Stir in the coriander and cook for a further 1–2 minutes. Add the tomatoes and beans and leave to simmer for 15 minutes, until the mixture is thick. Mash with a potato masher or a fork to break up the beans and tomatoes a bit. Season to taste.

To assemble the moussaka: put a layer of potatoes into a shallow ovenproof dish, using a third of the potatoes. Spoon half the bean mixture on top, then repeat the layers of potatoes and beans and finish with a layer of potatoes. Whisk together the fromage frais, milk and egg, season to taste, then pour over the potatoes. Sprinkle the grated cheese on top then bake, uncovered, for about 40 minutes, until golden brown. Serve hot.

Red bean potato moussaka

nuts

Nuts are versatile ingredients, equally at home in sweet and savoury recipes. Traditional vegetarian cookery uses them for nut cutlets, nut roasts and bakes, with different nuts to offer a range of delicious flavours, from sweet, creamy cashew nuts to aromatic pine nuts and intensely flavoured walnuts and pecans. Nuts can be added whole, chopped or ground to salads, vegetable and grain dishes; they thicken savoury sauces such as Satay sauce (page 84) and Pesto (page 85); they feature in many puddings, cakes and biscuits, and in marzipan, quite apart from their use as a nutritious snack.

Each nut is a little package of nutrients: they are a good source of protein, iron, B vitamins and vitamin E; almonds, Brazil nuts, hazelnuts and walnuts are particularly good sources of calcium. Trace elements such as zinc and selenium are needed by the body to interact with other minerals and vitamins; most nuts provide these, and Brazil nuts are so high in selenium that some health experts say it's a good idea to eat two of them every day to ensure an adequate supply. The downside, if you're watching your weight, is that most nuts are comparatively high in fat, although these are not the saturated fats that are most damaging to health.

The most important thing to remember when you're using nuts is to make sure that they are fresh. If their natural oils are allowed to become rancid, they will taste unpleasant and are potentially harmful to health. Buy in small quantities and always check the best-before date before you use them. Keep them in a cool, dry place or, better still, the refrigerator or freezer if you have room. Grind them by whizzing them in a food processor or a coffee grinder, a few at a time.

Cashew nuts may be sold unroasted or roasted and salted

Classic nut roast

This is moist, tasty and rich, good with a vegetarian gravy (page 83)and cooked vegetables, or cold with a salad. You can also use this mixture to make burgers – just form it into burger shapes instead of a loaf. I like to use cashew nuts and pecans, but you could try other combinations or a single type of nut, such as Brazil nuts, hazelnuts or walnuts.

SERVES 6
1 tablespoon olive oil
1 onion, peeled and chopped
2 garlic cloves, crushed
125 g/4 oz mushrooms, chopped into 3 mm/
   ⅛ inch pieces
2 teaspoons plain flour
300 ml/10 fl oz mushroom stock (page 30) or water
175 g/6 oz nuts, finely chopped or grated
175 g/6 oz fresh wholewheat breadcrumbs
1–2 tablespoons soy sauce
½ teaspoon dried rosemary
salt and freshly ground black pepper
2 tablespoons plain flour, or 6 tablespoons dried
   wholewheat breadcrumbs, for coating
4 tablespoons groundnut oil

Heat the oven to 190°C/375°F/Gas Mark 5. Heat the oil in a large saucepan, add the onion and garlic and fry gently for 5 minutes. Add the mushrooms and fry for a further 5 minutes. Sprinkle the flour on top and stir well, then pour in the stock or water and bring to the boil, stirring all the time. Let the mixture simmer for 2–3 minutes, then remove from the heat. Stir in the nuts, fresh breadcrumbs, soy sauce and rosemary, then season to taste.

   Turn the mixture out on to a board sprinkled with flour or dried breadcrumbs and, using your hands, form into a loaf shape. Roll the loaf in the flour or crumbs so that it is coated all over.

   Put the oil into a roasting tin and heat in the oven for a few minutes. Put the nut loaf into the tin and turn it to coat it all over with the hot oil. Bake for 40–45 minutes, until crisp, spooning some of the oil over the top of the loaf after about 30 minutes. Cut into thick slices to serve.

Nut burgers

A simple, everyday recipe. Use whatever nuts you have to hand. The burgers freeze well and can be fried from frozen.

MAKES 8
1 tablespoon olive oil
1 onion, peeled and chopped
1 teaspoon mixed dried herbs
2 tablespoons wholewheat flour
200 ml/7 fl oz vegetable stock or water
1 tablespoon soy sauce
½ teaspoon yeast extract
225 g/8 oz nuts, finely chopped or grated
175 g/6 oz fresh wholewheat breadcrumbs
salt and freshly ground black pepper
10 tablespoons dried breadcrumbs, for coating
vegetable oil for shallow-frying

Heat the oil in a large saucepan, add the onion and fry for 10 minutes, until soft and lightly browned. Stir in the herbs and flour and cook for 1–2 minutes, then pour in the stock or water and stir until thickened. Add the soy sauce, yeast extract, nuts, fresh breadcrumbs and salt and pepper to taste, then leave the mixture to cool.

   Divide the mixture into eight pieces, then form into flat burgers about 1 cm/½ inch thick. Coat on both sides with dried breadcrumbs, pressing them in well. Flatten the burgers by tapping them firmly on top and around the sides with a palette knife – this helps them to remain intact as you fry them.

   Fry the burgers in a very little oil for about 3 minutes on each side, until browned and crisp. Drain on paper towels and serve hot.

Little nut fritters
Form the mixture into small balls, pressing them together well. Coat them in very fine dried breadcrumbs or flour and deep-fry or shallow-fry. Serve as a nibble, with a piquant dip such as Yogurt and caper sauce (page 80). As a main course, serve them with the same sauce or a hot creamy Béchamel or Caper sauce (page 80).

Nut burgers, with tomatoes, red onions and chives

Mary's nut loaf

My friend Mary makes the most wonderful nut loaves, which are popular with vegetarians and meat-eaters alike; this is her recipe. It's important to grate the nuts really finely and to purée the mixture thoroughly in a food processor. The nut loaf slices well when hot or cold and can also be frozen after cooking. It's excellent served with a Mushroom sauce or Vegetarian gravy (page 83), roast potatoes and vegetables.

SERVES 6

40 g/1½ oz butter, plus extra for greasing the tin
1 onion, peeled and chopped
2 celery sticks, quite finely sliced
125 g/4 oz mushrooms, thinly sliced
200 g/7 oz cashew nuts or ground almonds, or a
  mixture
50 g/2 oz bread (without crusts)
1 heaped teaspoon plain flour
70 ml/2½ fl oz milk
several sprigs of fresh parsley, thyme, marjoram
2 eggs
50 g/2 oz pine nuts
1 tablespoon fresh lemon juice
salt and freshly ground black pepper
freshly grated nutmeg

Heat the oven to 180°C/350°F/Gas Mark 4. Prepare a 450 g/1 lb loaf tin by lining it with a long strip of nonstick baking paper to cover the base and the two narrow ends; grease the uncovered sides of the tin with a little butter.

Melt the butter in a saucepan, add the onion and celery, cover the pan and leave to cook over a low heat, stirring occasionally, until the vegetables are nearly soft, about 15 minutes. Add half the mushrooms and cook for a further 4–5 minutes.

Meanwhile, grate the cashew nuts in the food processor: do this thoroughly so that they are really fine. Tip the nuts into a large bowl and add the ground almonds. Whiz the bread in the processor to form fine crumbs, and put these into another (small) bowl.

When the vegetables are cooked, stir in the flour and cook for a minute, then pour in the milk and stir until thickened. Remove from the heat and pour into the food processor.

Purée until smooth, then add the fresh herbs and the eggs and whiz again. Tip this mixture into the bowl with the nuts and mix together. Add the pine nuts, lemon juice and as many of the breadcrumbs as you need to make a soft dropping consistency (usually I find about 40 g/1½ oz is enough). Finally, add the rest of the mushrooms, and season well with salt, pepper and nutmeg.

Spoon the mixture into the prepared tin, smooth the top level and cover with a piece of foil. To ensure that the mixture cooks gently and has a good texture, stand the loaf tin in a deep roasting tin and pour in hot water to come half-way up the sides of the loaf tin. Bake in the oven for about 1 hour, or until the loaf is firm and a skewer inserted into the centre comes out clean. You may like to remove the foil for the last 15 minutes or so of cooking time to brown the top slightly.

Remove from the oven and leave the loaf in the tin for 5 minutes, then slip a knife around the edges and invert the tin on to a warmed serving dish. Serve hot or cold.

Variations
You can vary the flavourings: I've known Mary to flavour it with a little fennel instead of the celery, and some caraway seeds instead of the herbs.

Brown nut loaf
Replace the cashews and ground almonds with brown nuts: hazelnuts and a few walnuts. Instead of the milk use 200 g/7 oz of canned chopped tomatoes. Use basil instead of the other herbs and add 1 teaspoon of yeast extract with the eggs.

Nut loaf en croûte
For a special occasion, try wrapping the baked and cooled nut loaf in puff pastry. Use the recipe on page 150, rolled out to about 3 mm/⅛ inch thick, or a packet of ready-rolled frozen puff pastry. Roll it around the nut loaf, tucking in the ends, trimming as necessary and putting the seam side underneath on a baking sheet. Make some slits in the pastry to let the steam out, decorate with pastry trimmings, brush with a little beaten egg, and bake at 200°C/400°F/Gas Mark 6 for 25–30 minutes, or until the pastry is puffed, golden brown and crisp. Serve at once.

White nut roast with herb stuffing

I think of this as a vegetarian alternative to light meats such as chicken or turkey and it's a favourite with my family for Christmas, served with all the usual trimmings.

SERVES 8–10
50 g/2 oz butter, plus extra for greasing the tin
1 large onion, peeled and chopped
1 teaspoon dried thyme
1 tablespoon plain flour
300 ml/10 fl oz milk or soya milk
225 g/8 oz mixed white nuts, grated (cashew nuts, blanched almonds and/or pine nuts)
125 g/4 oz fresh white breadcrumbs
2 egg whites
salt and freshly ground black pepper

FOR THE HERB STUFFING
175 g/6 oz fresh breadcrumbs
125 g/4 oz butter
4 tablespoons chopped fresh parsley
grated rind of ½ lemon
2 tablespoons grated onion
1 teaspoon each marjoram and thyme
2 egg yolks

TO GARNISH
parsley sprigs
lemon wedges

Heat the oven to 190°C/375°F/Gas Mark 5. Grease a 900 g/2 lb loaf tin with butter and line with a strip of buttered greaseproof paper to cover the base of the tin and extend up the narrow sides.

Melt the butter in a large saucepan, add the onion and fry over a low heat for 10 minutes, until soft. Add the thyme and flour, cook for a minute or two, then add the milk and stir until thickened. Remove from the heat and add the grated nuts. Season to taste with plenty of salt, pepper and nutmeg.

Whisk the egg whites until they stand in stiff peaks, then delicately stir the whites into the nut mixture.

For the stuffing, mix all the ingredients together and season to taste.

Spoon half the nut mixture into the prepared tin and spread in an even layer. With your hands, form the stuffing into a flat layer that will fit over the top of the nut mixture;

put it into the tin. Cover the stuffing with the rest of the nut mixture and level the top. Cover with buttered foil and bake for 1–1¼ hours, or until the loaf is firm and a skewer inserted into the centre comes out clean. You may like to remove the foil for the last 15 minutes or so of cooking time to brown the top slightly.

Remove from the oven and leave the loaf in the tin for 4–5 minutes, then slip a knife around the edges and invert it on to a warmed serving dish. Decorate with the parsley sprigs and lemon wedges.

Variation
For a vegan version, leave out the eggs. You will need to add up to 125 g/4 oz more breadcrumbs to the nut layer to make it firm enough to hold its shape; the stuffing will be fine if you just leave out the yolks.

vegetarian protein foods

While many foods provide protein in the vegetarian diet, what these foods have in common is that they do not occur naturally, like nuts and beans, but are manufactured products. Some, such as tofu (bean curd), have been made for thousands of years, others are more recent inventions; all are high in protein.

In a way, these foods are all meat substitutes. Some can be used as direct replacements for meat in traditional Western recipes, and even taste rather similar. Others have a character of their own, and are treated differently in recipes. They are a useful addition to the repertoire of vegetarian ingredients.

Tofu is a versatile food, useful in both savoury and sweet dishes

using vegetarian protein foods

Quorn

Quorn is a vegetable protein, invented in Britain in the 1980s. The basic ingredient is produced by culturing microfungi. The Vegetarian Society has not approved Quorn because it contains egg white from non free-range hens; I share these reservations. but many people find Quorn a useful ingredient.

Quorn chunks are firm and pale, with a texture similar to chicken, and Quorn is also available as mince; both forms are ready to use from the chilled foods section of the supermarket. Quorn can be used in a similar way to meat, although you need less of it because it is quite filling.

Seitan

Seitan has an ancient pedigree, having been made in China for many centuries. It is made by washing the starch out of wheat flour, leaving the gluten, which has a chewy, slightly fibrous texture resembling meat. It is then cooked in well-flavoured vegetable stock.

It is sold, canned or packaged, in some Asian stores and health food shops. Sliced or minced, it can take the place of meat in stews, casseroles, pies and burgers.

Tempeh

Tempeh has been produced for many centuries in some parts of Indonesia. It is made from cooked soya beans that are fermented by a special mould, which increases their already high nutritional value. Look for tempeh in the freezer of health food shops. It has a knobbly appearance and a distinctive flavour, which is something of an acquired taste. Tempeh can be fried or used in stews and casseroles.

Textured vegetable protein (TVP)

Textured vegetable protein made from soya beans was developed in the 1960s. It is made by extruding the soya into fine strands and then bonding them together to make a texture similar to meat. TVP is available in many forms; I think the most useful products are the frozen mince, which you will find in any large supermarket, and the dried TVP in both mince and chunks. You can buy these in flavoured or natural versions and most of them just need a five-minute soak in hot water to make them ready for use. There is also a type, available from some health food shops, called Smoky Snaps, that you can use straight from the packet: these have a bacon-like flavour and a crunchy texture, good in dishes such as omelettes and quiches.

Some vegetarians like to use TVP but prefer to stick to the unflavoured varieties. My own view is that if you're buying something that is so similar in texture to meat, you might as well buy a meaty flavoured one (made with vegetarian flavourings). I don't use these products very much, although I think they are very useful for people who want to become vegetarian for moral reasons but miss the flavour and texture of meat.

Tofu (bean curd)

Tofu is a white curd that the Chinese have been making from soya beans for centuries. It doesn't taste of much but absorbs flavourings well and can be used in both sweet and savoury dishes. The best tofu is sold fresh in Chinese shops; store it, submerged in water, in the refrigerator and it will keep for several days if you change the water daily.

Packs of firm tofu are now available from the chilled foods sections of supermarkets and other food shops. You can also buy a soft tofu, called 'silken tofu', vacuum-packed so it will keep without refrigeration. The soft one is mainly useful for making dips and creams. Firm tofu can be used in this way, but can also be sliced and used in many other dishes.

Ready-marinated tofu chunks are available from Asian stores and supermarkets; as the name suggests, these have been marinated and then fried, so they do contain more fat than plain tofu. However, they are delicious and, in my experience, popular even with professed tofu-haters. They could be used in recipes that call for Quorn or TVP chunks.

Other recipes for using tofu appear in the chapters on Starters, Dressings, and Puddings.

Baked (or grilled) marinated tofu

Serve this with plain boiled rice and steamed vegetables for a delicious low-fat supper. Yellow bean sauce is available from Chinese shops, or any large supermarket.

SERVES 2

275 g/10 oz firm tofu

1 tablespoon yellow bean sauce

1 tablespoon soy sauce

2 teaspoons sugar

1 teaspoon salt

½ a green chilli, deseeded and chopped

1 garlic clove, crushed

walnut-sized piece of fresh ginger, grated

juice of ½ lime

1 spring onion, chopped

Slice or cube the tofu into bite-sized pieces and place in a shallow ovenproof dish. Mix together all the remaining ingredients, then spoon the marinade over the tofu, turning the pieces gently to make sure that they are all coated. Cover the dish with cling film and leave for at least 30 minutes, preferably longer, say 2 hours, or even overnight.

Heat the oven to 200°C/400°F/Gas Mark 6, or heat the grill. Bake the tofu in the oven, uncovered, for about 20 minutes. Or cook it under the grill for about 7 minutes, turning the pieces over to cook both sides.

Curried tofu, TVP or Quorn

This is a fruity, English-style curry rather than being authentic, but it is a delicious way of jazzing up vegetable protein foods. Serve it with boiled or pilau rice and mango chutney. The quantities are based on one packet of Quorn or marinated tofu; to make a curry for four, simply double everything. You can also use dried TVP chunks – hydrate them according to the packet instructions and then weigh them.

SERVES 2

1 tablespoon olive oil

1 small onion, peeled and chopped

1 small green pepper, deseeded and cut into 5 mm/¼ inch pieces

1 garlic clove, crushed

1 teaspoon grated fresh ginger

1 teaspoon curry powder

½ teaspoon turmeric

about 175 g/6 oz ready-marinated tofu, Quorn chunks, or frozen TVP chunks

1 tablespoon plain flour

375 ml/12 fl oz vegetable stock or water

1 tablespoon fresh lemon juice

1 tablespoon mango chutney

2 tablespoons double cream or soya cream

Heat the olive oil in a large saucepan, add the onion, stir, then cover the pan and leave to cook gently for 5 minutes.

Add the pepper, stir, cover and cook for a further 5 minutes. Stir in the garlic, ginger, curry powder and turmeric, then add the tofu, Quorn or TVP and stir well to mix. Sprinkle in the flour, stir, then gradually stir in the stock. Bring the mixture to the boil, then turn the heat down, cover the pan and leave to cook very gently for about 20 minutes, or until the vegetables are tender.

Stir in the lemon juice, mango chutney and cream, season to taste and serve hot.

Butter bean curry
Use 425 g/15 oz canned butter beans, drained, instead of the Quorn, tofu or TVP.

Tofu stir-fry

This is easy to make and pretty to look at.

SERVES 2

275 g/10 oz firm tofu
1 tablespoon olive oil
1 bunch of spring onions, trimmed and sliced
2 small carrots, scraped and cut into matchsticks
1 red pepper, deseeded and chopped or sliced
125 g/4 oz mushrooms, wiped and sliced
salt and freshly ground black pepper

FOR THE MARINADE

1 tablespoon olive oil
1 tablespoon dry sherry
2 tablespoons soy sauce
1 garlic clove, crushed
1 tablespoon grated fresh ginger

Drain the tofu and pat dry on paper towels, then slice and place in a shallow dish. Mix together all the ingredients for the marinade and pour over the tofu. Turn the tofu gently in the marinade to make sure it is all coated, then cover with cling film and leave for at least 1 hour, or overnight.

To cook the stir-fry, heat the oil in a large saucepan or wok, add the vegetables and stir-fry over high heat for 2–3 minutes, until heated through. Add the tofu and its marinating liquid and stir-fry for a further 1–2 minutes, until hot. Taste and adjust the seasoning and serve at once.

Vegetarian stroganoff

The classic dish of beef with mushrooms, onions and soured cream can easily be adapted for vegetarians. Serve it with boiled rice and a green salad.

SERVES 2

1 large onion, peeled
25 g/1 oz butter
1 tablespoon olive oil
about 175 g/6 oz ready-marinated tofu, Quorn chunks, or frozen TVP chunks
225 g/8 oz mushrooms, sliced
150 ml/5 fl oz dry white wine or cider
salt and freshly ground black pepper
150 ml/5 fl oz soured cream
squeeze of lemon juice
freshly grated nutmeg

TO SERVE

paprika pepper
chopped fresh parsley

First prepare the onion: cut it in half through the stalk end, then put each half flat on a board and slice across, so that you end up with thin half circles. Heat the butter and olive oil in a large, heavy-based saucepan, add the onion and cook gently for 5 minutes, until the onion is golden and beginning to soften. Remove the onion from the pan with a draining spoon and put it on to a plate.

Turn the heat up high and add the tofu, Quorn or TVP; let them brown, stirring them around often. Turn down the heat and return the onion to the pan, along with the mushrooms, wine or cider and some salt and pepper to taste. Cover the pan and leave it to cook over a low heat for 30 minutes.

Stir in the cream and a squeeze of lemon juice; taste and check the seasoning and add a good grating of nutmeg. Cook for a few minutes more to heat the cream through, but don't let it boil.

Bean stroganoff

Use 425 g/15 oz canned white beans – butter beans, haricot beans or cannellini beans – instead of the Quorn, tofu or TVP.

Tofu stir-fry

143

Shepherd's pie

This recipe was given to me by my friend Chryssa and is loved by meat-eaters and vegetarians alike. Chryssa recommends beef-flavoured TVP mince, which you can find in the freezers of supermarkets and some health food shops. If you use a dried mince, check the packet instructions to make the correct amount of hydrated (soaked) mince. Serve the Shepherd's pie with buttered cabbage, and extra Vegetarian gravy (page 83), if you like.

SERVES 4–6

2 tablespoons olive oil

1 onion, peeled and chopped

1 carrot, peeled and grated or cut into 3 mm/ ⅛ inch dice

1 garlic clove, crushed

1 bay leaf

½ teaspoon dried thyme

400 g/14 oz canned tomatoes, chopped

about 150 g/5 oz TVP mince

1 vegetable stock cube, crumbled

125 g/4 oz frozen peas

125 g/4 oz frozen sweetcorn

3 tablespoons Smoky Snaps (see page 140)

1 tablespoon sweet chutney or pickle

about 1 teaspoon vegetarian gravy powder – not granules (optional)

salt and freshly ground black pepper

FOR THE TOPPING

1 kg/about 2 lb potatoes, peeled and cut into 2.5 cm/1 inch chunks

knob of butter or vegan margarine

a little milk or soya milk

Heat the oven to 200°C/400°F/Gas Mark 6.

To cook the potatoes for the topping, put them into a saucepan with cold water to cover them, bring to the boil and leave them to simmer for about 15–20 minutes, until they are tender when pierced with a skewer.

Meanwhile, for the filling, heat the oil in a large saucepan, add the onion, stir, then cover and cook over a fairly low heat for 7 minutes, but don't let the onion get too brown. Add the carrot, garlic, bay leaf and thyme, stir and leave to cook for about 5 minutes. Add the tomatoes, then the mince and the stock cube and cook for a further 5–10 minutes or so

until the liquid has disappeared. Remove the pan from the heat and stir in the peas, sweetcorn, Smoky Snaps and pickle. The mixture should be firm enough to support a layer of mashed potato on top. If your mixture seems too liquid, you can thicken it either by stirring in a little vegetarian gravy powder, or by popping the pan back over the heat and letting the mixture bubble for a bit longer to drive off the extra liquid.

When the potatoes are done, drain and mash them with a potato masher. Add a knob of butter, salt and pepper to taste and enough liquid to give a creamy consistency (you can use a little of the cooking liquid, or milk, preferably warmed first). Beat the mashed potatoes with a wooden spoon until they are light and fluffy.

Put the vegetable mixture into an oiled ovenproof dish and level it with the back of the spoon. Then spoon the mashed potatoes on top, spreading them into the corners of the dish. Draw the prongs of a fork over the potatoes, to give an attractive and crisp finish, dot a few little pieces of butter on top, then bake in the oven for about 30 minutes, until the potato is golden brown.

Old-fashioned stew

You can cook this over a low heat on top of the stove or in a moderate oven – either way, slow cooking produces a warming casserole with a rich-tasting gravy. Serve with a quick-cooking green vegetable such as cabbage.

SERVES 4

about 325 g/12 oz Quorn or frozen TVP chunks
2 tablespoons plain flour
salt and freshly ground black pepper
6–7 tablespoons groundnut, soya or rapeseed oil
1 large onion, peeled and sliced
750 ml/1¼ pints vegetable stock
2 tablespoons Smoky Snaps (see page 140)
4 small carrots, sliced into 5 mm/¼ inch rounds
2 celery sticks, cut into 5 mm/¼ inch slices
2 leeks, washed and cut into 5 mm/¼ inch slices
2 large potatoes, peeled and cut into 2.5 cm/1 inch chunks
1 bay leaf
1 sprig of thyme or ½ teaspoon dried thyme
3 tablespoons soy sauce

If you want to cook this in the oven, heat the oven to 180°C/350°F/Gas Mark 4.

Put the Quorn or TVP on a plate and sprinkle with the flour and some salt and pepper, turning the chunks so that they are all coated with the flour and seasoning.

Heat 2 tablespoons of the oil in a large saucepan or casserole. When it's really hot, add the pieces of Quorn or TVP and fry them, a few at a time, for 3–4 minutes or until they are brown. Take them out with a draining spoon and put them on a plate.

In the same pan, heat a further tablespoon of oil if necessary, add the onion and fry briskly until lightly browned, about 5 minutes.

Put the fried chunks back into the pan and pour in the stock, stirring over the heat until the mixture has thickened. Then add all the remaining ingredients.

If you are cooking the stew in the saucepan on top of the stove, cover with a lid and leave over a very low heat for 1 hour. Alternatively, put the casserole in the oven, cover tightly with a lid or foil and bake for 1 hour, until the vegetables are tender. Taste and adjust the seasoning before serving.

Stuffed tofu

In this dish, slices of tofu are sandwiched with a tasty stuffing and then baked. The tofu takes on the flavour of the stuffing. (You will need a food processor for this recipe.) Serve with Vegetarian gravy (page 83) and lightly cooked seasonal vegetables.

SERVES 2

275 g/10 oz firm tofu
½ an onion
2 slices of day-old white bread
a good handful of fresh parsley, stalks removed
1 teaspoon dried oregano
grated rind of ½ lemon
15 g/½ oz butter or vegan margarine
salt and freshly ground black pepper
a little cornflour for coating
a little olive oil

Heat the oven to 200°C/400°F/Gas Mark 6. Drain the tofu, then pat dry on paper towels. Cut the block of tofu into quarters, then, using a sharp knife, slice each quarter in half horizontally, making eight thin slices. Leave the slices to drain on paper towels while you make the stuffing.

Cut the onion into chunks, then put these into a food processor with the bread, parsley, oregano, lemon rind and butter or margarine. Whiz until you have a smooth mixture that holds together, then season to taste with salt and pepper.

Divide the stuffing into four pieces and sandwich each piece between two of the tofu slices. Spoon a little cornflour into a shallow dish and turn the tofu 'sandwiches' in the cornflour to coat them evenly.

Brush the tofu on both sides with a little olive oil, place on a baking sheet and bake for about 30 minutes, turning them over after 20 minutes. Serve hot.

pastry and pizzas

Why are so many people nervous about making pastry? It's not difficult and it's so rewarding – and much nicer than anything you can buy. The one exception is filo pastry, which is really beyond the scope of this book. I don't know anyone who makes their own – even the thought of handling the packet type seems to scare some people off, although it's nothing to worry about, as I hope you'll agree when you try Spanakopita, a Greek spinach and cheese pie (page 154).

The pastries I am including in this section are shortcrust, the most useful basic pastry; choux, which is the basis of a wonderful cheesy vegetarian main course dish, Gougère (page 154), as well as éclairs and profiteroles; soured cream pastry, which is rapidly becoming a modern classic in dishes such as Goats' cheese and mint tartlets (page 150); and finally puff pastry, which is more complex, but perfectly within the range of any cook with the ridiculously easy recipe in this chapter.

I've also included a recipe for homemade pizza. Making your own pizza may seem unnecessary when they're so widely available, but it's very satisfying to make your own and much easier than you might think, so why not give it a go? For more about cooking with yeast, see page 180.

It's true that some people avoid eating pastry because it is high in fat, but if it's the main course of a meal, and the rest of the meals of the day are low in fat – plenty of fruit, salad, steamed vegetables, plainly cooked pasta or grains – there's no need to worry, especially if you include some fibre-rich wholewheat flour in the mixture. Wholewheat flour has traditionally been used in vegetarian cookery and I prefer it for homemade pastry, although it must be made with a light touch. I often use a mixture of 100 per cent wholewheat flour and plain unbleached white flour for a light yet wholesome result.

You can use butter, vegetable margarine, white vegetable fat, or a mixture; it's really a question of personal preference. Personally I use butter, for its superb flavour.

NOTE *It used to be the convention that a quantity of pastry given in a recipe, for example 225 g/8 oz shortcrust pastry, referred to the weight of the flour used to make the pastry – the actual weight of the pastry would of course be more. Now recipes often suggest the use of ready-made pastry (either homemade or bought) and give the weight for that, so this is something you need to watch out for.*

Gougère (page 154) with Wild mushroom ragout (page 99)

basic pastry recipes

The metric/imperial weights in these recipes are not equivalents. When making pastry, it's particularly important to stick to one set of measurements or the other to get the correct proportions of flour to fat.

Shortcrust pastry

MAKES PASTRY WEIGHING ABOUT 400 G/ 13 OZ

250 g/8 oz wholewheat flour (or a mixture of
   wholewheat and white flour)
½ teaspoon salt
125 g/4 oz cold, firm butter or vegan margarine, cut
   into pieces
3 tablespoons cold water

If you have a food processor, just put in the flour, salt and fat and whiz for a few seconds until the fat and flour have combined to produce a mixture that looks like coarse breadcrumbs. Then add the water and process again, very briefly, until the mixture forms a ball of dough. Stop then – it's important not to over-process the pastry.

To make the pastry by hand, sift the flour into a bowl through a large sieve. With wholewheat flour, there will be some bran left behind in the sieve – just tip this into the bowl. Add the salt and fat, then, using your fingertips, rub the fat into the flour until the mixture looks like fine breadcrumbs, using as light a touch as you can and lifting the mixture into the air as you work to incorporate as much air as possible. Sprinkle the cold water on top and gently press the mixture together to form a dough.

Cover the dough or wrap it in greaseproof paper and chill it for 30 minutes (or longer), to give the gluten in the flour time to react with the water and make the dough pliable.

Let it come back to room temperature, then knead it lightly on a floured board. Form the dough into a rough round, square or oblong, depending on the shape you want. Roll out the dough using a floured rolling pin and short strokes, and making sure that it does not stick to the board or to the rolling pin – lightly sprinkle the dough with flour as necessary.

To transfer the pastry to the tin, lift the pastry board to the edge of the tin, then slide the pastry off the board and on to the tin. If you are using the pastry to line a tart or flan tin, roll it out to a little larger than you need, transfer it to the tin, then press the pastry down into the base of the tin to make sure no air is trapped, especially around the edges. Be careful not to stretch the pastry as you press it in – just ease it in gently – or it may shrink as it cooks. Then trim the edges and prick the base with a fork (again, this helps to prevent the pastry from rising up because of trapped air; don't worry, the holes will close up as the pastry cooks). Put the tin into the refrigerator to rest for a further 30 minutes – this will prevent it from shrinking down the sides of the tin as it cooks.

Cheese shortcrust

Add 75–125 g/3–4 oz of finely grated strongly flavoured Cheddar cheese to the mixture at the breadcrumb stage. You could also add a pinch or two of cayenne pepper.

Walnut shortcrust

Add 25–50 g/1–2 oz of finely grated or chopped walnuts to the mixture at the breadcrumb stage. You might need a drop more water to make it hold together.

Herb or curried shortcrust

Add 1 tablespoon of finely chopped fresh herbs (or 1 teaspoon dried) or 1–2 teaspoons of curry powder to the mixture at the breadcrumb stage. Robust, strong-tasting herbs like rosemary, thyme, marjoram, oregano and sage work best.

Soured cream pastry

MAKES PASTRY WEIGHING ABOUT 350 G/
12 OZ
175 g/6 oz wholewheat flour (or a mixture of
  wholewheat and white flour)
good pinch of salt
150 g/5 oz cold, firm butter, cut into pieces
6–7 tablespoons soured cream

If you have a food processor, put in the flour,
salt and fat and whiz for a few seconds until
the fat and flour have begun to combine but
you can still see bits of butter. Then add the
soured cream and process again, briefly, until
the mixture forms a ball of dough. Stop then –
it's important not to over-process the pastry.

To make the pastry by hand, sift the flour
into a bowl through a large sieve. With
wholewheat flour, there will be some bran left
behind in the sieve – just tip this into the
bowl. Add the salt and butter, then, using your
fingertips or a fork, mix the fat into the flour
roughly so that you can still see some bits of
butter. Add the soured cream and gently press
the mixture together to form a dough.

Wrap the pastry in greaseproof paper, cling
film or polythene and chill until you need it.
Let it come back to room temperature before
you roll it out.

Choux pastry

I like to use white flour for this, but I've found
that it doesn't make any difference whether I
use plain or self-raising. The most important
things are (1) don't refrigerate the mixture
before using it, and (2) cook it thoroughly in a
hot oven until it's really crisp and well-
browned, almost, but not quite, to the point of
being overdone.

SERVES 4–6
50 g/2 oz butter, cut into pieces
125 ml/4½ fl oz water
65 g/2½ oz plain flour, sifted on to a sheet of paper
2 eggs

Put the pieces of butter into a small saucepan
with the water. Put the pan over a
medium–high heat to allow the butter to have
completely melted by the time the water
comes to the boil. Pour in the flour and wait
for a moment until the water seethes up over
it, then take the pan off the heat and
immediately start to beat the mixture – an
electric hand whisk is best for this but you
could use a balloon whisk.

When the mixture is smooth and very thick,
add one of the eggs and beat again until the
mixture is absolutely smooth, then repeat
with the second egg. Cover with a plate or
some cling film and leave until completely
cold, but don't put it in the refrigerator.

When you want to use the choux pastry,
spoon it on to a baking sheet lined with
nonstick baking paper and bake until the
pastry is puffed up, very brown and crisp. This
takes about 25 minutes for a heaped
dessertspoon-sized bun – but see individual
recipes for exact timings. Remove from the
oven and pierce with a sharp knife to let out
the steam.

Puff pastry

For years I shied away from making puff pastry because I found it too time-consuming and complicated. Then a reader sent me this wonderfully easy method. Do try it and see for yourself how delicious puff pastry can be. The quantity I've given can easily be doubled. You can store the finished puff pastry in the refrigerator for up to a week, or in the freezer for two to three months.

MAKES PASTRY WEIGHING ABOUT 625 G/ 1 LB 6 OZ

250 g/9 oz plain 'strong' white flour, plus extra for rolling out
250 g/9 oz butter or hard margarine
150 ml/5 fl oz cold water
1 tablespoon fresh lemon juice

It's important to have everything really cold, so first of all sift the flour into a large bowl and put this into the refrigerator, along with the packet of butter or margarine and the water in a jug; leave to chill for at least 1 hour.

Cut the chilled butter or margarine into 5 mm/¼ inch cubes and put them into the bowl with the flour. Separate the cubes with your fingers and mix them lightly with the flour, without rubbing them in, so that they are just coated with flour and separated.

Take a tablespoon of water out of the jug, discard it and add the lemon juice in its place. Pour this liquid into the flour mixture and mix it lightly until it leaves the sides of the bowl. Don't attempt to mix in the butter – you need a mixture that is full of lumps of butter.

Turn the lumpy dough out on to a floured board and shape it into a rough oblong brick. Using small, jerky movements of the rolling pin, not long, sweeping ones, roll out the dough to an oblong about 1 cm/½ inch thick. Fold the top third of the dough down to within a third of the bottom edge and fold the bottom third up, then bang the rolling pin on the edges of the dough to seal in air.

Give the pastry a quarter turn to the right so that you have the loose edge on the right, like the cover of a book. Repeat the rolling, folding and quarter-turning process four more times, then put the folded dough into a polythene bag and pop it into the refrigerator for at least 1 hour, longer if you have time – the longer the better.

When you're ready to use the pastry, take it out of the refrigerator and leave it at room temperature until it is pliable enough to roll. Then roll it out, being careful to roll it in the same direction to keep the layers intact.

Goats' cheese and mint tartlets

These light tartlets make an excellent first course, or they can be served with salad as a main dish.

SERVES 6 AS A FIRST COURSE, 3 AS A MAIN COURSE

Soured cream pastry (page 149)
150 g/5 oz soft goats' cheese
2 free-range eggs
2 tablespoons chopped fresh mint
salt and freshly ground black pepper

Make the pastry, wrap and chill for at least 30 minutes.

Heat the oven to 200°C/400°F/Gas Mark 6. Take the pastry out of the refrigerator and leave it at room temperature until it is soft enough to handle.

On a floured board, cut the pastry into six equal pieces, form each into a ball and roll out to fit a 10 cm/4 inch individual tart tin. Press the pastry gently into the tins, then chill them while you make the filling.

Put the goats' cheese into a bowl with the eggs and whisk together, then stir in the mint and season to taste. Place the uncooked tarts on a large baking sheet and divide the cheese mixture between them. Bake in the preheated oven for 10–15 minutes, or until the filling is set and the pastry crisp and golden brown. Serve hot or warm.

Goats' cheese and mint tartlets

Spicy potato pasties

These flaky pasties make a delicious snack –
or serve them with a salad or some cooked
vegetables and make a meal of them.

MAKES 6

Soured cream pastry (page 149)
2 tablespoons olive oil
1 large onion, peeled and chopped
325 g/12 oz potatoes, boiled in their skins and
    cooled
1 fresh chilli, deseeded and chopped very finely
1 garlic clove, crushed
1 tablespoon finely grated fresh ginger
1 teaspoon mustard seeds
1 teaspoon ground cumin
1 teaspoon ground coriander
125 g/4 oz frozen peas
3 tablespoons finely chopped fresh coriander
salt and freshly ground black pepper
a squeeze or two of fresh lemon juice

Make the pastry, wrap and chill while you
make the filling.

Heat the oil in a large saucepan, add the
onion, cover the pan and fry gently for 10
minutes or until soft.

Meanwhile, skin the potatoes and cut them
into 5 mm/¼ inch dice. Add the chilli, garlic,
ginger and spices to the onions and cook for 1
minute, stirring, then add the potatoes and
peas. Cook for a further 2–3 minutes, then
remove from the heat and add the fresh
coriander and salt, pepper and lemon juice to
taste. Leave the mixture to cool.

Heat the oven to 200°C/400°F/Gas Mark 6.
Take the pastry out of the refrigerator and
leave it at room temperature until it is soft
enough to handle.

Divide the pastry into six pieces. Roll each
piece out quite thinly and cut out a circle
about 15 cm/6 inches in diameter: I cut
around a saucer with a sharp knife.

Spoon some of the potato mixture on to
each pastry circle, fold the pastry over into a
pasty shape and press the edges together with
a fork. Make a couple of small holes in each
pasty to allow steam to escape, place them on
a baking sheet and bake for 20–25 minutes.
Serve hot or cold.

Spinach and potato pasties
*Replace the peas with about 300 g/11 oz of frozen
chopped spinach, thawed, then squeezed well to
remove excess liquid. (No need to cook it before
mixing it with the potatoes.) You can leave out the
spices if you like, and flavour the spinach with
freshly grated nutmeg instead.*

Mushroom tart

This can easily be made for vegans. These
quantities are right for a 20 cm/8 inch tart but
this recipe is also very effective made as four
individual 10 cm/4 inch tartlets. For a large
tart – 30 cm/12 inches, which is great for
entertaining – double all the quantities.

SERVES 6

50 g/2 oz butter or vegan margarine
700 g/1½ lb button mushrooms, wiped clean with a
    damp cloth
2 garlic cloves, crushed
2 teaspoons cornflour
150 ml/5 fl oz single cream or soya cream
salt and freshly ground black pepper
freshly grated nutmeg
squeeze of lemon juice
chopped fresh parsley

FOR THE SHORTCRUST PASTRY

175 g/6 oz plain flour (half white and half
    wholewheat)
pinch of salt
75 g/3 oz cold, firm butter or vegan margarine
2½ tablespoons cold water

Make the pastry (see page 148), wrap in
greaseproof paper and chill in the refrigerator
for 30 minutes.

Roll out the pastry on a floured surface and
use it to line a shallow 20 cm/8 inch fluted tart
tin. Gently but firmly press the pastry down
into the base of the tin, then trim the edges
and prick the base with a fork. Put the pastry
into the refrigerator for a further 30 minutes.

Heat the oven to 200°C/400°F/Gas Mark 6.
Put a circle of greaseproof paper in the base
of the tart and put some dried beans or dried
crusts on top, to weigh it down and prevent
the base from rising as it bakes. Bake for 15
minutes, until the pastry is set. Remove the

paper and beans, put the tart back into the oven and bake for a further 5 minutes, until the base is crisp.

While the pastry is cooking, prepare the filling. Melt the butter or margarine in a large saucepan, add the mushrooms and garlic and cook, uncovered, for 15–20 minutes, or until the mushrooms have produced a lot of liquid and this has then mostly disappeared. Stir the mushrooms from time to time.

Put the cornflour into a small bowl and mix to a paste with the cream; pour this into the pan with the mushrooms and stir over the heat until thickened. Remove from the heat and season to taste with salt, pepper, nutmeg and a squeeze of lemon juice. Spoon this mixture into the hot cooked pastry case and serve immediately or keep it warm in the oven until you're ready. Sprinkle the parsley on top before serving.

Vegetable flan with cheese pastry

You can vary the vegetables in this flan according to taste and season. Sweetcorn is a popular addition.

SERVES 6
4 small carrots
1 bunch of spring onions
8 sun-dried tomatoes, drained of oil
1 fresh tomato
2 tablespoons chopped fresh herbs
salt and freshly ground black pepper
300 ml/10 fl oz single or soured cream
2 eggs and 1 extra egg yolk
50 g/2 oz mature Cheddar cheese, grated
FOR THE CHEESE PASTRY
175 g/6 oz plain flour (half white and half
  wholewheat)
2 pinches of cayenne pepper or chilli powder
pinch of salt
75 g/3 oz cold, firm butter
50 g/2 oz mature Cheddar cheese, grated

Make the pastry (see page 148), wrap in greaseproof paper and chill in the refrigerator for 30 minutes.

Roll out the pastry on a floured surface and use it to line a 3 cm/1¼ inch deep, 22 cm/

9 inch tart tin. Gently but firmly press the pastry down into the base of the tin, then trim the edges and prick the base with a fork. Put the pastry into the refrigerator to rest for a further 30 minutes.

Heat the oven to 200°C/400°F/Gas Mark 6. Put a circle of greaseproof paper in the base of the flan and put some dried beans or dried crusts on top, to weigh it down and prevent the base from rising as it bakes. Bake for 15 minutes, until the pastry is set. Remove the paper and beans, put the pastry case back into the oven and bake for a further 5 minutes, until the base is crisp. Remove from the oven and set aside. Turn the oven down to 180°C/350°F/Gas Mark 4.

While the pastry is cooking, prepare the filling. Scrub or scrape the carrots, then slice them into even-sized pieces, cook in a saucepan of boiling water for 2 minutes, then drain well. Trim and chop the spring onions. Chop the sun-dried tomatoes and slice the fresh tomatoes.

Arrange all the vegetables in the pastry case and sprinkle with the fresh herbs and some salt and pepper. Whisk together the cream, eggs and egg yolk. Season, then pour this mixture over the vegetables. Sprinkle the grated cheese on top. Bake for 35–40 minutes, until the egg mixture is set. The flan is best served at room temperature, so let it cool for 45–60 minutes before serving – it will then also be easier to cut.

Cauliflower quiche
Bake the pastry case until crisp, as above, but when you take it out of the oven, don't turn down the oven temperature.

For the filling, divide a medium-sized cauliflower into florets and cook these in a little boiling water for about 5 minutes, until they are just tender; drain well.

Prepare a batch of Cheese sauce (page 80); make it quite thick, and season well with mustard and cayenne pepper. Mix the cauliflower florets with the sauce, check the seasoning, then spoon the mixture into the cooked pastry case. Sprinkle with grated cheese and pop the flan back into the oven for 10–15 minutes until piping hot and golden brown on top.

Gougère

This golden ring of cheesy choux pastry is much easier to make than it looks, and is very adaptable. It's delicious served with Roasted Mediterranean vegetables (page 103), Ratatouille (page 101) or Wild mushroom ragout (page 99) for a special main course (illustrated on page 146). For a summer lunch you could serve it with a herby green salad, a tomato or grilled pepper salad and a glass of chilled white wine.

SERVES 4–6
double quantity of Choux pastry (page 149)
175 g/6 oz strong Cheddar or Gruyère cheese, grated
good pinch of cayenne pepper

Make the choux pastry as described on page 149, stirring in two-thirds of the cheese and the cayenne pepper after you've whisked in the second egg. Leave it to get completely cold, but do not put it in the refrigerator.

When you're ready to bake the gougère, heat the oven to 220°C/425°F/Gas Mark 7. The best thing on which to make this is a large flat ovenproof dish, measuring about 30 cm/12 inches in diameter. Or you could line a baking sheet with nonstick baking paper marked with a 30 cm/12 inch circle (draw the circle on one side of the paper, then turn it over). Put heaped dessertspoonfuls of the mixture on to the paper inside the circle or around the edge of the dish. Sprinkle with the rest of the cheese, then bake on the shelf above the middle of the oven for 40–50 minutes, until the gougère is puffed up, very crisp and a deep brown. If necessary, transfer from the baking paper to a warmed serving dish. Serve immediately.

Spanakopita

One of my favourite dishes, which I've made a lot over the years and gradually refined to this most labour-saving version, using frozen spinach that you don't even have to cook first. It freezes well before baking, so is a good dish to prepare ahead. Although traditionally made in a rectangular dish and served in squares, I find that it's easier to divide and serve if you use a round dish – everyone gets some of the outside. I like to serve it with a green salad with fresh herbs, and perhaps new potatoes.

SERVES 6
3–4 tablespoons olive oil
1 large onion, peeled and chopped
900 g/2 lb frozen chopped spinach, thawed
175 g/6 oz feta cheese, crumbled
salt and freshly ground black pepper
300 g/11 oz filo pastry

Heat the oven to 200°C/400°F/Gas Mark 6.

Heat 1 tablespoon of the oil in a saucepan, add the onion, stir, then cover and leave to cook over a low heat for 7 minutes, until the onion is tender.

Drain the thawed spinach in a large sieve or colander, pressing out the excess water. Put the spinach into a bowl and add the onion, feta cheese and salt and pepper to taste.

Open the packet of filo pastry and cover the sheets loosely with a piece of polythene or a damp cloth to prevent them from drying out. Brush a 25 cm/10 inch round flan dish with olive oil, then lay a piece of filo pastry in it, allowing the edges to hang over the sides of the dish (don't worry if the pastry tears a bit as you put it into position – there will be other layers to cover it). Brush with olive oil, then place another piece of pastry on top. Continue until you have six layers of filo pastry.

Spoon the spinach mixture on to the pastry, spreading it out to the sides. Cover with six more sheets of filo pastry, brushing each sheet with olive oil, including the top sheet. To neaten the edges, roll them over towards the centre and tuck them inside the rim to make an attractive edge. Make a few small cuts in the top of the pastry to let the steam out then bake for 40–45 minutes. Serve hot or warm.

Goats' cheese in puff pastry

These make an easy and unusual main course. Serve them with Cumberland sauce (page 84) and steamed vegetables or salad.

They freeze perfectly, so even if you're making them for two people, it's worth preparing the full quantity and then freezing two before baking.

SERVES 4
½ quantity of Puff pastry (page 150) or
   350 g/13 oz ready-rolled puff pastry
2 x 100 g/3½ oz firm goats' cheese logs
a little beaten egg to glaze

Heat the oven to 220°C/425°F/Gas Mark 7.

Roll out the pastry to about 45 x 25 cm/18 x 10 inches. Cut out eight circles, each 10 cm/4 inches in diameter. Slice each goats' cheese in half horizontally. Place a piece of goats' cheese on four of the pastry circles, cut side of the cheese uppermost so that it won't ooze out as it cooks. Brush the edges of the pastry with cold water, put the other pastry circles on top and press the edges firmly together.

Prick the tops to allow steam to escape and decorate with pastry trimmings. Brush with beaten egg, then place on a baking sheet that has been brushed with water and bake for 15 minutes, until golden brown. Serve hot.

Spanakopita

Cheese, tomato and onion pizza

Pizza dough will keep in the refrigerator for a couple of days, wrapped in cling film, so you can take a piece of dough when you need it, roll it out, put on your topping and bake.

MAKES FOUR 30 CM/12 INCH PIZZAS
400 g/14 oz strong brown bread flour
½ teaspoon salt
1 sachet of easy-blend yeast
a little olive oil
FOR THE TOPPING
Fresh tomato sauce (page 82)
450 g/1 lb tomatoes, cut into thin slices
1 onion (use a red onion if you like), peeled and
    sliced into thin rings
225 g/8 oz cheese, grated
2 teaspoons dried oregano or 1 tablespoon
    chopped fresh parsley
a little olive oil

Put the flour, salt and yeast into a large bowl. Pour in 300 ml/10 fl oz tepid water. Mix to a dough that leaves the sides of the bowl clean, then turn the dough out on to a clean work surface and knead until the dough feels smooth and silky: this takes about 5 minutes.

Oil the bowl, put the dough back into it, turn it in the oil so that it is coated, then stretch a piece of cling film over the top. Leave until the dough has doubled in size: as little as 45 minutes in a warm room, or up to 2 hours or more in a cold place. The dough can also be put into the refrigerator overnight.

Knead the dough briefly (this is often referred to as 'punching it down') and let it rise again. It will be quicker this time – but if you're not ready for it, you can punch it down again, and put it into the refrigerator or freezer to use later if you wish.

Heat the oven to 200°C/400°F/Gas Mark 6. Oil one or two large baking sheets.

Take a quarter of the dough and roll it out into a thin circle about 30 cm/12 inches across (or take an eighth of the dough and make a 20 cm/8 inch circle). Make the number of pizzas you want and transfer to the baking sheets.

Spread a thin layer of tomato sauce on each pizza, then cover with slices of tomato and onion, some grated cheese and a sprinkling of oregano or parsley, using a quarter of the ingredients on each 30 cm/12 inch pizza. Sprinkle a little olive oil over the top – a teaspoon or so on each pizza – and bake for 15–20 minutes, or until the pizza is crisp at the edges, the dough is cooked right through in the centre, and the top is lightly browned. It's wonderful straight from the oven but also good warm or cold.

Mixed pepper pizza
Omit the tomato slices and use 1 red, 1 green and 1 yellow pepper, sliced into thin rings.

Tomato and roasted garlic pizza
Omit the cheese and onion. Instead of the onion, use 8 sun-dried tomatoes that you have drained and cut into strips. Then add some halved garlic cloves (about 10 or 12 large cloves should be about right) and drizzle with olive oil.

Mushroom and garlic
Omit the tomato slices, onion and cheese. Cut 450 g/1 lb of mushrooms into thick slices. Heat 1 tablespoon of olive oil in a large saucepan, add the mushrooms and cook over a moderate–high heat until they are just tender and their liquid has evaporated. Add 2 cloves of garlic, chopped, 2 tablespoons of chopped fresh parsley and some salt and pepper. Spread over the tomato sauce.

Cheese, tomato and onion pizza

puddings

Most puddings are naturally vegetarian and so there are plenty of recipes to choose from. In this chapter I'm including simple fruit puddings, crumbles, pies and tarts, ice creams and cheesecakes, some chocolate puddings and a classic pavlova.

There are two ingredients that vegetarians need to watch out for: suet and gelatine, both of which are derived from animal carcasses. Some traditional baked and steamed puddings such as jam roly poly, Christmas pudding and mince pies are often made with suet. Gelatine is used to set cold puddings such as mousses, jellies and chilled soufflés. Recipes using these ingredients can be made vegetarian: in the case of suet, vegetarian suet is now widely available, or you can substitute grated butter or hard vegan margarine. Gelatine is a little more difficult to substitute because although there is a vegetarian setting agent, made from a seaweed called agar agar, it behaves rather differently to animal gelatine. You have to use a method that I have explained fully in the recipe for Apricot jelly (page 174).

Tender, juicy pears make an excellent dessert. If they are not quite ripe, poach them in fruit juice, water or wine

cooking fruit

Baking

In this simple cooking method you just trim the fruit as necessary (you don't have to peel it, just remove the core of apples or pears, or halve and stone peaches or apricots), put it into a baking dish with flavourings and a little liquid – water or apple juice – cover and bake in a moderate oven, 190°C/375°F/Gas Mark 5, until the fruit is tender. Baked apples (page 165) and Fruits baked with orange and ginger (page 162) are examples of this method.

Stewing

To stew fruit, you add only the minimum amount of liquid, so this is a good method for naturally juicy fruit such as blackcurrants, blackberries, gooseberries, juicy plums, apples and rhubarb. Prepare the fruit by removing the stems, stones or cores, and peeling if necessary. Put it into a heavy-based saucepan with 2 tablespoons of water to each 450 g/1 lb of fruit. Cover and heat gently until the juices run and the fruit is tender – about 10 minutes – then sweeten with honey or caster sugar to taste. Alternatively, instead of the water, you can use fruit juice, or butter or vegan margarine for apples, and add some raisins, sultanas or other chopped dried fruit for natural sweetness.

Poaching

Similar to stewing, the difference lies in the amount of liquid used – poaching means cooking the fruit very gently in plenty of liquid and is the best method for firm fruits such as pears, apricots and plums. The poaching liquid can be apple juice, water and/or red wine (as in Ginger poached pears, page 161) or a sugar syrup, which you make by dissolving 85 g/3 oz sugar in 300 ml/½ pint of water and boiling for 2 minutes. This is enough to poach 450 g/1 lb of fruit. Put in the fruit, let the liquid come back to the boil, then cover and leave to simmer very gently until the fruit is tender right through to the centre when pierced with a skewer. This takes longer than you might think: about 15–20 minutes for apricots or plums and 30 minutes for whole pears. When the fruit is tender, remove it from the pan with a draining spoon, turn up the heat and boil the liquid rapidly for a few minutes until it has reduced in quantity and become syrupy, then pour this over the fruit.

Whether you're stewing or poaching, you can flavour the fruit by adding thin pieces of lemon or orange rind, a vanilla pod (which can be rinsed afterwards, dried and used again – keep it pushed into a jar of caster sugar), a piece of cinnamon stick, a few cardamom pods, a clove or two or, for gooseberries, a head of fresh elderflowers.

Tofu cream

Whizzing tofu in a food processor makes it light and creamy. The nicest tofu to use is the kind you buy fresh from a stockist of Chinese or Japanese foods; see page 140 for information on storage. Otherwise, use either a vacuum-packed silken tofu or firm tofu – you need to add a bit more liquid to the firm one when you purée it. You can make this cream as thick or thin as you want, depending on the amount of liquid you add; and you can vary it by using fruit juice instead of water and adding ripe fruits such as strawberries, or cooked fruits.

SERVES 2 AS A PUDDING, 6 AS A TOPPING
300 g/11 oz tofu
honey or sugar to taste
½ teaspoon vanilla extract
1–3 tablespoons (or more) water or apple juice

Put the tofu into a food processor with a little sugar or honey and the vanilla extract and whiz to a smooth purée, adding a little water or apple juice if necessary to get the consistency you want. Chill until needed.

Fruit fool

To make a fruit fool, you simply fold yogurt, custard or cream – or a mixture – into a roughly equal volume of stewed and puréed fruit or mashed very ripe fruit. You can purée the fruit so that it's really smooth or leave it with some texture.

For a vegan version, use Tofu cream (above) or soya yogurt as a base.

Classic fools use slightly tart fruits – gooseberries, redcurrants, raspberries – to cut the richness of the cream or custard base. However, strawberries and mangoes also make good fools.

Dried apricots, soaked for a few hours, gently poached in their soaking liquid until very tender, then puréed, make a delicious pudding when combined with thick Greek yogurt (and some whipped cream for a richer mixture), honey to sweeten and a scattering of toasted flaked almonds.

Yogurt, honey and dates

The success of this simple mixture depends on having top quality ingredients.

SERVES 4
50 g/2 oz almonds (in their skins)
225 g/8 oz fresh dates
500 g/1 lb thick strained Greek yogurt
4 tablespoons clear honey such as acacia
4 tablespoons thick cream, preferably Jersey

First blanch the almonds by putting them into a small saucepan, covering with cold water and bringing to the boil. Let them boil for 1 minute, then remove from the heat and drain. Slip the almonds out of their skins with your fingers, then cut the almonds into long thin pieces with a sharp knife.

Stone and halve the dates. Divide the dates between four bowls or glasses, or put them into one large bowl. Spoon the yogurt over the dates, drizzle the honey over the yogurt and finally top with the cream and almonds.

Ginger poached pears

This is a good way of preparing pears, particularly if they are too hard to eat raw. They will keep, well covered, in the refrigerator for at least 24 hours.

SERVES 4
4 pears
grated rind and juice of 1 orange
300 ml/10 fl oz red wine
50 g/2 oz caster sugar
1 piece of preserved stem ginger, finely chopped

Peel the pears, keeping them whole with the stems still attached. Put them into a deep saucepan with the orange rind and juice and the red wine. Bring to the boil, then reduce the heat and simmer gently until the pears are cooked right through, about 30 minutes.

Remove the pears from the pan using a draining spoon and put them into a shallow dish. Add the sugar and ginger to the liquid and boil for 4–5 minutes, until it is syrupy, then pour it over the pears. Serve hot or cold.

Apple and strawberry crumble

This is a particularly delicious combination of flavours. Serve it with cold creamy Greek yogurt or vanilla ice cream.

SERVES 6
grated rind and juice of 1 lemon
1 kg/2¼ lb Cox apples
4 Golden Delicious apples
25 g/1 oz butter
450 g/1 lb strawberries
50 g/2 oz caster sugar
FOR THE CRUMBLE TOPPING
225 g/8 oz plain flour (white or wholewheat)
50 g/2 oz cornflour
125 g/4 oz cold butter or hard vegan margarine
50 g/2 oz demerara or granulated sugar

Put the lemon juice and rind into a saucepan large enough to hold the apples. Peel and core the apples and slice them directly into the pan, turning them in the lemon juice to prevent them from discolouring. Add the butter, pushing it down to the bottom of the pan. Cover the pan with a lid and cook over a low heat for about 20 minutes, until the apples are tender. Stir from time to time to prevent sticking. Remove from the heat.

While the apples are cooking, remove the stems from the strawberries and halve or quarter the strawberries if they are large. Put them into an ovenproof dish and sprinkle with the caster sugar.

Next make the crumble topping. Sift the flour and cornflour together into a bowl. If you are using wholewheat flour, add the bran left in the sieve. Cut the butter into small pieces, add these to the flour, then, using your fingertips, rub the butter into the flour until the mixture looks like breadcrumbs. Stir in the sugar and keep in the refrigerator until you are ready to finish the crumble.

Heat the oven to 200°C/400°F/Gas Mark 6. Spoon the apples into the dish on top of the strawberries, then spread the crumble topping evenly over the apples. Bake for 30–40 minutes, until the crumble is golden brown and crisp on top. Serve warm.

Apple and blackberry crumble
Replace the strawberries with blackberries.

Pear and blueberry or raspberry crumble
Use pears instead of apples and blueberries or raspberries instead of strawberries.

Fruits baked with orange and ginger

This is my version of a recipe by the creative vegetarian cookery writer, Nadine Abensur, in *The New Cranks Recipe Book* (Weidenfeld & Nicolson, 1996). It is a lovely way of preparing fruits without any added sugar.

SERVES 8
1 orange
3 eating apples
3 sweet pears, not too ripe
18 dried apricots
18 dried figs
18 dried prunes, stones removed
200 ml/7 fl oz apple juice
5 cm/2 inch piece of fresh ginger, grated

Heat the oven to 180°C/350°F/Gas Mark 4.

Scrub the orange, then remove some thin strips of peel using a zester or the fine side of a grater. Squeeze the juice out of the orange.

Cut the apples and pears into quarters and remove the cores, but keep the peel on. Put them into a casserole or baking dish and pour over the orange juice.

Add the apricots, figs and prunes, the apple juice and grated ginger. Cover with foil or a lid and bake for 1 hour. Stir in the orange peel and serve hot, warm or cold, with some creamy Greek yogurt if you like.

Apple and strawberry crumble

Double-crust blueberry pie

A classic fruit pie for a wintry day. Serve it with cream or custard.

SERVES 6
Shortcrust pastry (page 148)
600 g/1¼ lb blueberries, washed
150 g/5 oz caster sugar
1 tablespoon cornflour
milk or soya milk to glaze

Heat the oven to 200°C/400°F/Gas Mark 6. Grease a 24 cm/9½ inch pie plate. On a lightly floured board, roll out half the pastry to form a circle and use to line the pie plate as described on page 148.

Put the blueberries on top of the pastry to within 1 cm/½ inch of the edges, then brush the edges with water. Mix together the sugar and cornflour and sprinkle this evenly over the fruit to sweeten it and thicken the juices as it cooks.

Roll out the remaining pastry and put this on top of the fruit. Press the edges of the pastry together, trim them so that they are even with the edge of the plate, then press around the edges with a fork. Make a steam hole in the centre. If you like, cut some shapes from the pastry trimmings and stick these on to the pie with cold water. Brush the pie lightly with milk, sprinkle with caster sugar, and bake for 30 minutes. Serve hot or cold.

Rhubarb pie
Replace the blueberries with 600 g/1¼ lb of trimmed rhubarb, cut into 2.5 cm/1 inch chunks.

Baked apples

A good old-fashioned pudding, and one that you can vary quite a bit by using different fillings for the apples.

SERVES 4
4 large cooking apples
85–125 g/3–4 oz filling (see below)
a little butter or vegan margarine (optional)
1 tablespoon clear honey (optional)

Heat the oven to 190°C/375°F/Gas Mark 5.

Remove the apple cores, keeping the apples whole. The best way to do this is to use a corer, but if you don't have one you can cut out the core from the top and bottom of the apples, using a sharp knife. Then make a shallow cut right round the middle of each apple (around its 'equator') to prevent the skin from bursting as the apple cooks.

Stand the apples in a very lightly greased baking dish. Stuff the centres of the apples with your chosen filling – you need just under 25 g/1 oz of filling for each apple. If you wish, spoon a little honey – about a teaspoonful – over each apple and put a few little pieces of butter or margarine on top. Bake the apples for about 45 minutes, until they are soft but not collapsed. Serve hot, warm or even cold, with Greek yogurt or cream if you like.

Fillings
My favourite filling is simply a few sultanas or dried dates, packed into the apple – the dried fruit swells with the juice of the apple and becomes succulent and delicious.

Alternatively, you could use a combination of any of the following fruits, nuts and flavourings: raisins, sultanas, chopped dried figs, dates, prunes, dried apricots, peeled and chopped banana, chopped preserved stem ginger; chopped walnuts or almonds; brown sugar, honey; grated orange or lemon rind; ground ginger, cinnamon or mixed spice; brandy or orange liqueur – or you could use mincemeat.

Double-crust blueberry pie

Chocolate roulade

This is one of my favourite puddings. It also makes a lovely gooey birthday cake, to be eaten with a fork, for a chocoholic. The roulade will keep well in the refrigerator for several hours, and can also be frozen.

SERVES 6–8
5 eggs, separated (see page 63)
175 g/6 oz soft brown sugar
3 tablespoons hot water
175 g/6 oz plain chocolate, melted
icing sugar to dust
300 ml/10 fl oz double cream
4 tablespoons rum

Heat the oven to 200°C/400°F/Gas Mark 6. Grease a 22 x 33 cm/9 x 13 inch Swiss roll tin and line with nonstick baking paper.

Put the egg yolks into a bowl with the sugar and whisk until thick and pale. Mix the hot water with the melted chocolate, then gently stir this into the egg yolk mixture.

Whisk the egg whites until stiff, then fold these gently into the chocolate mixture, using a gentle cutting and turning movement to combine the two mixtures. Pour the mixture into the tin, spreading it out to the edges. Bake for 15 minutes.

Leave to cool in the tin for 10 minutes, then cover with a damp tea towel and leave for a further 10 minutes.

Remove the cloth and turn the cake out on to a piece of greaseproof paper dusted with icing sugar. Remove the nonstick paper from the cake, then leave to cool completely.

Whisk the cream until thick, then stir in the rum. Trim the edges of the roulade, then spread the cream over it, taking it to within 1 cm/½ inch of the edges. Carefully roll up the roulade, starting with one of the narrow sides and using the paper to help. It may crack, but that is part of its charm. Dust with icing sugar.

Variations
You can vary the filling by adding chopped crystallized ginger or marrons glacés; or you could spread the roulade first with a layer of sweetened chestnut purée and then the cream.

Chocolate torte

This is best made at least 12 hours before you want to serve it, to allow the chocolate to firm up. It can be kept for 24–48 hours in the refrigerator, as long as you leave it in its tin or keep it well covered. It's rich, so a little goes a long way, but if you want to serve a lot of people you can double all the ingredients and make it in a 30 cm/12 inch round tin. It's good served with single cream or crème fraîche.

SERVES 6–8
400 g/14 oz plain chocolate (at least 50% cocoa solids)
125 g/4 oz amaretti biscuits
a little neutral-flavoured oil, such as groundnut oil
300 ml/10 fl oz single cream
2 tablespoons rum
TO DECORATE
50 g/2 oz chocolate

Break the chocolate into a bowl, set the bowl over a pan of steaming water and leave until the chocolate has melted, stirring once or twice until smooth.

Crush the amaretti biscuits to fine crumbs in a food processor or in a polythene bag with a rolling pin. Brush a 20 cm/8 inch straight-sided tart tin with oil, line the base with a circle of nonstick baking paper and brush again with oil. Sprinkle the crushed biscuits evenly in the base of the tin – this will be the top of the torte.

When the chocolate is smooth, add the cream and rum and whisk until the mixture becomes thick and pale. This takes a few minutes with an electric whisk, or a little longer by hand. Spoon the chocolate mixture on top of the crushed biscuits and smooth it to the edges of the tin with the back of a spoon. Cover the tin with cling film, then put it into the refrigerator for at least 12 hours.

Prepare the chocolate for the decoration by drawing a potato peeler down the length to make curly shavings.

To turn out the torte, remove the cling film and slip a knife around the edge of the tin. Invert a serving plate over the tin and turn it over. Remove the paper, then sprinkle the chocolate shavings on top of the torte.

Variation

For a vegan version, make sure that the chocolate and biscuits are vegan, and use soya cream instead of single cream. This means using biscuits other than amaretti, which are made with egg whites. I prefer almond-flavoured biscuits, but digestives or ginger biscuits are good too.

Chocolate pots

This is an unconventional recipe for this classic dish because it contains no eggs – you can make a very good vegan version by substituting soya cream for the single cream.

SERVES 4

300 g/10 oz plain chocolate (at least 50% cocoa solids)
300 ml/10 fl oz single cream or soya cream

First draw a potato peeler down the length of the chocolate a few times to make some chocolate curls to decorate the pudding: keep these on one side.

Break the rest of the chocolate into pieces, put it into a deep bowl and set the bowl over a pan of steaming water. Leave until the chocolate has melted, stirring once or twice until smooth.

Pour in the cream, then whisk until the mixture is thick and pale; this will only take a minute or two. Spoon the mixture into individual bowls or glasses, decorate with the reserved flaked chocolate and keep in a cool place until required.

Quick syrup sponge

Here is a modern version of an old favourite – steamed syrup sponge made quickly and easily in the microwave.

SERVES 4

2 generous tablespoons golden syrup
125 g/4 oz butter or margarine, softened
125 g/4 oz caster sugar
125 g/4 oz self-raising flour
½ teaspoon baking powder
2 eggs

TO SERVE

extra golden syrup
custard

Put the golden syrup into the base of a microwaveable pudding basin with a clip-on lid.

Put the butter or margarine, sugar, flour, baking powder and eggs into a bowl and beat, using an electric or hand whisk, until light and creamy. Add a tablespoon of water to loosen the mixture if it's too stiff to drop easily off the spoon. Spoon the mixture on to the syrup in the bowl and cover with the lid.

Microwave at Full power for 5–6 minutes, until the mixture has risen and feels firm in the centre when touched. Turn out and serve with more syrup to taste, and custard.

Treacle tart

Be careful not to eat this straight from the oven, or the hot treacle will burn your mouth. Cool it down with some single (or soya) cream, crème fraîche or creamy Greek yogurt.

SERVES 4–6
325 g/12 oz golden syrup (see recipe)
Shortcrust pastry (page 148)
100 g/4 oz fresh wholewheat breadcrumbs
juice of ½ lemon

Heat the oven to 190°C/375°F/Gas Mark 5. Put the tin of golden syrup into the oven to warm as the oven heats up – make sure the lid isn't on too tightly.

On a lightly floured board, roll out the pastry to form a circle and use to line a shallow 18–20 cm/7–8 inch tin as described on page 148.

The easiest way to weigh out the golden syrup is to put the breadcrumbs into a bowl that will fit on top of your scales, then pour the warm syrup into the bowl until you have 325 g/12 oz of syrup – this does the job with the minimum amount of stickiness. Add the lemon juice, stir, then pour or spoon this mixture into the pastry case.

Re-roll the pastry trimmings about 3 mm/⅛ inch thick and cut into strips, then criss-cross these over the tart to form a lattice. Bake for about 25 minutes, until the pastry is crisp and lightly browned. Serve warm.

Tarte Tatin

If you put this pudding into the oven just before you start your meal, it can bake while you eat and you can then enjoy it fresh from the oven. You can use a special tarte Tatin dish – one that can be heated on top of the stove, then put into the oven – or a 20 cm/8 inch round baking tin.

SERVES 4
½ quantity Puff pastry (page 150), or
  1 quantity Soured cream pastry (page 149), or
  325 g/12 oz ready-rolled puff pastry
40 g/1½ oz butter
40 g/1½ oz sugar
5 medium-sized Cox apples
juice of ½ lemon

Heat the oven to 200°C/400°F/Gas Mark 6.

Roll out the pastry and cut out a circle 1 cm/½ inch bigger all round than the top of the tin you are going to use for the tart.

Spread the bottom of the tarte Tatin dish or a frying pan with the butter and sugar. Peel and quarter the apples and sprinkle them with lemon juice. Put the apple quarters in the pan and cook over a high heat to caramelize the butter and sugar, for about 6 minutes, until the apples are slightly brown.

Unless you're using a tarte Tatin dish, you should now transfer the apples to a 20 cm/8 inch round baking tin; make sure you also transfer as much of the gooey butter and sugar mixture as possible. Whichever tin you're using, the apples need to be arranged curved side down.

Put the pastry on the top of the apples, tucking it down into the apples at the sides. Make some steam holes in the pastry using a sharp knife, then bake for 20 minutes.

To serve, loosen the edge with a knife, then turn upside down on to a plate – the apples will be on top. Leave for a couple of minutes before serving.

Tarte Tatin

Quick no-cook cheesecake

The name says it all, really . . . you can make this in about 10 minutes. You will need an 18 or 20 cm/7 or 8 inch plain flan ring, which you can buy at any cook shop.

SERVES 4
50 g/2 oz butter
175 g/6 oz ginger biscuits
200 g/7 oz medium-fat or low-fat soft white cheese
50 g/2 oz caster sugar
grated rind of ½ lemon
2 tablespoons fresh lemon juice
2 tablespoons double cream

TO DECORATE
a few curls of lemon zest, or some small
  strawberries, or fresh mint sprigs

Melt the butter in a saucepan over a low heat. Meanwhile, crush the biscuits to fine crumbs, either by whizzing them in a food processor or by putting them into a polythene bag and crushing with a rolling pin. Remove the melted butter from the heat and stir in the biscuits until they are all coated.

Put the flan ring on to the plate from which you want to serve the cheesecake. Spoon the crumb mixture into it; press it down firmly with the back of a spoon or the base of a jam jar and put it into a cold place – I pop mine into the freezer.

For the topping, put the soft cheese into a bowl with the sugar, lemon rind and juice and the double cream. Stir vigorously for a minute or two until very thick. Spoon the mixture on top of the biscuit base in the flan ring, spreading it to the edges.

You can serve it almost immediately, as it sets quickly, or leave it in the refrigerator until you want to eat it; simply lift the flan ring off, and decorate the top with a few curls of lemon zest, strawberries or mint leaves.

Lime cream pie

This is a version of the classic American Key lime pie. It needs to be made several hours in advance to give it time to set. It can be kept, well covered with cling film, for 24 hours in the refrigerator.

SERVES 8–12
75 g/3 oz butter
200 g/7 oz digestive biscuits
300 ml/10 fl oz double cream
a small can (218 g) of condensed milk
grated rind and juice of 2 limes

TO DECORATE
slivers of lime zest

Melt the butter in a saucepan over a low heat. Meanwhile, crush the biscuits to fine crumbs, either by whizzing them in a food processor or by putting them into a polythene bag and crushing with a rolling pin. Mix the crumbs with the butter, then put the mixture into the base of a 20 cm/8 inch springform cake tin and press down well.

For the filling, whisk the cream until it is thick but not stiff, then add the condensed milk and whisk again, until it's very thick. Add the lime juice and rind and stir – the mixture may look as if it's going to separate at first, but don't worry, it won't; just keep on stirring gently until it's very smooth and thick.

Spoon this mixture on top of the biscuit base, then smooth and level it with the back of a spoon or a spatula. Cover and chill for several hours.

To serve, unclip and remove the outside of the springform tin and decorate the pie with slivers of lime zest.

Traditional baked cheesecake

This simple, creamy cheesecake is open to plenty of variations. To be really wicked you could serve it with extra cream to pour over it.

SERVES 8–12
50 g/2 oz butter
175 g/6 oz digestive biscuits
400 g/14 oz medium-fat soft white cheese
150 ml/5 fl oz double cream
75 g/3 oz vanilla sugar or caster sugar with a few
  drops of vanilla essence
grated rind of ½ lemon
2 eggs
4 tablespoons soured cream

Heat the oven to 160°C/325°F/Gas Mark 3. Grease a 20 cm/8 inch springform cake tin.

Melt the butter in a saucepan. Put the biscuits into a polythene bag and crush them to fine crumbs with a rolling pin, or whiz them in a food processor. Mix the crumbs with the butter, then put the mixture into the springform tin and press down well. Put this into the refrigerator or freezer to chill while you make the topping.

Put the soft cheese into a bowl with the double cream, sugar, grated lemon rind and eggs and whisk together until smooth. Pour the mixture over the biscuit base, put it into the oven and bake for about 1–1¼ hours, until the cheesecake is firm in the centre.

Turn off the oven and leave the cheesecake to cool in the oven. When it is completely cool, spread it with the soured cream, then put it into the refrigerator to chill.

To serve, slip a knife around the cheesecake to loosen it, then unclip and remove the outside of the springform tin.

Variations
Add 50 g/2 oz of chopped crystallized ginger, sultanas, chopped candied peel or chocolate chips to the mixture before baking.

Instead of the soured cream, you could top it with soft fruit such as strawberries or raspberries and spoon warmed redcurrant jelly over to give a shiny glaze.

Tiramisu

This means 'pick-me-up' in Italian: with its strong black coffee and brandy, it should have the desired effect!

SERVES 4–6
200 g/7 oz mascarpone cheese
2 eggs, separated (see page 63)
50 g/2 oz caster sugar
150 ml/5 fl oz strong black coffee
4 tablespoons Marsala or brandy
125 g/4 oz sponge fingers
2 teaspoons cocoa powder

Beat the mascarpone with the egg yolks and half the sugar. Whisk the egg whites until they stand in soft peaks, then whisk in the remaining sugar. Mix a tablespoon of the whites with the yolk mixture, then fold in the remaining yolk mixture

Mix the coffee and Marsala or brandy in a shallow dish, then dip the sponge fingers into the mixture, holding them in for a few seconds so they absorb some of the liquid but do not become soggy.

Use half the fingers to line the base of a trifle dish, then cover with a layer of the mascarpone mixture and sift over half the cocoa. Repeat the layers, then chill for at least 30 minutes before serving.

NOTE *Since this recipe uses uncooked eggs, it is not suitable for anyone in the groups vulnerable to salmonella poisoning: the very young and very old, pregnant and breastfeeding women, and anyone who is ill.*

Summer pavlova

A pavlova always makes an eye-catching and popular finale to a special meal, and it's surprisingly easy to make.

SERVES 8

4 egg whites
225 g/8 oz caster sugar
1 teaspoon cornflour
¼ teaspoon vinegar
½ teaspoon vanilla extract

FOR THE FILLING

225 g/8 oz strawberries
125 g/4 oz raspberries
125 g/4 oz blueberries or redcurrants
25 g/1 oz caster sugar
450 ml/15 fl oz double cream
150 ml/5 fl oz Greek yogurt

Heat the oven to 150°C/300°F/Gas Mark 2. Line a baking sheet with nonstick baking paper. Draw a 20 cm/8 inch circle (around a dinner plate or cake tin) on the paper, then turn it over so that the marking is on the underside of the paper.

Whisk the egg whites in a clean, grease-free bowl until they are so stiff that you can turn the bowl upside down without them falling out. Whisk a quarter of the sugar into the egg whites. When this has been absorbed, whisk in another quarter, and so on, until all the sugar has been added. Then gently stir in the cornflour, vinegar and vanilla. Pile the meringue mixture on to the baking sheet, spreading it out to fit the marked circle, with a dip in the centre. Bake the pavlova at the bottom (or coolest part) of the oven for 1 hour, until the meringue base and sides are crisp. Remove from the oven and leave to cool on a wire rack. Don't worry if it cracks a bit – that is normal.

While the meringue is cooking, prepare the topping. Wash and drain the fruit. Remove the stems from the strawberries, then halve or quarter them, depending on their size. Put all the fruit into a bowl and sprinkle with 25 g/ 1 oz caster sugar. Cover and leave for 1 hour.

Just before you want to serve the pavlova, place it carefully on a serving plate. Whisk the cream in a large bowl until soft peaks form, then fold in the yogurt, which will thicken the mixture. Spoon the cream mixture on top of the pavlova, making a dip in the centre. Drain off any liquid that the fruits have produced, then spoon them on top of the cream.

Lemon tart

Rich yet refreshing, lemon tart is delicious for pudding or served as a cake.

SERVES 4–6

3 eggs
85 g/3 oz caster sugar
grated rind of 1 lemon
50 g/2 oz unsalted butter, softened
juice of 3 lemons
icing sugar to dust (optional)

FOR THE SHORTCRUST PASTRY

150 g/5 oz plain flour
75 g/2½ oz butter
1 tablespoon cold water

Make the pastry (see page 148), wrap and chill for 30 minutes. Roll it out and use to line a 20 cm/8 inch loose-bottomed tart tin (not the very shallow kind). Trim the edges, then place in the refrigerator to chill while you make the filling.

Heat the oven to 180°C/350°F/Gas Mark 4.

Break the eggs into a bowl and add the caster sugar and lemon rind, then whisk them together until they are thick and pale. Add the butter, a little at a time, whisking after each addition until it has all been incorporated, then stir in the lemon juice. Pour this mixture into the (uncooked) pastry base. Bake for about 30 minutes, or until set. Leave to cool, then chill before serving. If you like, dredge the tart with icing sugar just before serving.

Summer pavlova

Apricot jelly with strawberries

You can now buy packets of vegetarian gelatine in most supermarkets, or you can buy it in the form of gelozone powder or agar agar flakes from some health food shops and macrobiotic or Japanese stockists. It makes a softer-textured jelly than the firm, springy type made with animal-derived gelatine.

SERVES 6
225 g/8 oz strawberries
caster sugar to taste
600 ml/1 pint apricot juice
1 sachet of Vege-gel, 2 teaspoons gelozone or
  2 tablespoons agar agar flakes

Wash the strawberries, remove the stems and slice if necessary, then divide them between six glasses or bowls. Sprinkle them with a little caster sugar if you think they need it.

If you are using Vege-gel, put the powder in a saucepan, gradually add the apricot juice, stirring all the time, then bring to the boil. For the other types of vegetable gelatine, put the juice into the saucepan and bring to the boil before sprinkling the powder or flakes over the top, whisking as you do so. In either case, cook the mixture for 1 minute after it has boiled, then remove from the heat. Sweeten the mixture a little to your taste if necessary.

If you're using glass bowls, let the mixture cool enough to prevent it from cracking the bowls, then pour it over the strawberries, and leave to set. (It will set much more quickly than conventional jelly.) I like to serve it with cream or soya cream.

Variations
You can use any type of fruit juice or 'fruit drink' to vary the flavour. If you want to make a pineapple jelly, use canned pineapple cubes rather than fresh pineapple, which reacts with the gelatine and prevents it from setting.

Raspberry ice cream

Fruit ice creams are easy to make, but the proportions are important because you need enough sugar to prevent the mixture from freezing too hard. Even so, this ice cream needs to be removed from the freezer 30 minutes before you want to serve it, to give it time to soften.

SERVES 4
225 g/8 oz fresh raspberries, washed, or frozen
  raspberries, thawed
175 g/6 oz caster sugar
300 ml/10 fl oz double or whipping cream

Purée the raspberries in a food processor, then pass them through a nylon sieve to remove the pips. (You need to use a nylon sieve because a metal one might react with the fruit and give a metallic flavour.) Add the sugar to the raspberries.

Whisk the cream until it is thick but not too stiff. Using a plastic spatula, gently combine the cream and the raspberry purée: this is done using a technique known as folding – cut the spatula across the centre of the mixture, reaching to the bottom of the bowl, turn the bowl slightly and gently scoop up the spatula to place some of the mixture on top. Continue until no large lumps of cream are visible, but do not overmix.

Pour the mixture into a plastic container and put it into the freezer. Chill a mixing bowl at the same time if you have room in your freezer. When the mixture is half solid, take it out of the freezer, tip it into the chilled bowl and whisk well to break up the ice crystals. Put the mixture back into the freezer and freeze until it's solid.

Vegan raspberry ice cream
You can substitute soya cream for the dairy cream, but do not whisk it before mixing it with the raspberry purée.

Strawberry ice cream
Strawberries make an even simpler ice cream, since you don't need to sieve them.

Classic vanilla ice cream

This is an economical recipe for real vanilla ice cream. It's wonderful with a warm chocolate sauce (see below).

SERVES 4

1 egg
40 g/1½ oz caster sugar
150 ml/5 fl oz milk or vanilla-flavoured soya milk
1 vanilla pod or ½ teaspoon vanilla extract
150 ml/5 fl oz double cream

The basis of this recipe is a thin custard made from the egg, sugar and milk, and you need to make this first. Break the egg into a bowl and whisk until foamy. Put the caster sugar into a small saucepan with the milk and the vanilla pod if you're using this and heat gently to boiling point, then pour over the egg, stir, and tip the mixture (including the vanilla pod) back into the saucepan. Stir over a very low heat for a few minutes until the mixture has thickened slightly – it's ready when it coats the spoon thinly when you take it out of the mixture. Don't try and hurry this process because if the mixture gets too close to boiling it will separate. This won't affect the flavour of the ice cream but will give it a grainy texture.

Leave the custard to get completely cold. Then remove the vanilla pod, scraping off any custard clinging to it. (Rinse the vanilla pod, leave it to dry in the air. then bury it in a jar of caster sugar to use again.) If you're not using a vanilla pod, add the vanilla extract to the custard at this point. Whisk the cream until it is thick but not too stiff, then fold this into the custard, using a plastic spatula in a gentle cutting and turning movement to combine the two mixtures.

Pour the mixture into a plastic container and freeze until firm round the edges. Turn the mixture into a bowl and whisk well to break up the ice crystals. Put the mixture back into the container in the freezer and freeze for another hour. Repeat this process until the mixture has frozen solid, about 3 hours. Remove it from the freezer 30 minutes before you want to serve it, to let it soften a little.

Mint ice cream

For this you need to flavour the milk with mint instead of vanilla. Add 25 g/1 oz of roughly chopped fresh mint leaves to the milk and sugar; bring almost to the boil, then remove from the heat, cover and leave for 30 minutes for the flavours to infuse. Then strain the milk, pressing the mint against the strainer to extract as much flavour as possible, and continue as above. You could colour this ice cream pale green using food colouring if you like – and add some good-quality chocolate chips for a superior mint-choc-chip ice!

Easy ice cream

This is a 'cheating' ice cream, but the result is excellent.

SERVES 8

600 ml/1 pint whipping cream
400 g/14 oz can condensed skimmed milk
1 teaspoon vanilla extract

Put the cream into a large bowl and whisk until thick, then pour in the condensed milk and the vanilla extract and whisk again until blended. Pour the mixture into a plastic container and freeze until firm – there's no need to whisk this mixture while it is freezing because ice particles do not form in it.

Chocolate sauce

A quick sauce that will make even bought ice cream special.

SERVES 4

175 g/6 oz good-quality plain chocolate (at least 50% cocoa solids)
150 ml/5 fl oz single cream

Bring a saucepan of water to the boil, then remove from the heat. Break the chocolate into a jug, add the cream and place the jug in the saucepan. Leave the chocolate to melt, stirring frequently to blend it with the cream.

baking

As with puddings, most baking recipes are suitable for vegetarians; the main things to look out for are the use of vegetarian fat (not lard, suet or dripping) and free-range rather than battery eggs. This chapter includes bread and scones, biscuits and brownies, and a selection of cakes.

Vegetarian baking used to be very much along wholefood lines: wholewheat flour and unrefined dark brown sugar. I still like to use these wholesome ingredients, but selectively rather than exclusively. For instance, I use half wholewheat flour and half plain flour in shortbread. In fact I nearly always use a proportion of wholewheat flour unless the recipe is very light, for example sponge cakes.

The more basic the dish is, the more likely I am to use 100 per cent wholewheat flour, organic and stoneground if possible – certainly for bread, and for chapattis, and nearly always for scones. My feeling is that if you're going to the trouble of making these yourself, you might as well make them as nutritious as possible, as well as good to eat. Biscuits and cakes, which are meant to be treats, are a different matter, although I do think that wholewheat fruit cake and parkin are good and they contain genuinely nourishing ingredients so are by no means 'empty calories'.

People love homemade biscuits, even if they're as simple as good old-fashioned flapjacks! I don't make them often because I feel that, being high in fat and sugar, they need to be kept in the category of treats rather than everyday foods . . . but on occasion they're lovely.

Carrot cake (page 184)

Scones

Scones are perfect for the beginner at baking: they're quick, easy to rustle up on the spur of the moment and wonderful to eat, warm from the oven, with honey or jam or, for a special treat, cream as well.

MAKES 8
225 g/8 oz plain flour (wholewheat, white or a half-and-half mixture)
2 teaspoons baking powder
50 g/2 oz cold, firm butter or vegan margarine
25 g/1 oz sugar (white or brown)
about 150 ml/5 fl oz milk or soya milk

Heat the oven to 220°C/425°F/Gas Mark 7.

Sift the flour and baking powder together into a bowl. With wholewheat flour, there will be some bran left in the sieve – just tip this into the bowl. Add the butter or margarine and use your fingertips to rub it into the flour, then stir in the sugar. Pour in slightly less than the full amount of milk and use a knife or your fingers to mix to a soft but not sticky dough, adding more milk if necessary.

Turn the dough out on to a floured board and knead lightly, then gently press out to a depth of at least 1 cm/½ inch. Cut out the scones with a 5 cm/2 inch round cutter and place them on a floured baking sheet.

Bake the scones for 12–15 minutes, until they are golden brown and the sides spring back when lightly pressed. Cool on a wire rack, or serve immediately. They are best eaten the same day they are made.

Cheese scones
Leave out the sugar and add ½ teaspoon of dry mustard powder and 40 g/1½ oz of grated cheese to the mixture. Sprinkle another 40 g/1½ oz of grated cheese on top of the scones before baking.

For another savoury version, add 6–8 chopped sun-dried tomatoes or some chopped olives and 1 teaspoon of dried oregano or thyme.

Fruit scones
Add 50–125 g/2–4 oz of raisins, sultanas or mixed dried fruit to the mixture. If you like, add ½ teaspoon of mixed spice or ground cinnamon.

Chapattis

Chapattis are easy to make and ideal for serving with curries or chilli bean dishes.

MAKES 12
250 g/9 oz plain flour
1 teaspoon salt
a little vegetable oil

Sift the flour into a bowl with the salt, pour in about 150 ml/5 fl oz cold water and mix to a soft dough. Turn the dough out on to a floured surface and knead for 5–10 minutes – the longer, the better. Cover the dough with a damp cloth and leave it to rest for 30 minutes.

Heat the grill to high, knead the dough again briefly, then divide it into 12 pieces. Form each into a ball, then roll them out with a rolling pin into 3 mm/⅒ inch thick circles.

Lightly grease a heavy-based frying pan, using a pad of paper towels dipped in oil, and place it over a medium heat.

Put a chapatti into the hot frying pan and when little bubbles begin to form in it, turn it over and cook the other side for a few seconds.

As each chapatti is done, transfer it to the grill, leaving about 15 cm/6 inches between it and the heat. When it puffs up, turn the chapatti over to do the other side, then put it into a warmed dish.

As soon as all the chapattis are done, serve immediately. (They will sink, but the puffing-up process makes them light.)

Soda bread

Soda bread is so easy to make and really delicious while it's still warm. It's certainly best eaten the day it's made, although you can toast it the next day. I do not put any salt in this bread because I find that the bicarbonate of soda gives it a salty taste – but you could add up to a teaspoonful, along with the baking powder, if you wish. I like to use a mixture of white and wholewheat flour.

MAKES 1 LOAF

450 g/1 lb plain flour (wholewheat, white or a half-and-half mixture)
1 teaspoon salt (optional)
2 teaspoons bicarbonate of soda
2 teaspoons cream of tartar
50 g/2 oz butter or vegan margarine
about 300 ml/½ pint buttermilk, or milk or soya milk plus 1 tablespoon vinegar

Heat the oven to 220°C/425°F/Gas Mark 7 and sprinkle a baking sheet with flour.

Sift the flour, salt, bicarbonate of soda and cream of tartar into a large bowl, tipping in any residue of bran left in the sieve from the wholewheat flour. Add the butter and rub it into the flour with your fingertips, until you cannot see any flecks of butter.

If you are using ordinary milk or soya milk, put it into a small saucepan and heat to tepid, then stir in the vinegar to sour it. Remove from the heat. Add the buttermilk or soured milk to the flour mixture and mix to a dough with your hands. It needs to be a soft mixture that leaves the sides of the bowl clean; add a bit more milk if necessary – a soft mixture makes a light loaf.

Turn the mixture out on to a lightly floured board and knead lightly for a few seconds until the dough is smooth. Then shape it into a round with your hands and put it on the floured baking sheet. Make a cross-shaped cut on top (which will help it to rise), then bake in the centre of the oven for about 30 minutes, until crisp and golden brown. Remove from the oven and cool on a wire rack – or eat while it is still warm, with butter and honey!

Blueberry muffins

Muffins are a wonderful breakfast or tea-time treat. They are best eaten on the day they are made, but they are easy and fun to make. You can use a 9-hole or 12-hole bun or muffin tin, depending on the size of muffins you are making, and line it with paper cake cases if you like.

MAKES 10 SMALL OR
6–7 LARGE MUFFINS

100 g/3½ oz plain flour
1 teaspoon baking powder
40 g/1½ oz caster sugar
1 egg, beaten
2 tablespoons milk
50 g/2 oz butter or vegan margarine, melted and left to cool
100 g/3½ oz fresh blueberries

Heat the oven to 220°C/425°F/Gas Mark 7. Line a deep-holed bun tin or muffin tin with paper cake cases if you are using these.

Sift the flour and baking powder into a bowl, then stir in the sugar.

Using a fork, whisk together the egg, milk and melted butter. Pour this mixture into the dry ingredients and stir briefly to form a lumpy batter; do not overmix. Add the blueberries and stir in gently. Put good spoonfuls of the mixture into the bun tin or paper cases and bake for about 20 minutes, or until the muffins are well risen and firm to the touch.

Apple and cinnamon muffins

Instead of the blueberries, add 1 apple, peeled and grated, and ½ teaspoon of ground cinnamon to the mixture.

Spiced carrot muffins

Sift ½ teaspoon of ground mixed spice with the flour and baking powder. Replace the blueberries with 1 small carrot, peeled and grated, and 50 g/2 oz of raisins.

Easy bread

Even if you've never baked anything before, you can make this bread. It's made by the one-rise method, which does not require any kneading. It is mixed, put into the tin to rise, then baked. You can use either fresh or dried yeast; I like to use fresh yeast whenever I can because I find it a pleasant product to handle and it seems to work more quickly than dried yeast. When working with any type of yeast there are two cardinal rules: the yeast must be really fresh, and the mixture must never get very hot until the point when it goes into the oven.

MAKES ONE 1 KG/2¼ LB LOAF OR
TWO 450 G/1 LB LOAVES

450 g/1 lb wholewheat flour
2 teaspoons salt
25 g/1 oz fresh yeast, or 2 teaspoons dried yeast,
  or 1 sachet (7 g) easy-blend yeast
1 teaspoon sugar
a little vegetable oil or butter

Sift the flour and salt into a large bowl and leave in a warm place, perhaps a cool oven, to warm. This isn't essential but it speeds up the rising process – but don't let the flour get too hot, just nice and warm.

Meanwhile, crumble the fresh yeast into a small bowl with the sugar and pour in 150 ml/5 fl oz tepid water. If you're using dried yeast, put the water and sugar into the bowl first, then sprinkle the yeast on top and stir. If you're using easy-blend yeast, just add it to the flour and salt in the bowl – there's no need to dissolve it first. Leave the yeast until it has frothed up like the head on a glass of beer; this takes about 5 minutes.

While you're waiting for the yeast, grease a 1 kg/2¼ lb loaf tin or two 450 g/1 lb loaf tins generously with butter or oil.

Add the frothy yeast mixture to the flour and add enough tepid water to make a mixture that is just too slippery to knead – start with 150 ml/5 fl oz water (300 ml/ 10 fl oz if you're using easy-blend yeast), then add a little more if necessary.

Flatten the dough into a rectangle and gently fold it over to make a rectangle to fit the tin; or divide it in half and make two folded rectangles if you're using small tins. Put the dough into the tin or tins with the fold underneath. Push it down into the sides and corners to give a domed shape to the loaf.

Cover with a clean tea towel wrung out in hot water and leave it in a warm place until the loaf has risen almost to the top of the tin and virtually doubled in size: this will take about 30 minutes in a warm room, longer – up to an hour perhaps – if the temperature is on the cool side. While the bread is rising, heat the oven to 200°C/400°F/Gas Mark 6.

Bake the bread for 45 minutes if you've made one large loaf, or about 35 minutes for two small ones, or until the bread is brown and firm to the touch and sounds hollow when you slip it out of the tin and tap it on the base with your knuckles. You can crisp the base and sides a bit more if you wish by putting the bread back into the oven for a few minutes after you've taken it out of the tin. Leave to cool on a wire rack.

Variation
For a lighter loaf, replace up to half of the wholewheat flour with strong white bread flour and make in the same way.

Soft rolls

These light rolls are made by the traditional bread-making method, so the mixture does have to be kneaded, but it's a very easy recipe. I like to use easy-blend yeast for these, although you could use fresh or dried yeast as described in the Easy bread recipe (left).

MAKES 8–10 ROLLS

150 ml/5 fl oz milk or soya milk
50 g/2 oz butter or vegan margarine
225 g/8 oz wholewheat flour
225 g/8 oz strong white flour
1 teaspoon salt
1 teaspoon sugar
1 sachet (7 g) easy-blend yeast

Put the milk, butter or margarine and 150 ml/5 fl oz water into a saucepan and heat gently until the butter has melted; remove from the heat and leave until tepid.

Meanwhile, sift the flours together into a large bowl, tipping in any residue of bran left in the sieve from the wholewheat flour. Add the salt, sugar and yeast, then make a well in the centre and pour in the milk mixture. Use your hands to mix to a dough, then turn the dough out on to a lightly floured surface and knead for 5 minutes, until it is smooth.

Put the dough into a clean, lightly oiled bowl, cover with a clean damp tea towel or some cling film stretched across the top of the bowl, and leave in a warm place for about 1 hour, until doubled in volume.

Heat the oven to 220°C/425°F/Gas Mark 7. Punch down the dough with your fist, then knead it again lightly for 1–2 minutes. Divide the dough into eight or ten pieces and shape them into rounds. Put them on to a floured baking sheet, leaving plenty of space between them. Cover loosely with a damp tea towel or a piece of lightly oiled polythene and leave in a warm, draught-free place for 15–20 minutes, until well risen.

Bake for 15–20 minutes, then leave to cool slightly on a wire rack; serve warm.

Date and banana teabread

This is good served in thick slices, buttered, or spread with cream cheese.

MAKES 1 LARGE LOAF

125 g/4 oz self-raising flour
125 g/4 oz plain wholewheat flour
1½ teaspoons baking powder
125 g/4 oz butter
125 g/4 oz Barbados sugar
1 egg
2 bananas, peeled and mashed
125 g/4 oz dried dates (not 'sugar-rolled'), chopped
4 tablespoons milk or soya milk
2 tablespoons demerara sugar

Heat the oven to 180°C/350°F/Gas Mark 4. Line a 900 g/2 lb loaf tin with a strip of nonstick paper to cover the short sides and the base; brush with oil.

Sift the flours and baking powder together into a bowl, tipping in any residue of bran left in the sieve.

Beat the butter and Barbados sugar together until light and fluffy – by hand, or using an electric whisk, food processor or food mixer. Beat in the egg, then add the bananas and beat until everything is well blended. Then lightly fold in the flour and dates, using a metal spoon. Add enough milk to make a soft mixture that drops easily off the spoon when you hold it above the bowl. Spoon the mixture into the loaf tin and sprinkle the demerara sugar over the top.

Bake for 1–1¼ hours, or until a warmed skewer inserted into the centre comes out clean. Turn out on to a wire rack to cool, then remove the paper and turn the loaf the right way up.

Shortbread

This crisp, light shortbread is good on its own, or served with summer fruits, such as strawberries and whipped cream.

MAKES 12 PIECES
175 g/6 oz butter
50 g/2 oz caster sugar
175 g/6 oz plain flour (white, or a mixture of wholewheat and white)
50 g/2 oz semolina

Heat the oven to 150°C/300°F/Gas Mark 2.

Beat the butter and sugar together until evenly blended. Sift in the flour and semolina, adding any residue of bran left in the sieve, and mix together to form a dough.

Transfer the mixture to a 20 cm/8 inch tart tin, press it down with the back of a spoon, then prick it thoroughly all over, to let the steam out as it bakes and keep it crisp. Bake for about 1¼ hours, until it's just beginning to turn golden; it's best if it only barely colours – don't let it overcook. Mark it into sections with a knife while it's still warm, then leave it in the tin to get completely cold and crisp.

Flapjacks

These are very sweet and gooey – but at least the oats are good for you!

MAKES 12–15
175 g/6 oz sugar (muscovado, caster or demerara)
175 g/6 oz butter or vegan margarine
2 tablespoons golden syrup
225 g/8 oz rolled oats

Heat the oven to 190°C/375°F/Gas Mark 5. Lightly grease an 18 x 28 cm/7 x 11 inch Swiss roll tin.

Put the sugar, butter or margarine and golden syrup into a saucepan and melt over a low heat. Remove from the heat and stir in the oats. Pour the mixture into the tin, level the top, then bake for about 20 minutes, until set.

Leave the mixture to cool slightly, then mark it into slices and leave to get completely cold before removing them from the tin.

Date or apricot flapjacks
Add 50 g/2 oz of chopped dates or dried apricots when you stir in the oats.

Peanut butter cookies

I've experimented with many recipes for these popular cookies; this is one I find works well.

MAKES 12–15
125 g/4 oz plain white flour
1 teaspoon baking powder
70 g/2½ oz butter
70 g/2½ oz soft brown sugar
70 g/2½ oz caster sugar
½ teaspoon vanilla extract
1 egg
50 g/2 oz peanut butter
50 g/2 oz salted roasted peanuts, chopped

Heat the oven to 180°C/350°F/Gas Mark 4. Grease one or two large baking sheets.

Sift the flour and baking powder together on to a plate or a piece of greaseproof paper.

Beat the butter with the sugars and vanilla extract until the mixture is light and fluffy – you can do this by hand, with an electric whisk, in a food processor or food mixer. Add the egg and peanut butter, and beat again until light. Fold in the flour and finally the chopped peanuts.

Roll teaspoonfuls of the mixture into small balls, then flatten and place on the baking sheets, allowing plenty of space for the cookies to spread. Bake for 12–15 minutes. Leave to cool slightly on the baking sheets, then transfer to a wire rack to cool completely.

Chocolate chip cookies
Add 100 g/3½ oz of chocolate chips to the mixture when you stir in the peanuts.

Best brownies

This is my invention, a brownie recipe with no flour at all. The result is wonderfully light, yet gooey. The recipe can also be made without the nuts – instead, you can use the same quantity of white chocolate, chopped.

MAKES 12

150 g/5 oz good-quality plain chocolate (at least 50% cocoa solids)
50 g/2 oz butter
2 eggs
50 g/2 oz brown sugar
50 g/2 oz walnuts or hazelnuts, roughly chopped

Heat the oven to 180°C/350°F/Gas Mark 4. Line a 20 cm/8 inch square baking tin with nonstick baking paper.

Break the chocolate into a bowl set over a pan of steaming water; leave until the chocolate has melted, stirring once or twice, until smooth. Stir in the butter.

Meanwhile, break the eggs into a bowl and add the sugar, then whisk at high speed until the mixture is very thick and the shape of a little of the mixture remains for several seconds: an electric whisk is best for this – if you do it by hand, it will take 10 minutes of hard whisking!

Pour the chocolate mixture on top of the whisked eggs and fold in, then gently fold in the nuts. Pour the mixture into the prepared tin, then bake until slightly risen and crusty-looking, about 25 minutes. The brownies will remain moist in the centre. Leave to cool completely in the tin, then turn out, remove the paper and cut into squares.

Best brownies

Carrot cake

There seem to be two different types of carrot cake: a very light one that is really a lemony sponge, and a moist, spicy one. This comes into the latter category.

MAKES ONE 18 CM/7 INCH ROUND CAKE
175 g/6 oz self-raising flour
1 teaspoon baking powder
2 teaspoons ground cinnamon
175 g/6 oz caster sugar
175 g/6 oz butter, softened
3 eggs
125 g/4 oz carrot, grated
50 g/2 oz walnuts, chopped

FOR THE TOPPING
50 g/2 oz butter, softened
125 g/4 oz icing sugar
grated rind of ½ lemon
juice of ½ lemon
a few chopped walnuts, to decorate

Heat the oven to 160°C/325°F/Gas Mark 3. Grease two 18 cm/7 inch sandwich tins with butter, then line the base of each with a circle of greased greaseproof paper.

Sift the flour, baking powder and cinnamon together into a bowl. Add the sugar, butter and eggs and beat with a wooden spoon for 2 minutes, or in a mixer for about 1 minute, until the mixture is smooth, thick and glossy, then add the grated carrot and walnuts and beat again briefly to incorporate them.

Spoon the mixture into the prepared tins, scraping the bowl with a plastic spatula. Level the tops, then bake, without opening the oven door, for 30 minutes.

Test whether the cakes are done by pressing them lightly in the centre with a fingertip; if the sponge bounces back, it's done. If not, bake for a further 5 minutes. Leave the cakes in the tins to cool for 1 minute, then turn out on to a wire rack, carefully remove the greaseproof paper, and leave to cool completely.

To make the icing, put the butter into a bowl with the icing sugar and lemon rind and beat together until creamy, then add 1–2 tablespoons of the lemon juice to make a light paste that is soft enough to spread. Use half of the mixture to sandwich the cakes together and spread the rest on the top. Sprinkle with a few chopped walnuts.

Carrot cake

Sponge sandwich cake

This sponge is made by the all-in-one method, which means you can whiz it up in next to no time – the important thing is for the butter to be soft (but not melted) so that it whisks easily.

MAKES ONE 18 CM/7 INCH ROUND CAKE

175 g/6 oz self-raising flour
1 teaspoon baking powder
175 g/6 oz caster sugar
175 g/6 oz butter, softened
3 eggs

FOR THE FILLING AND TOPPING

4 tablespoons good quality raspberry jam
a little caster sugar

Heat the oven to 160°C/325°F/Gas Mark 3. Grease two 18 cm/7 inch sandwich tins with butter, then line the base of each with a circle of greased greaseproof paper.

Sift the flour and baking powder together into a bowl. Add the sugar, butter and eggs and beat with a wooden spoon for 2 minutes, or in a mixer for about 1 minute, until the mixture is smooth, thick and glossy.

Divide the mixture between the prepared tins, scraping the bowl with a plastic spatula. Level the tops, then bake, without opening the oven door, for 30 minutes.

Test whether the cakes are done by pressing them lightly in the centre with a fingertip; if the sponge bounces back, it's done. If not, bake for a further 5 minutes. Leave the cakes in the tins to cool for 1 minute, then turn them out on to a wire rack, carefully remove the greaseproof paper, and leave to cool completely. Sandwich the cakes together with the jam and sprinkle the top with caster sugar.

Variations

A lemon version is good – add the grated rind of 1 lemon to the mixture and sandwich the cakes together with a good-quality lemon curd.

For a chocolate sponge, replace 1 tablespoon of the flour with 1 tablespoon of cocoa powder and sandwich and ice with the mixture given in the next recipe.

Meg's chocolate cake

This beautiful cake was invented by my daughter, Meg; it is made without eggs and is suitable for vegans. She first made it in a Swiss roll tin and rolled it up as a Yule log one Christmas. Here, I've made it in two sponge tins then sandwiched it together.

MAKES ONE 18 CM/7 INCH ROUND CAKE

85 g/3 oz self-raising white flour
40 g/1½ oz cocoa powder
100 g/3½ oz ground almonds
175 g/6 oz caster sugar
6 tablespoons groundnut oil
1 teaspoon vanilla extract
150 ml/5 fl oz soya milk

FOR THE ICING AND FILLING

50 g/2 oz vegan margarine, soft but not melted
125 g/4 oz icing sugar
grated rind of 1 lemon
½ teaspoon vanilla extract
1–2 tablespoons soya milk
a little grated or flaked chocolate

Heat the oven to 160°C/325°F/Gas Mark 3. Grease two 18 cm/7 inch sandwich tins and line the base of each with a circle of greased nonstick baking parchment.

Sift the flour and cocoa powder together into a bowl. Add the ground almonds, caster sugar, oil and vanilla extract. Pour in the soya milk and 85 ml/3 fl oz water and mix well to form a smooth, fairly wet batter. Pour the mixture into the prepared tins, dividing it between them.

Bake for about 30 minutes, until the cakes spring back to a light touch in the centre. Leave to cool in the tins for 5 minutes, then turn them carefully on to a wire rack – they are quite delicate – and leave until completely cold before you peel off the paper.

To make the icing and filling, put the margarine into a bowl with the icing sugar and lemon rind and beat together until creamy, then add the vanilla extract and 1–2 tablespoons of soya milk to make a light paste that is soft enough to spread. Use half of the mixture to sandwich the cakes together and spread the rest on the top. Decorate with the grated or flaked chocolate.

Parkin

This traditional Yorkshire recipe for parkin does not include eggs, so it can easily be made vegan if you use soya milk – which I prefer in any case. Wrap it in greaseproof paper and foil and it will keep for a week or ten days, getting more deliciously sticky all the time.

MAKES 12–16 PIECES

125 g/4 oz plain wholewheat flour
2 teaspoons baking powder
2 teaspoons ground ginger
125 g/4 oz medium oatmeal
125 g/4 oz muscovado sugar
125 g/4 oz black treacle
125 g/4 oz golden syrup
125 g/4 oz butter or vegan margarine
175 ml/6 fl oz milk or soya milk

Heat the oven to 180°C/350°F/Gas Mark 4. Line a 20 cm/8 inch square tin with nonstick baking paper.

Sift the flour, baking powder and ginger together into a bowl, adding the residue of bran left in the sieve, and also the oatmeal.

Put the sugar, treacle, golden syrup and butter or margarine into a saucepan and heat gently until melted. Leave to cool until you can comfortably put your hand against the pan, then stir in the milk or soya milk.

Add this mixture into the dry ingredients in the bowl, mix well, then pour into the prepared tin. Bake for 50–60 minutes, until the middle of the parkin is firm to the touch. Lift the parkin out of the tin and put it on a wire rack to cool. Strip off the paper and cut the parkin into pieces.

Fruit cake

A moist, easy, eggless recipe, in which the combination of bicarbonate of soda and vinegar causes it to rise. It can be made for vegans if you use vegan margarine and soya milk. I like to use wholewheat flour but you could use plain white, or a mixture of the two.

MAKES ONE 20 CM/8 INCH ROUND CAKE

325 g/12 oz plain wholewheat flour
1 teaspoon mixed spice
175 g/6 oz butter or vegan margarine
175 g/6 oz soft brown sugar
325 g/12 oz mixed dried fruit (currants, raisins, sultanas, cherries and mixed peel)
grated rind of 1 orange
grated rind of 1 lemon
125 ml/4 fl oz milk or soya milk
2 tablespoons vinegar
¾ teaspoon bicarbonate of soda
25 g/1 oz flaked almonds

Heat the oven to 150°C/300°F/Gas Mark 2. Grease a 20 cm/8 inch deep cake and line it with a double layer of greased greaseproof paper, then grease again.

Sift the flour and mixed spice together into a bowl, adding the residue of bran left in the sieve. Rub the butter or margarine into the flour with your fingertips until the mixture resembles breadcrumbs, then add the dried fruits and the orange and lemon rind.

Warm half the milk in a small saucepan and add the vinegar. Dissolve the bicarbonate of soda in the rest of the milk, then add to the milk and vinegar mixture. Quickly stir this into the flour and fruit, mixing well so that everything is combined.

Spoon the mixture into the prepared cake tin and sprinkle the almonds on top. Bake for 2–2½ hours, until a skewer inserted into the centre of the cake comes out clean. Leave the cake in the tin to cool, then strip off the greaseproof paper.

Celebration cake

This is a wonderful, moist, rich fruit cake, superb for Christmas, birthdays or weddings.

MAKES ONE 20 CM/8 INCH ROUND CAKE
850 g/1 lb 14 oz mixed dried fruit (currants, raisins, sultanas and mixed peel)
50 g/2 oz glacé cherries, halved
5 tablespoons brandy
250 g/9 oz plain flour
1 teaspoon mixed spice
1 teaspoon freshly ground black pepper
½ teaspoon ground cinnamon
4 eggs
225 g/8 oz butter
225 g/8 oz soft brown sugar
grated rind of 1 lemon
grated rind of 1 orange
50 g/2 oz pecan nuts, chopped
50 g/2 oz flaked almonds

It's a good idea to begin a day in advance by putting the mixed fruit and cherries into a large bowl and sprinkling with 3 tablespoons of the brandy. Cover and leave for 12–24 hours for the brandy to soak in.

Prepare your tin by lining it with a double layer of greased greaseproof paper (or nonstick baking paper, which there's no need to grease), and tie a double layer of brown paper around the outside of the tin, extending 5 cm/2 inches or so above the tin.

When you're ready to make the cake, heat the oven to 120°C/250°F/Gas Mark ½.

Sift the flour, mixed spice, pepper and cinnamon together into a bowl or on to a plate. Whisk the eggs in a small bowl.

Put the butter and sugar into a large bowl and beat until they are light and pale. (You can do this by hand with a wooden spoon, but of course it's easiest to use a food mixer or an electric whisk.) The mixture needs to be really fluffy because the quality of your finished cake depends on this stage. Add the beaten eggs to the butter and sugar, about a tablespoonful at a time, whisking well after each addition. If the mixture looks as if it's going to curdle, whisk in a tablespoonful of the flour mixture.

When you've beaten in all the egg, gently fold in the flour mixture. Then gently stir in the dried fruit mixture, orange and lemon rind and the nuts. Spoon the mixture into the prepared tin and smooth the top level, using the back of the spoon. Place a doubled piece of greaseproof paper, with a 2 cm/1 inch diameter circle cut in the middle, over the top of the brown paper, to prevent the top and sides of the cake from browning before the inside is done.

Bake the cake at the bottom of the oven (or in the coolest part) for 4½–5 hours or until a skewer inserted into the centre comes out clean. (Don't open the oven door until the cake has been baking for at least 4 hours or it might sink in the middle.)

When it's done, leave it to cool in the tin, then prick the top all over with a skewer and pour 2 tablespoons of brandy over it. Wrap the cake in a double thickness of greaseproof paper and store in an airtight tin. It will keep well and mature for 2–3 months; sprinkle a little more brandy over it occasionally during this time if you wish.

glossary of cooking terms

Al dente An Italian term meaning 'to the tooth', used to describe perfectly cooked pasta and rice: just tender, but still firm in the very centre, which you can test by biting them.

Au gratin A dish that has been topped with crumbs and/or grated cheese, or simply browned under the grill or in the oven.

Bain marie Also known as a water bath: a container (deep roasting tin or saucepan) half-filled with hot water and kept just below boiling point. The water diffuses direct heat, so pans are stood in the bain marie to keep delicate foods (such as hollandaise sauce) hot, and sometimes to prevent dishes from over-heating as they cook in the oven (as in Mary's nut loaf, page 136).

Bake To cook in the oven in dry heat.

Bake blind To bake pastry cases before they are filled. Press the pastry down well to exclude air and prick the base of the pastry thoroughly to let the steam out (the little holes will seal up as the pastry cooks). Some people put a piece of greaseproof paper on the pastry and weigh it down with dried beans or special ceramic baking beans to keep the pastry flat as it cooks. These should be removed after 15 minutes, when the pastry has set; the pastry should then be returned to the oven for a further 5 minutes, until it is crisp but still pale.

Baste To spoon fat over foods from time to time during cooking to prevent them from drying out and improve the flavour.

Beat To agitate a mixture rapidly with a whisk, wooden spoon or fork to break it up (for example tofu), soften it (butter) or incorporate air into it (egg whites).

Blanch Originally meant to immerse food in boiling water briefly to whiten it or loosen the skins (as in almonds, tomatoes) but now commonly used instead of parboil (see below) before freezing or reheating.

Boil To cook food in liquid at 100°C/212°F.

Bouquet garni Aromatic herbs used to flavour stock, soups and stews. A classic bouquet garni comprises parsley stalks, bay leaves and thyme, tied together with string so they can be removed after cooking. A bouquet garni could also include a stick of celery, a piece of leek, or other herbs.

Braise To cook food in a covered pan with enough liquid to cover.

Chill To cool food in the refrigerator without freezing it.

Chop To cut food into small pieces without mashing or crushing it.

Coddle To cook something in water just below boiling point. Usually applied to eggs (see page 63).

Cream To beat together butter or margarine and sugar, softening them and incorporating air, so that the mixture is light and fluffy.

Crimp To decorate and seal the edges of a pie or tart by pinching them together or pressing them with the prongs of a fork.

Curdle To separate, as if into 'curds and whey'; can refer literally, to sour milk, or to an emulsion (for example mayonnaise) when the oil has been added too quickly, or to creamed butter and sugar (in a cake mixture) when the beaten egg has been added too fast.

Deseed To remove the seeds, for example from chillies and peppers.

Dice To cut into small, regularly sized cubes.

Dredge To sprinkle food with sugar, flour, icing sugar, cocoa or chocolate powder. If you do not have a special shaker, sprinkle the powder through a sieve.

Dropping consistency A term used to describe the consistency of a cake or pudding mixture when it falls off a spoon held on its side above the bowl, within five seconds.

Egg and crumbing Dipping food first into beaten egg and then into dried breadcrumbs to make a coating, usually before frying in hot oil.

Emulsion A mixture of two liquids that do not dissolve into each other, such as vinegar and oil.

En croûte Food wrapped in pastry and then baked in the oven.

Fold To mix delicately, using a gentle, lifting movement to retain as much air in the mixture as possible.

Fry To cook food in hot fat or oil. Shallow-frying uses a small amount of oil, in a frying pan. Deep-frying uses enough oil to immerse the food, in a deep pan.

Garnish To add edible decorations to food, for example lemon slices or herb sprigs.

Glaze To give something a shiny coating, for example by brushing pastry with beaten egg or milk and sugar before putting it in the oven, or by brushing a fruit tart with warmed jam or jelly.

Grind To crush or grate foods (such as nuts or spices) very finely in a food mill, mortar and pestle or electric grinder.

Hull To remove the stem from soft fruits such as strawberries.

Infuse To flavour a liquid by soaking ingredients such as herbs and spices in it, often warming the liquid first.

Julienne Very thin strips of vegetables or citrus rind.

Knead To press, stretch and fold yeast dough to distribute the yeast thoroughly. A similar but much lighter motion is used to distribute the ingredients in pastries and other doughs.

Knock back or knock down To knead risen yeast dough to expel the air.

Marinade The liquid used to marinate (see below).

Marinate To soak ingredients in a mixture of liquid, oil and flavourings.

Mill To make food into a powder or paste (see **Grind**, above).

Pass To push food through a sieve.

Parboil To boil food briefly, for part of its cooking time. For example, roast potatoes are parboiled then roasted in fat. Other vegetables may be parboiled (often called blanching) to begin to soften them, so that the final cooking time of a dish is shorter (as in stir-fries, or Vegetables braised in oil and lemon, page 101).

Pare To peel thinly; usually applied to fruit and to citrus rinds.

Poach To cook food gently in liquid in an open pan.

Pressure cooking Cooking food in steam under pressure. It speeds up cooking times because the boiling point of liquids is lower at higher pressure.

Prove To leave yeast dough to rise after kneading.

Punch down See **Knock back**, above.

Reduce To boil food rapidly to evaporate the liquid and concentrate the flavours.

Refresh To immerse parboiled foods in cold water (or run them under the cold tap) in order to stop them cooking and set their bright colour.

Roast To cook food in an oven, usually in fat.

Rub in To blend fat and flour by lightly rubbing them together with the fingertips to produce a mixture that looks like breadcrumbs.

Sauté To cook food in a little fat in a frying pan, usually over a fairly high heat, tossing or turning it until it's evenly cooked.

Scald To heat liquid to just below boiling point, or to pour boiling water over ingredients to clean them.

Scallop To decorate the edge of a pastry dish by making little cuts in the pastry, then pulling it back towards the centre of the dish.

Seed See **Deseed**, above.

Seasoning Adding salt, pepper and sometimes other ingredients such as lemon juice and nutmeg to perfect the flavour of a dish.

Sieve To push food through a sieve to produce a smooth consistency.

Sift To shake dry ingredients such as flour through a sieve, to incorporate air and remove any lumps.

Simmer To cook food in liquid at just below boiling point.

Steep To cover food with hot or cold water and leave it to stand.

Stew To cook slowly in liquid kept just below boiling point.

Stir-fry To fry quickly in a small amount of hot fat while stirring constantly.

Stock Liquid flavoured by simmering vegetables and herbs in water then straining them out.

Syrup Concentrated solution of water and sugar.

Tepid Approximately blood heat, 37°C/98°F.

Whip, whisk To beat vigorously with a whisk.

Zest The coloured outer layer of citrus fruits.

index

Author's acknowledgements
I'd like to express my warm thanks to everyone involved in the production of this book. To Susan Haynes for the original idea; my friends, family and my agent Barbara Levy, for their enthusiasm, support and, in some cases, recipes; the production team, especially art director David Rowley, designer Nigel Soper, Philip Webb for his beautiful photographs and Pete Smith for showing off my recipes at their best. In particular I'd like to thank my daughter Claire for reading the manuscript and making many helpful suggestions; and Maggie Ramsay for doing such a superb job on the editing.